# IMPROVING EVALUATIONS

# SAGE FOCUS EDITIONS

# IMPROVING EVALUATIONS

## EDITED BY
## LOIS-ELLIN DATTA AND
## ROBERT PERLOFF

 SAGE Publications    Beverly Hills/London

Royalties from the sales of this book are being donated to the Guttentag Memorial Fund of the Evaluation Research Society.

*For information address:*

SAGE PUBLICATIONS, INC.  SAGE PUBLICATIONS LTD
275 South Beverly Drive    28 Banner Street
Beverly Hills, California 90212    London EC1Y 8QE


Printed in the United States of America

**Library of Congress Cataloging in Publication Data**

Main entry under title:
Improving evaluations.

    (Sage focus editions; 12)
    Includes bibliographies.
    1.   Evaluation research (Social action programs)—Congresses. 1. Datta, Lois-ellin, 1932-   II. Perloff, Robert.   III.   Evaluation Research Society.   IV.   Series.
H62.I54       309.1'73'0926       79-13627
ISBN 0-8039-1240-4
ISBN 0-8039-1241-2 pbk.

FIRST PRINTING

# CONTENTS

## SECTION III.  IMPROVING MEASUREMENT

## SECTION IV.  THE ROLE OF EVALUATION

# DEDICATION

*This volume is dedicated
to
MARCIA GUTTENTAG*

*Founding President
Evaluation Research Society*

*A warm and caring colleague
. . . a powerful force for the improvement
and utilization of evaluations as a means toward the
betterment of society and of the human condition.*

# INTRODUCTION:
# ENHANCED LIVES, IMPROVED EVALUATIONS

Lois-ellin Datta and Robert Perloff

In mid-October of 1977, one year after she had presided at the founding of the Evaluation Research Society (ERS), Marcia Guttentag led the opening session of the society's first annual convention. Two weeks later, she suffered a fatal heart attack.

During that first ERS meeting, Marcia was particularly enthusiastic about developing a published series based on the ERS annual meetings.[1] The series—as she conceptualized it—was to be in style between a proceedings, in which the essence of almost every presentation is reported briefly, and an edited book, in which chapters of highest scientific excellence are selected. She hoped for a series which could be used in daily work and in evaluator training to keep evaluation growing and improving.

She particularly wanted to show the connections between evaluation theory and evaluation practice, and among improved theory, improved practice, and the enhancement of human lives. This belief, perhaps more than common endorsement of any technology of evaluation, brings together members of the Evaluation Research Society: a commitment to a just, humane, and humanly rich way of life and the belief

that evaluation can make a contribution to this kind of society worth
the energy and commitment of our own lives. This volume[2] is intended
as an experiment in this spirit, and as a memorial to Marcia's own spirit.

The four sections of the volume reflect interests prominent in Marcia
Guttentag's published work. The first section, "Obstacles to Evaluation," deals with the political forces influencing what questions are
asked, when, and by whom. Rossi begins the section by asserting that
evaluation research has fallen into a trap of accepting questions beyond
reasonable answering. Citing the negative income tax experiments
where political forces beyond the evaluator's control shifted the comparison conditions three times during the course of the five-year experiment, Rossi argues for evaluators' becoming more proactive in identifying the intersect where issues of public interest can be informed by
social science research. It is in this intersect that he sees the greatest
future contributions of evaluation. Abt looks at the buyer-seller relationship in evaluations, dissecting the limitations unnecessarily imposed
by the competitive procurement process in evaluation research. The
high cost of submitting proposals relative to the low probability of an
award drives out true competition. Once receiving the award, the
researcher often is forced to conduct a by-the-recipe study, despite
obvious needs for changes in design, measurement, analysis, and reporting from those planned. Abt argues for a change in procurement
procedures to better fit the dynamic world in which evaluations take
place. Wurzburg suggests that the impact of evaluation results on
federal policy is restricted because of certain features of the state of the
art of evaluation and because of frequently unstable environments in
which policy is created at the federal level. Finally, Simmons offers for
consideration fourteen obstacles in the path of evaluating human
service programs at the state level.

Writers in the second section, "Improving Evaluation Designs," share
a common concern with the question of causal inference or internal
validity: how to feel reasonably assured that effects, if any, are attributable to the change under study. The question arises from a Catch-22
quality of many evaluations: in most situations, causal inference is
strongest where true controls are possible. In most evaluations, however, true controls are thought to be difficult to obtain, and even when
they are possible aberrant control group behavior may make inference
more rather than less difficult. In her many struggles with this problem,

Guttentag was led to inverse probability as a mathematical model which best fit the political and philosophical beliefs she cherished and her view of what was realistic: a shifting, changing reality where those most directly affected by the evaluation findings should have greatest control over what was studied, and would have their values most prominently reflected in the results. While none of the articles in this section springs from the Multi-Attribute Utility Theory or Decision-Theoretic approach which she and her colleagues developed, the definition of the problem and the search for alternative solutions were topics she found exciting and important.

Saxe and Fine begin with a model for evaluation which embeds control group designs for answering specific questions within a larger evaluation model. They suggest that the either/or question of a control group versus the decision-theoretic approach is artificial and unproductive. Their case study illustrates one application of a combined model, an attempt to gain the strongest inference possible about impact in a study of television diagnosis in rural areas, while retaining the pragmatic convenience of the nonexperimental models for answering other questions. The three other papers in this section range from the true experimental design to statistical paradigms for drawing inferences. Bentler and Woodward present an approach to causal modeling in which process data are used to select the most plausible of alternative interpretations of changes associated with an intervention. Knapp describes another strategy: the use of time series data to rule out competing hypotheses and establish causality. Like Bentler and Woodward, Knapp identifies the limiting conditions of this approach, while arguing that it is a presently an underutilized and extremely powerful method. Tuchfeld, closing this section, offers an overview of statistical methods for measuring change. His survey of these methods presents several facets of the dilemma (faced squarely by Guttentag) between design and analysis in drawing causal inference.

"Improving Measurement," the third section of the volume, deals with three concerns. Windle's paper raises the question of how large an effect is needed in order to be practically, as well as statistically, meaningful. Although his examples are focused on mental health program evaluations, the often-neglected distinction between statistical significance (which is fairly easy to change by increasing Ns and the reliability of the measures) and practical significance could be applied

to other fields. Boruch and Gomez treat a second concern: the impact
of measurement unreliability on the power of evaluations to detect
differences when they actually exist, and what statistical approaches
can be applied to gain power. The third issue is the construction and
interpretation of measures in different fields. Allen and Sears, in a case
study of desegregation, illustrate the care needed in interpreting attitudinal data. Schwind, in the context of bank manager training, presents a
psychometric improvement on the use of task sampling for scale construction. Davenport and Nuttall, dealing with mental health programs
supported by Medicaid, suggest ways of thinking about values in a field
where a positive outcome may be an increase in clients rather than the
more usual decreases in number of cases and time spent on each.
Mushkin, facing a similar dilemma, illuminates hitherto murky areas of
thinking about costs and benefits of the new, life-sustaining health
technologies.

These areas, too, Marcia found exciting. Her own work at first glance
more frequently dealt with design and analysis than with improving
measures per se. Looked at in more detail, almost all her studies
grappled with trying to think clearly about what the numbers meant:
about conceptually establishing important social issues involved in *any*
of the content areas; about creating imaginative, sensitive approaches to
studying these conceptually salient questions; and about great care in
translating back from the computer printouts to meaningful implications for the people and programs reflected, however dimly, in the
quantitative data. In her own work, conceptual sense and creative
assessment were more dominant than psychometrics for its own sake.
While recognizing the need for valid, reliable measures, she would place
higher value on meaningful, interpretable data, a concern of the papers in
this section.

In "The Role of Evaluation," section four, the papers return to issues
raised in the first section, to the relation of evaluation to the social
order in which it is inextricably embedded. While the first section deals
with government-imposed obstacles to evaluation, the fourth section
turns to what evaluators may uniquely contribute to improving the
impact of data on policy and practice. Mitroff, Emshoff, and Kilmann
consider the role of assumptions in evaluations: the preference of many
evaluators for specificity in defining the program objectives and purposes despite the multi-purpose, multi-actor nature of even the smallest

program with the most narrowly defined purpose. They present a heuristic for dealing with this, which involves a systematic testing of strategic assumptions. Knapp, in his examination of organizational theory, offers an approach more attuned to human relations. He argues that most social systems in education pull toward the individual and away from the group. Evaluators, rather than seeking group consensus, he argues, should identify the opportunities for changes and design evaluations to reflect these concerns. Rich identifies a variety of critical issues that evaluators need to address, including the availability and utilization of appropriate methodological tools, the identification of training programs suitable for preparing evaluators to face the realities and challenges in evaluation tasks as scientists and practitioners, the continuing need to translate evaluation results into humane and relevant policy, the need to reduce instances of abuse and misutilization of evaluation data, and the development of ethical standards for evaluators. Finally, Davis and Salasin step back from these specific issues in their analysis of the relation between evaluation and change. They argue primarily that evaluators should accept a role as change agents. Rather than lamenting that evaluations are not utilized (when they are dropped from Olympus), evaluators should come down to earth, using presently available techniques for understanding readiness for change, and better meshing the evaluation studies with the situations as they find them—in their human and humane diversity, inconsistencies, and complexities.

In some ways, these chapters probably would have worried Marcia. She cared deeply about change, and spared neither herself nor others in the directness of her efforts to see justice done and individuals enabled to create their own lifestyle in their own life space. She hoped evaluation, by giving individuals information about themselves, their situation, and about approaches that worked, could be, if necessary, a terrible swift sword, but preferably a plowshare. She would have resisted whatever would have compromised with might against right, or placed evaluation in the position of background musician among the counselors of the princes. Yet in many other ways, these efforts, like her own, to find ways in which evaluations could be most useful in promoting humane, moral, life-enhancing change—both within the profession and in society—were like her own, and might well have earned her brightest smile and her heartiest "Good work."

## NOTES

1. As this volume goes to press, we see the realization of Marcia Guttentag's aspirations in the establishment of the forthcoming (commencing in fall 1979) Sage Research Progress Series in Evaluation—a joint undertaking of the Evaluation Research Society and Sage Publications, under the able editorship of Susan Salasin. The series will consist of brief, theme-oriented volumes (developed in part from papers presented at each year's ERS meetings) for the use of evaluation researchers, practitioners, and students.

2. The essays in this volume were selected not only for their quality but also for their relation to the volume's major themes. We are grateful to the contributors—both those who wrote new essays for this volume and those who cooperated so cheerfully with us in the revision process. The volume's royalties will be donated to the Society's Guttentag Memorial Fund to further advance us toward the goals which Marcia Guttentag sought to reach.

# SECTION I
## OBSTACLES TO EVALUATION

# 1

## PAST, PRESENT, AND FUTURE PROSPECTS OF EVALUATION RESEARCH

Peter H. Rossi

Although some form of evaluative activities always has been undertaken by the federal government, it is only within the last decade that systematic and widespread evaluations have become a consistently present feature of the national scene. Enough experience has now been accumulated concerning the field that an attempt to assess where we have been and where we are going appears to be in order. That is the purpose of this paper.

The perspective from which this paper is written is that of an academic and an outsider to the federal evaluation scene. I have undertaken evaluation researches and have administered evaluation research activities. I have also written some on the topic and taught a lot more. But I have never been on the federal agency side of the fence except to be a consultant, usually taking part in the rfp ("request for proposal") reviewing process. An academic outsider has some advantages and some disadvantages that stem from his perspective. The main disadvantage is that of being slightly out of date. Insiders know what is going on right now, whereas outsiders usually know what happened a year or more ago. The advantages are ones which provide a comparative perspective and hence perhaps a larger view of what is going on. I have dealt with a variety of federal agencies, whereas many insiders may have dealt with at most one or two. I may also have read more evaluation study reports in connection with my teaching and writing. I am also not constantly under the gun and have had more time to make this assessment than an insider ordinarily enjoys. On balance, I would characterize my viewpoint as being that of an academic outsider who does not have to make his living from evaluation research but has been more than just a voyeur getting his kicks from observing others in action.

There are so many things that have been included under one or another usage of the term evaluation that it is essential to present my own understanding of that field so that we both can be clear about the activities under discussion. Evaluation research covers in my view the following activities: (1) *monitoring programs:* the collection of data usually from administrative records or administratively required reports from program operators that permit a description of the program, the clientele served, expenditures of funds, characteristics of program personnel, services rendered, and so on. Although I have stressed monitoring as an internally generated data system, there are also types of monitoring that might be carried out by an external agency, i.e., on contract to a research firm or university. Thus, a human services delivery program might hire a social anthropologist to report on what is going on in a more informal but perhaps more insightful fashion. And, (2) *outcome evaluations:* attempts to systematically assess the effects of the program, not the effects of competing factors. An outcome evaluation applies a set of criteria for assessing a program, ones, it is hoped, that are relevant to the program's expressed purposes.

There are activities that are sometimes included in evaluation research that are excluded in my usage of the term: (1) *policy analysis,* assessments of the potential benefits of alternative policies that are being considered; and (2) *Modeling,* attempts to understand the processes that underlie a particular phenomenon. Both policy analysis and modeling are essential activities feeding directly into decision making. Leaving them out of the field of evaluation research mainly reflects that these activities are less bounded by social science data and hence ought to be considered separate from monitoring and outcome evaluation.

# THE CURRENT STATE OF FEDERAL
# EVALUATION EFFORTS

Although there have always been some research activities of the federal government that might have been called evaluation research, even in the restricted sense in which I have used the term, the contemporary upsurge of evaluation activity really starts in the 1960s. The first years' federal efforts were truly pitiful as those of you who went through that period must recall. Not only were the agencies—even sophisticated ones like OEO and the Department of Labor—stumbling about but also the evaluation research community was in its infancy and barely knew how to crawl. It should be recalled that the most cited reference of evaluation research, Campbell and Stanley's little volume on research designs (1966), was first published in 1963 embedded in a handbook of educational research and not published as a separate work until 1966.

There have been enormous improvements in both the federal evaluation effort and the evaluation research community since the early 1960s. In the early period there was almost no appreciation for powerful research designs. When several researchers suggested that the Job Corps might be best evaluated by a randomized controlled experiment, the proposal was immediately and vigorously rejected. The Job Corps staff did not or would not understand how randomization would have helped to assess conclusively program effects or how the process when used in the context of a surplus of applicants over and above the Job Corps Center's capacity was no more cruel or capricious than the method of selection then employed.

There are many signs of improvement. First of all, the personnel in charge of evaluation units within the agencies are now much more knowledgable about research, resulting in a much higher quality of rfp's and less capricious project management. As a measure of the improvement, there are now more than a dozen randomized controlled experiments that have been completed or are currently underway, including four field experiments on negative income tax plans, two experiments using housing vouchers, an experiment on comprehensive medical insurance, and several experiments on criminal justice procedures.

Second, an evaluation community has emerged whose members are drawn together by their shared interest in evaluation research. The established professional societies in the social sciences have begun to pay some considerable attention to evaluation research at their annual meetings. New professional societies such as the Evaluation Research Society have been started during the past few years and have already become established. Professional journals devoted largely to evaluation research have been established and have quickly become economically viable: *Evaluation Quarterly* started in 1977, had nearly 4,000 subscribers before the end of its first year in existence.

The presence of an evaluation research community will do much to further shore up trends toward better research. Professional meetings provide opportunities for the exchange of problems and solutions. They also provide the basis for the development of a consensus on what is the current state of the art. Most of all, we will also have someone else to lean upon in dealing with clients, fellow researchers, and with the obstinate problems with which evaluation research must necessarily deal.

There are now first-rate firms that engage almost exclusively in federal research and perhaps as many as 300 firms who respond to evaluation rfps. Evaluation research has become a respectable activity among academics, a development that only partially reflects the present labor market for new social science Ph.D.s. For example, the three annual Summer Evaluation Research Institutes run at the University of Massachusetts each year received several hundred applications for the 25 or 30 places.

The trend toward improvement shows no sign of slackening. The federal agencies are becoming increasingly sophisticated and the research community increasingly able to deliver a better product. The complaints which follow then should be regarded as starting from the base of an assessment of considerable improvement but one with still some major defects.

There are some areas in which I believe there are still serious deficiencies in the federal evaluation effort.

First of all, too many evaluation tasks as set out in rfp's are simply impossible to undertake without serious compromise of scientific standards, provided with funds that are inadequate to the task, or set in a time frame that is impossible to meet. Over the past three years, my colleagues and I have screened several hundred rfp's searching for examples we could use for didactic exercises in the Summer Institute. We were able to find less than a dozen that we could use (see Bernstein and Freeman, 1975) applying the principle of whether the task as stated could be responded to with a sensible research plan. It may well be the case, as John Tukey once said, that "if something is worth while doing, it is worth while doing superficially!" But, in most cases it seemed to me that one would have to be methodologically naive, on the verge of slipping below the poverty level, a scientific hypocrite, or a combination of the above to have responded to most of the rfp's we reviewed.

The reverse side of this picture is the correspondingly low level of the vast majority of evaluation researches. Several evaluation researchers connected with Russell Sage Foundation have been screening evaluation research reports to find examples of well-executed projects that we could review in a special section of *Evaluation Magazine* to be devoted to drawing attention to evaluation researches of high quality. We also have not been able to find more than half a dozen after reviewing more than a hundred reports. Perhaps most of the reports reflect the tasks that were set in the rfp's to which they were a response, but it is also the case that most had such major technical defects that it is difficult to imagine that the firms and persons involved knew what they were doing. It almost appears as if the evaluation research industry is about at the stage that the garment industry was around the turn of the twentieth century. At that time almost anyone with a week's rent and a sewing machine could set himself up as a garment manufacturer. Today anyone with an IBM selectric typewriter and a month's rent can set himself (or herself) up as a research firm and respond to rfp's.

I am sure that this judgment appears to at least some of you as the harsh pronouncement of an evangelical methodological purist. But let me assure you that the standards we were applying were quite minimal ones, considerably lower than those we would demand of a passing M.A. thesis. The fact of the matter is that most evaluations are still not worth much more than no evaluation at all.

A second criticism of the current evaluation research effort of the federal government is that the evaluation effort is still much of an afterthought. The best time to plan an evaluation is before the outset of a program. A program that has been underway for two or three years can scarcely be evaluated very well. It is difficult to reconstruct exactly the program content over those years. Program administrators regard an evaluation task imposed upon them after the program has gone into full swing as an inquisition at worst and as a bureaucratic imposition at the least, but most important the better research designs require some measures be taken either before the start of the program or while the program is getting under way and a comparison with some comparable groups not receiving the treatment.

A third criticism pertains to the goals of social programs. The vagueness of goals and their internal contradictions still plague the attempts to evaluate. Evaluation researchers understand that the main sources of vagueness lie outside the federal agencies and stem from the styles of writing legislation and from the necessity to appeal to a wide constituency for support. Yet the agencies often have a hand in writing legislation and hence bear some of the responsibility. Much of the difficulty in designing good evaluation research stems from this distressing vagueness of goals, and a good deal of the rancorous conflict that arises after an evaluation report has been issued arises from the fact that vagueness in program goals always provides an excuse for dismissing an evaluation as irrelevant to some of the goals of the program.

Finally, I should mention that monitoring, an evaluation function that is perhaps most properly carried out within administrative and operating agencies, is also at a low level. All too often it is impossible to find out such simple facts as where programs are located, how many people are being served, and what services are being rendered. This is not because there are restrictions on the dissemination of such information but because the reporting system is either nonexistent or set up in such a fashion that the information cannot be retrieved. I venture that no one knows with certainty where the money dispensed under Title I of ESEA went or for what it was used. I should also mention that there are programs which are monitored much better; for example, the Small Business Administration has a very good system for retrieving information on disaster loans.

This last point illustrates a more general statement that should be made, lest any take offense at my assessments of the federal evaluation establishment. There is considerable variation from agency to agency and within agencies from research project to research project. DHEW has funded some of the best evaluation research yet, but some of the constituent agencies within DHEW have sent out some of the worst rfp's I have seen. The same degree of variability obtains for the research firms that perform the evaluation research whose reports I have reviewed. You can count on a very high level of performance from such firms as Mathematica, Research Triangle Institute, Westat, and Abt, or from such university-based research centers as Michigan's Institute for Social Research and Chicago's National Opinion Research Center, but the remainder of the 400 or so establishments that also bid on rfp's are too often several standard deviations below that level of performance. (The specific firms cited here are only some of the examples of very good firms. Similarly, there are other university-connected research centers that are as prominent in quality as the two cited.)

If this assessment be progress, then from what state of depravity did the field progress? The major difference between the early days of 1960 and the present lies in the variability of the present. There are some extremely good evaluation researches that have been undertaken and there are agencies that have a considerable degree of sophistication.

But now let us turn to the future.

## A BLUE SKY PLAN FOR FEDERAL EVALUATION RESEARCH

My vision for the future reform of federal evaluation research efforts has two parts to it. In the first place, there are changes that can be made in current practice that involve mainly shifts in funds and emphases. The second part consists of new institutions that I would like to see started.

## MAKING PROGRAM GOALS MORE SPECIFIC

It has now become almost trite to express the hope that program goals should be formulated in terms specific enough that the corresponding evaluation plan can actually be carried out. At the risk of verging on the trite, I would like to emphasize the importance of that point. It may help, however, to stress in what ways the goals of programs should be made more specific. To begin with, I want to emphasize that becoming more specific does not mean stressing any one goal exclusively. A program can have a multiplicity of goals and still be evaluated. Thus a negative income tax plan may have the multiple goals of reducing administrative complexity, reducing perverse incentives to work effort among the working poor, and bolstering family stability.

All these are goals specific enough to be evaluated, or, at least, it is possible to think of the criterional measures that could be applied that would correspond more or less to these goals.

Nor does it mean that the goals have to be so specific that the criteria measures (e.g., scores on the Metropolitan Reading and Mathematics Tests) are clearly laid out. Achieving consensus on the appropriateness of specific criteria measures can be left to the evaluators to negotiate. It should be noted that not enough effort has gone into efforts to find out whether criteria measures would be acceptable to policy makers. Coleman mentions that he and his colleagues spent a large amount of time reading over the congressional hearings connected with the Civil Rights Act of 1964 to find out what legislators meant by the phrase "equality of educational opportunity," decided that the congressmen were confused, and went off to devise the measures that went into the now-famous Coleman Report (Mosteller and Moynihan, 1972). I have asked Coleman whether he had thought of checking back at any point with the authors or supporters of the legislation, and he indicated that he had not.

From my own experiences I know how difficult it is to yield any autonomy in the devising of research designs and analyses and how tempting it is to hide behind the shield of technical expertise and professional autonomy. But applied social research is not merely a technical matter, being suffused throughout by political and value considerations, and hence is too important to be left to researchers to carry out without restrictions.

Joseph Wholey and his associates at the Urban Institute have worked out quite sophisticated techniques for eliciting from administrators and policy makers what were the intended goals of programs or projects. Wholey et al. (1975) suggests that before evaluations be undertaken a clear understanding be worked out with these two groups about what criteria will be applied in evaluations.

Finally, I am not at all sure that legislators and other policy makers are aware of the extent to which they have written enabling legislation in language that is too obscure to lead to clear mandates for evaluation of the ensuing program. For example, did the legislators and other persons who wrote into various acts the necessity to produce environmental impact statements realize that they were imposing upon others tasks which were in many cases impossible to achieve? Is it not possible that no one told them that although there have been many speculative accounts of the impact of major highways, no one has firm information of what running a highway through a neighborhood does to neighborhoods of different locations? Who knows how much money has been thrown away in the production of federal highway impact statements that are based mainly on a careless reading of Jane Jacobs, the massaging of some out-of-date Census statistics, and appeals to sweet reason?

How do we get better statements of the purposes of social programs so that the programs can be evaluated properly? It seems to me that not enough effort has gone into influencing the writing of legislation on the part of those who will bear the responsibility for the ensuing evaluations. We need to bring to the attention of legislators and other policy makers that current practices lead down a primrose path to self-destruction. We also need to bring these same groups into the decision-making process that surrounds the evaluation research itself. I think it would have been proper for Coleman to go back to those who were responsible for the writing of the 1964 Civil Liberties Act and to ask them whether his interpretation of their mandate was consonant with what they had in mind when they wrote a requirement for the Commissioner of Education to conduct a survey of educational opportunity into the act. Maybe we would have had a different Coleman report if that had been the case. My hope is that it would have been better or at least more relevant to policy needs.

## PRACTICING EVALUATION BIRTH CONTROL

Two of the major criticisms given earlier of the current federal evaluation scene are that a very large proportion of the rfp's issued describe impossible tasks and that a very large proportion of completed evaluation researches are of unacceptably low quality. It appears to me that most rfp's should not be issued at all on the grounds that the research tasks specified cannot be done well and that most evaluation researches should be led over to the nearest shredder and recycled into paper napkins. A recent estimate (Abt, 1976) I have heard is that the amount of federal funds going into evaluation research is on the order of one billion dollars. If that is the case, then one could save enough by the judicious application of evaluation birth control to fund more adequately evaluations that are worthwhile doing or the kind of basic research that would make some of the evaluations possible.

Assuming for the moment that it would be possible to call a halt to the lower-grade evaluations that are currently being funded, what could the money saved be used for? I have several suggestions, some of which are in the form of institutional innovations that I will discuss later on, and some, things that can be done right now.

First of all, I would like to see more basic research on some of the problems that lie behind the social programs. For example, I think we have learned so much more about the nature of poverty and the kinds of events which lead to families sinking below the poverty line through James Morgan's (1974) five-year longitudinal study of 5,000 American families that we are now in the position of being able to design a welfare system which is more adequate to the needs that poverty represents. Specifically, Morgan shows that the traumatic events that shift families across the poverty line have to do mainly with the changes in household composition that accompany household formation, dissolution, and the addition or subtraction of family members from the household.

Another example concerns the kinds of information that we need in order to be able to make sensible impact statements about proposed highways, power plants, dams, and similar large-scale development projects. It is possible to make statements that are empirically based about the impact of such projects, provided that the basic research involved is undertaken (see, e.g., Chernoff, 1976).

A second use for the funds released by judicious pruning of current evaluation researches is to fund more adequately those types of evaluation activities that can be undertaken well. A major use of this sort would be to fund more generously the monitoring activities of federal programs. It is somewhat disgraceful that it is not at all clear what is being done in the drug abuse clinics that are supported by federal dollars, or that the distributional characteristics of the Food Stamp plan are not known, along with a lot of other facts about the way in which the Food Stamp plan works out in practice. Such examples could be multiplied almost without limit. It is important to understand what it is that a good monitoring program can do and what it cannot do. The main purpose of a monitoring program is to provide descriptions of a program—how it is administered, who are clients, and what do clients receive? Of course, monitoring does not tell how effective a program is in achieving its goals. That is the job of outcome evaluation studies.

I realize that one of the major difficulties that stands in the way of adequate program monitoring is that it is hazardous to rely on operating organizations to generate data on their own operations. The nation's school systems have been remarkably effective in sabotaging all efforts to find out what it is that Title I funds are being used for (McLaughlin, 1975). National Youth Corps grass roots administrators often did not adequately document on the forms supplied by the Department of Labor information that would enable one to understand who was getting benefits. And so on. But monitoring need not necessarily be a task given only to program administrators. It would have been possible to monitor the NYC program on a sample basis using outside organizations as contractors.

A special type of generalized monitoring should also receive some support. As most of you know, over the past few years a movement has arisen to develop a set of social indicators, analagous to economic indicators, that would monitor the state of the nation with respect to the noneconomic or social aspects of our society. This monitoring activity promises to be useful in detecting potential sore points in our social structure that might develop into the social problems of the future and also in ascertaining the extent to which existing social programs are achieving adequate coverage of the population in need.

Evaluation birth control would have the salutary effect of reducing considerably the size of the evaluation research community and raising the level of quality of evaluation research. Without the ten to fifty thousand dollar research contracts to assess the unassessable, most of these firms would go out of business. Incidentally, this might also put a lot of local and state evaluation administrators out of business since a good deal of the evaluation research conducted by local and state agencies is of extremely low quality.

## CHANGING THE TIMING OF
## EVALUATION RESEARCH

For most of the social programs that constituted the backbone of the War on Poverty, evaluations were afterthoughts that occurred a number of years after the programs were under way. Thus Head Start was evaluated starting in 1968 after almost three years of Head Start experience. Similar delays characterized the evaluation efforts that looked into the Community Action Program or Jobs Corps. An after-thought evaluation suffers from several serious disabilities. First of all, it is difficult to reconstruct afterwards what the state of affairs would have been without the program. Secondly, it is almost impossible to construct a reasonable facsimile of a control group, as the Head Start evaluation discovered. Finally, program administrators are quite prone to regard an evaluation imposed upon them three years into a program as an intrusion and possibly a threat.

An adequate evaluation of an ongoing social program has to be started at the same time that the program is instituted. There are several models that might be employed. For programs like Head Start and the Job Corps, neither of which were initially intended to achieve total coverage of their eligible target populations, experimental designs with randomized assignments to treatment and control groups could have been instituted. For programs that will achieve full coverage almost immediately (as in the case of proposed reforms in the welfare pro-gram), it is possible to build in planned variations in the program analysis which will help to improve the efficiency and efficacy of the program, and to obtain before-program measures of the state of the target population. In this connection, it was heartening to note that the Family Assistance Plan, introduced by the Nixon administration in 1970 and 1971, did contain provisions for planned variations, even though the rest of the bill did not appear to many of us to be a remarkable departure from the existing welfare system.

One of the big mysteries in programs such as Head Start and Job Corps is that it is no longer possible to find out what those programs were actually like back in 1965 when they first started. The impression is that they were of considerable heterogeneity, but this is just an impression since contents of Head Start projects were undocumented. An evaluative effort that started at the outset of the program and contained a monitoring component would have enabled the Head Start evaluators to distinguish between Head Start Centers on the basis of what was done to the children who attended. Valuable information on potentially effective programs was not collected, and hence the pro-gram had to be evaluated as an undifferentiated black box.

Starting the evaluation at the outset raises the interesting organizational question of where does evaluation fit in the table of organization that links together funding sources and operating organizations, as well as the equally interesting question of how much authority over a program should be wielded by evaluation researchers. It is my view that evaluation is a function of the funding source and that the evaluator's authority to enter a program and make measurements derives from the funding source. Evaluators are not particularly knowledgable a priori about what works and hence should have little or nothing to say about program operations. However, the right of an evaluation researcher to enter an organization, take measurements, examine records and documents should be one that is built into the contract between a funding source and an operating organization. Evaluators should have rights similar to those of auditors but with a different content to the documents that must be made available to them.

Perhaps the model of an evaluation that is on the ground at the outset is that of the current study of the use of unemployment compensation payments to released prisoners started under Department of Labor auspices in Georgia and Texas. This is a demonstration program that is designed as an experiment with approximately 1,000 prisoners in each state randomly designated as receiving payments similar to unemployment compensation for varying periods of time with an additional several hundred released prisoners being placed in control groups, both groups to be followed for two years to observe their adjustment to civilian life and especially their re-arrest rates and recidivism. By 1978, it should be possible to draw very strongly supported inferences concerning the efficacy of this program.

## SOME PROPOSED NEW INSTITUTIONS
## FOR EVALUATION RESEARCH

The first proposed new institution is suggested as a device to lower the rancorous nature of evaluation research controversies. As things stand now, the release of a major evaluation research report tends to be followed within the space of a few months by a rejoinder from some source that objects to its findings. Indeed, there is a new occupation spawned by evaluation research—the traveling technical expert who for a price is willing to draw his technical big guns and fire upon the research report. Since no piece of research is ever definitive and current evaluation practice produces research in which almost any one with the slightest technical knowledge can find something to criticize, the technical expert is usually someone with enough stature to draw attention because his guns are bigger and usually shoot with more accuracy. Within the space of another few months, the researchers reply. Perhaps there will be another round and maybe still a third volley and counter-volley. Witness the controversies surrounding the Coleman Report, the New Jersey-Pennsylvania Negative Income Tax Experiment, and Head Start as examples of the rancorous conflict that surrounds the release of evaluations that run counter to someone's intuition. The problem with these conflicts is that because they tend to be long and drawn out and because the parties involved are acknowledged partisans, the controversies mainly cast doubt upon an evaluation but leave the audience with only an impression of controversy without any closure.

As a proposal, when a program of some consequence is evaluated, several evaluations should be sponsored simultaneously, each being given the mission to try to make a good case either for the program or against the program with respect to some agreed-upon criteria. Thus, in the case of Head Start one evaluation team would be given the mission of trying to prove that Head Start had an effect and the other the mission that it did not have an effect. I would even go so far to suggest that an important qualification for evaluators is that they have made statements on the public record in favor of or against the program in question.

In addition to the competing evaluation teams, I would also propose a review panel to be composed of persons nominated by each side and by the sponsoring agency. The purpose of the review panel would be to make judgments about how well documented and researched the competing claims are.

It is important to keep in mind the strictures placed around this institution. First, it should only be used in the evaluation of very important programs. Second, both teams have to agree on what are the criteria on which the program is to be evaluated. Third, the evaluators are to be selected on the basis of their technical competence in the first place and on their ideological preferences in the second place. Fourth, the two competing evaluations are to be issued simultaneously after which each team is to be allowed free access to the data collected by the other.

This would be an expensive operation. It should at least double the costs for evaluating major programs. It may also be the case that we evaluation researchers are so craven that no bids would be received from the evaluation community. Nevertheless, such open competition would result in better research that is more likely to be accepted by the public and especially by program administrators and policy makers. Furthermore, it would be only in the unusual case that the competing teams would come up with radically different conclusions.

A second new institution I would like to propose is the National Center for Social Experimentation or one with some similar name. The NCSE is to be designated as a body that either would undertake itself or contract out social experiments on social programs that might be considered by policy makers a decade or so ahead. It is to be an independent consortium of universities—perhaps like the national laboratories—provided with long-term federal financing, staffed by social scientists, and governed by a ruling board of policy makers and social scientists.

My reasoning for proposing the NCSE is as follows. The best evaluation researches are randomized controlled experiments testing out policies that have yet to be enacted, such as the Negative Income Tax Experiments, the Housing Voucher Experiment, Contract Learning, and Health Insurance. The federal government has taken a very bold step in funding these experiments. Indeed, they are the highlights of the federal evaluation experience of the past decade. Randomized controlled experiments have many desirable features. Most important of all, they do yield results which come closer to being definitive than those yielded by any other method of evaluating. They do have some drawbacks, however. For one thing, they take a long time; it was six years before we saw any firm results from the first negative income tax experiment. Second, they are expensive since they involve not only research costs but the costs of running a program for a number of years, albeit on a very restricted scale compared with national programs that are enacted.

But one of the major drawbacks to randomized controlled experiments under the present scheme of things is that they tend to be undertaken far too late in the policy formation process. The same climate of politics that makes it possible for an agency to contemplate funding a field experiment is also the same climate of opinion that is ready to consider the policy itself. Thus, shortly after the first negative income tax experiment was funded, the Nixon administration proposed the Family Assistance Plan, a variant of the Negative Income Tax plans. Similarly, long before results will be available from the Health Insurance experiment, the administration will undoubtedly introduce a bill authorizing some version of a national health insurance plan. And so on.

A useful program of social experimentation has to be one that is planned about a decade in advance so that it is possible to have findings when our government is ready to consider the policy. Because any existing administration is too preoccupied with the policy issues of the moment and of the next moment it is not likely that the social experiment for the social policies of the future will get much attention. Thus, the government agencies concerned with energy policies ought to be funding field experiments now (or even better two years ago) on the potential yield in energy savings of a variety of energy conservation measures, but there are only a few field experiments going on in utility pricing policies. Hence, I suggest a quasi-independent body to administer and possibly carry out the proposed program of forward-looking field experimentation.

A criticism that is often made of the field experiments currently under way is that they are too conservative in the range of treatments they are testing. This conservatism results mainly from the researchers' sticking to what they consider to be the range of politically feasible alternative policies, a judgment that is often based on assessment of the political line-ups of the current time. Freed from the myopia of current decision makers, the proposed NCSE is likely to design experiments that will yield better knowledge of the effects of programs, since extreme versions of programs are likely to be considered as part of the treatments.

## CONCLUSIONS

There are several important points made in the body of this paper. First of all, there has been an appreciable increase in both the quantity and quality of evaluation research in the federal establishment. Second, despite the improvement, the general level of federally sponsored evaluations is such that nothing would be lost and perhaps an opportunity gained by simply not funding most of the rfp's that come out routinely and instead using the money to support alternative evaluation activities that show more promise. Third, the activities recommended for increased support are as follows: increased support for program monitoring, starting evaluations at the outset of a program, competing evaluations, and finally some sort of national center for social experimentation.

Evaluation research has become fashionable. The fact that many persons attending the first annual meeting of the Evaluation Research Society are from agencies that are not heavy users of evaluation is a sign that such is the case. Fashion might turn into fad, one that will fade away when it has run its natural course as an attention-getting innovation. If evaluation research is to remain an important tool informing the making and the unmaking of policy, it has to be sufficient to that important task. It cannot do so unless it incorporates the best we know in the way of social science technical knowledge.

# REFERENCES

ABT, C. (1976) "Toward the benefit/cost analysis of U.S. government applied social research." Cambridge, MA: Abt.

BERNSTEIN, I. and H. FREEMAN (1975) Academic and Entrepreneurial Research. New York: Russell Sage Foundation.

CAMPBELL, D. T. and J. STANLEY (1966) Experimental and Quasi-Experimental Designs for Research. Chicago: Rand McNally.

CHERNOFF, M. (1976) "Assessing the social impact of interstate highway construction in urban areas." Ph.D. dissertation, University of Massachusetts.

McLAUGHLIN, M. W. (1975) Evaluation and Reform: The Elementary and Secondary Education Act of 1965. Cambridge, MA: Ballinger.

MORGAN, J. et al. (1974) Five Thousand American Families: Patterns of Economic Progress. Ann Arbor: Institute for Social Research.

MOSTELLER, F. C. and D. P. MOYNIHAN (1972) On Equality of Educational Opportunity. New York: Basic Books.

WHOLEY, J. S., J. N. NAY, J. W. SCANLON, and R. E. SCHMIDT (1975) "Evaluation: when is it really needed?" Evaluation Magazine 2, 2: 89-93.

# 2

## WHAT LIMITS THE IMPACT OF EVALUATIONS ON FEDERAL POLICY?

Gregory Wurzburg

All the good will and rhetoric notwithstanding, the hopes of evaluators to affect policy formulation must remain just that: hopes. The link between evaluators and policy makers is a tenuous one because of limitations imposed by the state of the art and by the environment in which policy is formed.

## THE STATE OF THE ART

The state of the art of evaluation is primitive—"Neanderthal," in the words of one observer. Furthermore, there is good reason to believe that many questions evaluators would like to answer are simply unanswerable for reasons beyond the control of evaluators. The programs whose effects evaluators are trying to assess are often very imprecise implements for intervention. Objectives are not always spelled out; and when they are, they are not spelled out in terms of readily observable phenomena. Some indicators are only crude proxies for the effects of public policy initiatives. Even if they were capable of doing that, measurement problems undercut the validity of conclusions. Underlying assumptions, failing to reflect the true state of the world, further reduce the certainty of any conclusions. None of these problems is new or surprising. They are hazards of the trade and are reflected in any agenda of methodological issues that evaluators tackle. The applicability of cost-benefit paradigms to welfare decisions, the problems of using control groups, and the role of operations research in evaluation are considerations requiring continual examination.

But state of the art problems aside, there are other forces impinging on evaluation findings as they assume potential for an impact on decision making. What might be referred to as the institutional environment in which social program evaluations take place is even more important than methodological adequacy in determining the ways evaluation findings affect policy.

## THE INSTITUTIONAL ENVIRONMENT

Taking evaluation out of a vacuum and putting it into the context of an institutional environment, evaluation findings are nothing more than another piece of evidence for decision makers to weigh before making their choices. In that environment factors other than "methodological adequacy" determine the extent to which evaluation findings are used and shape the way they are used. Some of these factors are a function of constitutional or statutory provisions. Others are a function of tradition, prejudice, procedures, and political forces.

One important focus for studying the institutional environment in which evaluations are used is the legislative versus executive role. This focus is interesting for its constitutional implications and because there have been some recent and dramatic changes here.

The separation between the executive branch and the legislative branch is a constitutional one that was intended to carve out distinct complementary roles and a separation of powers, creating a system of checks and balances. Congress, reflecting the will of the people, formulates policy and passes law to implement the policy. The executive branch carries the burden of executing the will of Congress: implementing the policy mandated in law. There have been two subsidiary evaluation roles that have evolved alongside the constitutional roles.

The executive branch has evaluated its efforts to assess the operations of its programs and the impact they have had. Congress has assumed an oversight role, checking on the executive branch to see how well it is carrying out the will of Congress.

While there is a constitutional rationale for how the evaluation roles in the two branches have developed, there are some less obvious reasons that have proven more persuasive in giving impetus to the evaluation activities. On the legislative side, "congressional oversight" was first recognized as a legitimate legislative activity in the Legislative Reorganization Act of 1946. Aside from establishing an oversight role in the committee system, it gave the General Accounting Office a mandate to guard the federal purse strings and to report directly to the Congress. However, for a long time financial auditing was undramatic, the General Accounting Office was not the most colorful group in town, and congressional oversight was more bark than bite—little more than a pro forma exercise. The explosion of social spending in the 1960s changed much of that, however. The government became deeply involved in activities that were politically controversial and whose outputs were not always discrete, measurable units. Congress, not being a consensus organization, suddenly raised a multitude of questions—some curious, some hostile—that had to be answered. The oversight role assumed a more serious dimension and the General Accounting Office was compelled to do more than count dollars and track down invoices. Although the Congress was receiving evaluation findings at that time from the executive side, some were viewed with frank suspicion. There was a feeling that Congress was not getting a straight story or, at the very least, that Congress was not getting an independent story. When the Economic Opportunity Act was amended in 1967, Congress included specific provisions for the General Accounting Office to evaluate activities carried out by the Office of Economic Opportunity and other measures authorized under the EOA. Those results, reported in 1969, were in fact instrumental in rescuing some parts of the OEO programs from the axe of Richard Nixon and Howard Phillips.

On the executive side, the era of transition from a policy of federal activism to attempts at retrenchment was also interesting for what it showed about how evaluations were used for more than straight knowledge development. While Congress was taking evaluation more seriously as a check on the word of the executive branch, it became apparent that evaluations were also being used as an executive tool for supporting administration policy. This became especially noticeable by contrast after Lyndon Johnson, architect of the Great Society, left office to be succeeded by Richard Nixon, elected on a platform critical of the social initiatives, their functions, and performance. Suddenly the Job Corps, a positive experiment under LBJ, was a program of dubious merit. Head Start became a misdirected effort, and the entire concept of Legal Services and Community Action for the poor was considered counterproductive if not un-American. In the atmosphere of confrontation and conflict between the two branches, evaluators and experimental manipulators became the manipulated. The impact evaluations had was shaped largely by who ordered them and when the results surfaced. The debate over income support policies for the poor is a good illustration.

## THE CASE OF THE FAMILY ASSISTANCE PLAN

In order to test the impact of a guaranteed income on work behavior, OEO authorized in 1967 a sophisticated social experiment to test a variety of strategies, mixing different combinations of support levels and marginal tax rates. Social scientists were given a fairly free rein in setting up the project, running it, and gleaning lessons from it. But political reality obtruded quickly. In 1969, after the project had been underway less than a year, President Nixon proposed his own Family Assistance Plan that included a negative income tax feature. The Nixon administration turned to the New Jersey Graduated Work Incentive program for some empirical evidence on the relationship between guaranteed income and work behavior. When preliminary and questionable findings of the New Jersey experiment were leaked to the Senate Finance Committee to support FAP, supporters of the concept were quick to capitalize on those results that were so tentative as to be meaningless and were later found by GAO to be largely manufactured. While those favoring the president's proposal took advantage of very suspect evidence to support his position then, the administration chose to ignore later results that were both positive and more conclusive when Nixon's interest in FAP cooled off.

At about the time FAP was proposed, Congress, wanting an opinion of its own, set up its own evaluation team. Based in the Fiscal Policy Subcommittee of the Joint Economic Committee, that team worked three-and-a-half years on *Studies in Public Welfare*. While it might not be considered a true evaluation by some, *Studies* is a well-documented review of alternative income maintenance strategies and an analysis of what was considered the important issues in welfare policy. Although the report came down favoring income support strategies, it failed to spur legislation in that direction. It laid out the alternative approaches to welfare reform in detail that was too gruesome to be politically palatable. In the face of such discouraging prospects, the status quo won out, and nothing changed.

## AND OTHER EXAMPLES

At the beginning of President Nixon's second term, evaluators again fell prey to larger forces in another policy initiative of that administration. After deciding to cut back support of low-income housing measures, the administration ordered a review of those efforts, examining their effectiveness. The result, *Housing in the Seventies,* was used to justify a nearly complete suspension of housing programs for the poor and a moratorium on new measures. Congress moved its own evaluation machinery into position to respond. After oversight hearings and its own analysis of the administration position, the conclusion was that the administration assessment was a hatchet job. The final result was a congressional mandate for new housing initiatives in the form of the Housing and Community Development Act of 1974.

In another case Congress stepped in when the National Institute of Education continued to ignore the positive results of evaluations it was supporting, because the findings ran counter to administration policy. Claiming that the executive branch was thwarting the will of Congress, the Senate Appropriations Committee cut the proposed appropriation to NIE for fiscal year 1977 down to zero. Although the budget was subsequently restored, the conflict pointed up again the ambivalent connection between evaluation findings and policy.

## WEAPONS IN A WAR

The tone of mutual distrust that has tainted the executive-legislative relations in obvious ways since the war in Vietnam began to sour has been important in contributing to the growth of the evaluation trade. But one gets the sensation that evaluation is being provided for, not to collect "objective" evidence but as weapons in a war over constitutional prerogatives and party dominance. While Congress has been building in more and more requirements for executive departments and agencies to evaluate its efforts, Congress has taken measures to vastly increase its own capabilities. The Legislative Reorganization Act of 1970 called upon GAO to upgrade its evaluation capabilities so it could provide substantive assessments of the results of executive branch programs. This was to be over and above simply financial and management auditing. But the most dramatic measure came after tensions between the two branches approached a breaking point part way through President Nixon's second term. Congress, frustrated by executive intransigence and unreliable assessments of program results, preyed on a President weakened by Watergate and continuous losing struggles over impoundments to pass the Congressional Budget and Impoundment Control Act of 1974. Aimed at improving the fiscal responsibility of Congress, the measure included provisions for upgrading the evaluation capabilities on the Hill. Besides pushing GAO even more in the direction of performing substantive evaluation and policy analysis, the act created the Congressional Budget Office for doing some serious program and policy evaluation of its own. At the same time, the Congressional Research Service found itself involved more and more in evaluation activities, doing either its own reviews or critiquing those of others.

Although there are legitimate differences in perspective and different information needs that justify separate evaluation efforts for each branch, other reasons seem to have motivated the actions Congress has taken to upgrade its evaluation capabilities. It remains to be seen if policy makers will take their cues from evaluators, or if evaluators will take their cues from policy makers.

It is tempting to view all evaluation activities at the top policy-making level with a cynical eye, but there is a real danger of overlooking the less manipulative forces behind them. Some evaluation efforts are honestly undertaken with the hope that they will define the real policy issues and will make public debate more informed. The extensive provisions for evaluation under the new youth legislation signed into law only two months ago is a good case in point. The law recognizes the bankruptcy of past policies in effectively dealing with youth unemployment. Taking a shotgun approach that authorizes a broad range of experimental projects, the law makes generous allow-ances for evaluation work in an extensive search for effective solutions. But what the law also reveals is the bipolar nature of the general strategies. As programs fall into place, constituencies will begin to form and a polarizing process will begin. As much as most parties involved now say they look forward to evaluation findings, it remains to be seen whether evaluation findings will receive a genuine hearing from the Congress and the executive agencies. To the extent that political inter-ests cluster around different experimental approaches, evaluators will find stiff competition for a place on the congressional hearings agenda and in the Department of Labor policy circles. But to the extent that those political interests also approximate a larger social welfare func-tion, the evaluation role might be seen as superfluous. To the extent that political interests diverge from the public interests as the evaluator sees them, the evaluator may be no more than a voice in the night that no one hears.

# 3

## GOVERNMENT CONSTRAINTS
## ON EVALUATION QUALITY

Clark C. Abt

A basic question for evaluation research sponsors, consumers, and scientist-producers is, how are costs and benefits to be estimated in evaluating research on social programs? The answers given will depend a lot on one's involvement with the public good or the private good or the government good, which most emphatically is not necessarily identical with the public good. The government good is also not the same as good government. It is rather the private good of people in government. In fact, the subtitle of this essay might be: "There's a Right Way to Do Evaluation Research, a Wrong Way to Do Evaluation Research, and There's the Government's Way to Do Evaluation Research."

Ultimately optimistic, I believe that the good of each group is linked to the good of the other two. This should be particularly true in a participatory, pluralistic democracy where many of us change roles from public to private to government activities at frequent intervals.

## WHOSE GOOD?

The question of "whose good?" really pertains to the question in benefit/cost analysis of whose benefit and whose cost, and the awareness of that has changed the entire way we have been doing benefit/cost analysis in the last few years. It depends on how one's loyalties are distributed among people, science, one's concept of the public interest, the incumbent government research sponsors, and the research managers in and out of government. An experience for medicine provides an example.

One would think that the benefits and costs estimated by a surgeon for the patient would be consonant with those of the patient, but if you read, for example, some of the particular studies in a very interesting book, *The Benefits, Risks, and Costs of Surgery,* by Bunker, Barnes, and Mosteller, you will find example after example of different constituencies to the medical therapy having very different perceptions and estimates of the benefits and costs. I was first struck by this in a seminar on this topic when a distinguished surgeon who had seemed to me to be very benevolent up to that point pointed out that if a female patient of his had a mother and a sister who had had breast cancer, he would immediately strongly urge a prophylactic radical bilateral mastectomy.

That shocked some us; but when we explored it with him, it turned out that from the point of view of maximizing what he perceived were the patient's benefits and costs, that is, in *his* view, pure *duration* of life, he was being quite rational, because even relatively frequent (semiannual) screening is unlikely to catch some of the most virulent cancers which seem to be highly heritable. So he was not concerned at all about *quality* of life for the patient. Now from the patient's point of view, a different decision would probably have been made.

It has been pointed out that one of the problems of applying benefit/cost paradigms is that there are many constituencies in most social programs, and they have many different conceptions of benefits and costs. Not only are there the different current constituencies, but it has also been suggested that there are the intergenerational effects, people who have secondary impacts, and nonmarket effects that are very difficult to capture. What, then, is the applicability of benefit/cost paradigms to social program evaluation research in the United States today?

# MULTIPLE CONSTITUENCIES

There are multiple constituencies for program benefits and costs. Because these multiple constituencies require multiple analyses for the making of internally and externally valid inferences, benefit/cost analyses must be more complex and costly than they were previously thought to be. There are usually at least four distinct federal government constituencies: the presidential administration, the legislative (Congress), the bureaucracy of administering and sponsoring agencies, and the judicial system. Multiply this by relevant state and local government involvements, and add the crucially important several impacted citizen groups and the involved research communities; and there are usually between ten and twenty major constituencies who each have legitimate views of costs and benefits to be addressed.

If this is so, and if evaluation coverage of major social programs is very incomplete as it is now, evaluation quantity or productivity, or probably both, have to be increased because of the human resource limitation on doing a sufficiently valid job to be useful.

# EVALUATION PRODUCTIVITY

Productivity of most evaluation research (and this is almost conventional wisdom now) is low. Estimates of the valid and relevant research in the field range from 5% to 20% of it, depending on how you picked your sample and how tough your criteria are and how optimistic or pessimistic you are. Comparing ourselves with basic researchers—and we have reason to do so—those numbers look pretty good. It depends in part on one's relative weighting of validity and relevance. However, comparing ourselves with engineers or professional practitioners of an applied art, those numbers look terrible. We can and should increase that productivity from its current very modest level, even if comparison studies of other professions' research (e.g., legal research, accounting research) were to reach even more pessimistic findings.

Low *average* evaluation research quality and productivity are the result of external constraints—principally the government policies and regulations that impose perverse incentives and unnecessary costs on the process of producing evaluation research, reducing the net benefits from it to the public, the government, and the private practitioners, and, indeed, probably reducing the government's net benefits less directly.

## GOVERNMENT CONSTRAINTS

Government constraints on the freedom of evaluation research are a kind of self-fulfilling prophecy, and they will continue to depress quality and quantity until they are modified in some way.

Validity and productivity of evaluation research will probably not increase significantly, other factors remaining more or less stable, until both the quality and quantity increase, and that can be done most efficiently and with greatest political feasibility by reforming the research procurement policies and processes actively involving researchers themselves, rather than simply increasing budgets.

Government misregulation of evaluation research currently distorts the ideal balance between basic research, applied research, and evaluation research which partakes of both kinds. Government overregulation has been trying to shift practically all research activities into a mold of applied research, or even beyond applied research to almost a production mold, at the cost of quality and validity and productivity and finally even relevance. Many of us involved in government evaluation research are accustomed to trying to produce basic research on an engineering production schedule and budget, with some of the attendant difficulties. Now let me go into some of those specific difficulties and suggest a few ways in which they might be addressed.

## LACK OF FLEXIBILITY

Here are some of the costs that reduce evaluation research productivity for the government. First, there is a great lack of *flexibility*. Most evaluation research *must* be incompletely defined at the start, because one simply does not know exactly what will be done and needs to be done until the research is under way. Specifically, early definition is limited by a short design period and inaccessibility of descriptive data, which is the most important input into design. All research should be sequential, yet government wants it to proceed in the fashion in which articles are written in a textbook approach: problem-method-results-conclusion. Interim findings produce new questions and the need for applying new analyses and new techniques. Yet the entire contracting process works against the flexibility which that situation requires, and the contract administration system works against the need for frequent technical redirection. This hardly could be what the government really wants, and the benefits of this in terms of an alleged fiscal control seem less real and more illusory.

## INEFFICIENT OVERREGULATION

Another unnecessary cost is *inefficient overregulation.* Constraints on research contracting are quite enormous, and they may reduce the amount of good research done. There are long lists of special provisions, general provisions, audit tests, contracting officer approvals, and they are generally enforced by contracting officers who have a broad range of experience and training and who are very competent in their own art—usually dedicated and serious but untrained in research. This has the effect of raising a researcher's administrative costs, whether that research is done under grants or contracts, in universities or independent research organizations, and of reducing the time available by the researcher for technical work.

Even worse, few of these constraints address the overall efficiency or productivity of the work, because they were not really intended for the kind of research that is being administered. The procurement regulations that surround research contracting are drawn from the military material procurement system, and the federal procurement regulations are based on decisions of a board of people who are made up of Army, Navy, and Air Force procurement officials, quite untrained in the social sciences and inexperienced in the production and application of social science research, most of them with hardware engineering backgrounds. Yet this is the way that the research is administered.

All of this pertains to the issue of contracting for changes in the research as it proceeds. If those changes are very difficult to pursue, or are only pursued at great risk or great cost, there tends to be a very rigid process that cannot maximize the production of knowledge, which is the real product, or maximize the ratio of produced relevant knowledge to cost, which is the relevant measure of productivity.

Social science research delivers a knowledge product, not a piece of hardware, and needs to be managed from that point of view. There are typically constraints in the overwhelming majority of evaluation research procurements on the scope, content, and methodology of the research employed. Not just the total cost is constrained, as would be reasonable from a budgeting point of view, but also the *types* of costs and the *methods* employed. Everything is so very hemmed in that if a researcher is not to incur very substantial risks of not being able to cover costs or not being held in default, every change must be negotiated formally and worked out in writing. After a while, typical large evaluation research project directors spend something on the order of a quarter to a half of their time administering rather than researching, and that is a much larger fraction than is optimally productive of excellent research (especially given that the government likes scientist project directors).

## SENSIBLE WAYS OF REDUCING COSTS

The cost of doing evaluation research could be reduced by augmenting currently insufficient government management resources. Government contracting shops are understaffed to handle the load that proper contract administration entails. Even if evaluation researchers make the investment, there are great delays on the government side. Those who have had the experience pushing questionnaires through Office of Management and Budget clearance know that that process, if one is fortunate, takes three or four weeks, but typically takes three to five months, and sometimes a year. One is usually not permitted to pretest a decent sample, nor can one collect descriptive background data to guide plans. OMB is often seen as a living nightmare by social research scientists. These are bottlenecks in the government side of the administration that are a result of insufficient quality and quantity of resources. These delays in making changes that are necessary for rapid response to pressing policy or research needs cost the government a lot of money, directly and indirectly, and, most importantly, many lost scientific opportunities and efficiencies. My own estimate ranges from

*$10 million* to *$20 million* annually, not even counting the opportunity costs of lost or delayed scientific knowledge-producing opportunities. Of course, not necessarily all of this could be saved by even ideal administration, since some government regulations are productive and essential.

## LESS RESTRICTIVE DEFINITION

Another opportunity for reducing the cost of evaluation research is to change the restrictive definition of contract changes. In large complex evaluations multiple cycles are needed, in the same way that it is usually more efficient to have a pilot survey before a major survey. Multiple successive surveys are needed, and the research techniques evolve over time with the research process, because in the beginning one cannot completely anticipate what one is going to find. But the notion of change in government research contracting is very restrictive. Despite the fact that almost every evaluation research effort of any scope undergoes many small changes in the scope of the work as the research proceeds, because that is the nature of the work, the contracting vehicle recognizes only the grossest changes in output as legitimate changes to the contract. But the really significant output of the work, new knowledge, is not what is measured, partly because the people concerned with it are not trained to be concerned with that and partly because it is intrinsically difficult to measure. We need a more appropriate definition of research contract changes that recognizes alterations in research methodology as well as changes in deliverable, concrete outputs.

## GREATER COORDINATION

There is also the problem of inefficient, long-term investment with little or no coordination among government project officers in capitalizing on past investments in social science and evaluation research. Large staffs of highly trained and experienced professionals are brought together for one to five years to work on a project at government expense, the government makes an enormous investment in building such institutional organizational capabilities, and then when the work ends, often the team is disbanded, and if that particular organization housing that evaluation research team does not happen to have a superbly competent marketing capability to maintain that team together, it gets dispersed. This works to the great disadvantage of the university contractors who naturally tend to disperse physically over precisely those periods of the year when most of the government procurements come out. It distorts the market for the research, and it certainly makes it more difficult to maintain even a few years' job security for the researchers, still far short of some kind of tenure or civil service system.

## DISTINGUISHING RESEARCHERS
## AND CONSULTANTS

Another problem is the confusion, particularly in HEW, between researchers and consultants. Researchers are not consultants, and no number of administrative regulations saying so will ever make them that. The government has consistently confused management consulting, basic research, applied social research, personal services, and other types of government contracting. There are often understandable administrative reasons for this, such as the desire to pay lower fees, but these decisions come back to haunt us because they confuse the administration of the research.

Applied social research, and particularly the major component of it, which is evaluation research, is very different from consulting. It looks different, it reads different, it is done by different people, it produces different things, and while there is perhaps a tiny overlap on the margins, it is very different; and applying the same regulations to it makes policy research and evaluation research much less useful, and also damages the evaluation research community by an insistence on lots of handholding, fast results, with relatively less emphasis on methodological validity. The kinds of things that are operationally functional values in consulting are not necessarily functionally valid in research. This is not a criticism of consulting. Consulting is just a different world with different objectives, and it is a distortion of the research process to treat evaluation research as if it were just a form of consulting.

## PARSIMONY OF QUESTIONS

There is an excessive demand by government for findings on an *excessive number* of policy issues within sample size or budget constraints that threatens internal and external validity on all the research questions posed. Government sponsors, in order to mobilize budget support for the research, often try to or feel they have to promise results to diverse research constituencies or sources of legislative mandates, multiplying the number of so-called relevant findings required from the particular piece of evaluation research. Researchers in turn are rarely successful in convincing the sponsors that fewer research questions investigated with more thoroughness and validity (that is, basically larger cell sizes), larger samples on a smaller number of questions rather than very small samples on large numbers of questions, would improve the validity of the overall evaluation within constant cost constraints, rather than risking the loss of the whole study.

## A MORE STABLE PROCUREMENT CYCLE

The procurement cycle itself, and its timing, is an unnecessary or reducible cost. The cycle is not particularly stable. It has taken a kind of second harmonic shift in the last two years, with the three months or one-quarter shift in the fiscal year, and the instability both of the cycle's phase and of its frequency imposes enormous difficulties in the proposal procurements and reviews for both the government review panels and the researchers, particularly those in universities. This distorts the distribution of research skills among organizations, in that this particular instability works very strongly against the smaller research organizations and the solo researchers in the field who do not have the organizational resources to forecast and generate reserves to cope with these instabilities in the procurement cycle. Shifting to more serial, more evenly distributed rather than parallel procurements would improve the situation.

## IMPROVING EVALUATION POLICIES

All these costs are at least crudely quantifiable. There was a recent article in *Science* magazine on the costs of government regulation of universities, which was summed up to be something on the order of $2 billion annually, or roughly the equivalent of the annual investment in universities. We have not added up the costs and benefits of government regulation of evaluation research, but we should begin to do so, because we will then identify in quantitative terms some of these points made here qualitatively. The practical result for the evaluation research community of all these unnecessary costs is a feeling of discouragement about the inability to see applications of the research, and particularly about the high incidence of rather fateful social policy decisions affecting millions of lives being made without benefit of preliminary evaluation research or even applications of already on-the-shelf research results.

The employment insecurity of the researchers associated with these costs tends to limit the attractiveness of the field for some of the best minds, because the best minds generally have many other options. If the evaluation research career option is highly unstable, unpredictable, and risky, we will lose some of our best people from it. The apparent lack of concern by many government sponsors for the maintaining of evaluation research institutional capabilities, wherever they may be, over the longterm also works in the direction of employment insecurity and the reduction in the quality of the working lives and the working output of the evaluation researchers.

Evaluation researchers can help harmonize the productivity of evaluation research in the interests of the public good, the government good, *and* the private good by three major efforts. One is by obtaining wide *research community consensus on a hierarchy of preferred research designs and methods* of relatively common, often repeated, and typical evaluation research problems and promulgating these standards so that all government sponsors and reviewers will have to recognize minimum quality standards for valid research designs for evaluations. Not only will that raise the quality of the overall competition, but it will also provide external support for those evaluation researchers who find themselves in conflict with government reviewers or sponsors over the choice of the first or second best designs and who, I might add, most often lose in the battle for good designs. A second area in which the evaluation researchers can provide great help is *to collect, assess, screen, and disseminate successful examples of effective evaluation researches* that are valid, policy-relevant, and that have had positive social impacts. A third arena for productive action is to work for the *rational reform of government research procurement* management practices.

# 4

## OBSTACLES TO EVALUATING
## STATE HUMAN SERVICE PROGRAMS

Michael Simmons

Thanks to governmental mandates, there is a growing demand for evaluative research in state human service programs. These mandates include the Medicaid Management Information System (MMIS), which can aid in evaluative research; the Early Periodic Screening and Diagnostic Testing (EPSPT) program, which requires evaluation; and federally funded demonstration grants, in which independent evaluations also are required. Evaluative research, however, is relatively new, and there are as yet few criteria governing who is qualified to conduct evaluative research or what constitutes a "standard" evaluation. More importantly, idealized models for evaluative research sometimes appear to be in conflict with existing state human service delivery systems.

This paper discusses obstacles to evaluative research in state human service programs from the perspective of the practitioner. Taking real-world situations and relating them to evaluative research needs, there are at least fourteen ways in which the ideal and the real diverge in practice.

## UNDEFINED PROGRAM GOALS
## THWART MEASUREMENT

Many state human service programs lack clearly defined program goals. Many programs simply define "eligibles" and then restrict service delivery. Objective measures might focus on the quantity of services provided or the dollars expended. These objective measures might serve as indicators of some underlying, unstated goals. It might be argued that evaluations have a rich store of techniques to elicit those unstated goals. However, even application of decision-theoretic or other approaches to goal definition by service providers prove limited in the real world of many people, many programs, little time, and less money for local program evaluations.

## EMPHASIS ON
## STATUTORY REQUIREMENTS AND REGULATION

Each state human service program has a manual considered to be the agency's bible. The manual is a conglomeration of federal statutes, state statutes, case law, administrative law, court mandates, and agency regulations. Consider, for example, the impact of HEW penalties for errors in the Aid for Families with Dependent Children (AFDC) program. There are financial penalties to states for having a high error rate, so emphasis is placed upon compliance to statutory requirements for fear of having these financial penalties levied. This implicit bureaucratic concern for productivity is reflected in greater evaluation emphasis on input and process measures which lend themselves nicely to evaluative research. This stress on input and process measures in turn neglects outcome measures which are crucial to evaluative research.

## UNDEFINED OUTCOME MEASURES

Because program goals often lack definition, outcome measures often are poorly defined. While the goal often appears to be simply to provide services to "eligibles," many would contend that the major goal should be to improve their quality of life. If so, quantitative and qualitative outcomes for quality of life would have to be defined.

## MISLEADING DATA

The primary reason for data collection in state human service programs is not evaluation. The concept of exception reporting has recently come to the forefront of large human service delivery systems. Through this methodology, exceptions to the norms are identified and dealt with administratively. Data also are collected to prepare mandated state and federal reports. In some cases, such as in Title XX programs, the collection of data is an integral part of the federal reimbursement process. While these reports may seem the height of good accountability, the bureaucratic adage "Don't believe it until you see it in black and white" often fails to apply. The content validity of data collected frequently leaves a lot to be desired.

## CHANGING RECORD-KEEPING PROCEDURES
## AND PROGRAM POLICIES

There is little stability in bureaucratic procedures. Forms are changed; definitions are changed; codes are changed; and changes are changed. The process changes as does the verification and information to be recorded. Record-keeping procedural changes have resulted in poor documentation. Additionally, program policy changes affect the interpretation of data. Given the turnover in many state human service programs, it may prove difficult, if not impossible, to receive an accurate understanding of a change which occurred.

## NONUNIFORM RECORD KEEPING PRACTICES

Large scale state human service delivery systems usually have three or four levels of bureaucracy. There are the state human services secretariat, the departmental administrators, the regional administrators, and local offices. In some cases, what is expected at one level does not filter down, or is misinterpreted by another level, resulting in different practices in different offices within the same program. Also, various programs may define what records should be kept, but are often silent regarding the specifics of how the records are to be kept. Because of the lack of standards for record maintenance, there exists a multiplicity of record-keeping systems within local offices.

## MANY REPORTS, LITTLE UTILITY

Reports generally are financial or accounting in nature. For example, a report might show expenditures in a specific month as opposed to expenditures by the months in which the services were actually rendered. Additional problems found in reports generated include: duplicate counts of recipients, duplicate counts of cases, dual operating systems or prior approval for services, and reports which are not 100% inclusionary.

## LOW AVAILABILITY OF
## IMPORTANT PROGRAM INFORMATION

It often is difficult to understand the operational specifics of state human service programs. An evaluator needs to understand why things are done and for what purpose. Since the evaluator was not privy to curbside discussions which palyed a part in policy formulation, the evaluator must seek out the actors, and then decide who is credible.

## ADMINISTRATORS DISAGREE

Since many goals lack definition, administrators are free to pursue their interpretation of goals. Additionally, a change in organizational leadership, either formal or informal, influences human service priorities. Budgetary concerns must also be considered. The impact of these and other influences is that there may be disagreement among administrators regarding where the program is going and how the program should get there.

## BASIC QUANTITATIVE DATA
## ARE NOT AVAILABLE

Basic data pertaining to the actual number of people participating in a specific program, the number of children in that program, the total cost per person participating in the program, or the turnover rate of the program are not always available. Additionally, there are cases where costs or quantity of services rendered cannot be ascertained.

## CONCURRENT PROGRAM CHANGES

A change in services provided, eligibility determination, reporting practices, or bureaucratic red tape in one area has an impact upon the service delivery system. For example, deletion of a specific drug from a state Medicaid program may cause an increased use of a similar drug. Viewing the service delivery system holistically, constructive efforts in one area may be detrimental or counterproductive in another area. New knowledge or new practices may also affect the delivery of services. Thus, the concept of concurrent changes extends beyond the purview of the service delivery system.

## IN-HOUSE RESEARCH
## VERSUS THE BUREAUCRACY

State initiated studies are limited and usually respond to federal reporting mandates or the receipt of a federal grant. State human service programs also have a problem of attracting quality personnel skilled in evaluative research. When such a professional accepts an in-house research position, he or she is inevitably spread thin. The desire to follow pure research techniques might come into conflict with the bureaucracy's status quo, and results of studies may be suppressed due to bureaucratic politics.

### BEFORE-AND-AFTER
### AND AFTER-ONLY MODELS

Services are provided statewide. Although possibly legal, experimentation in the manner of delivery of services in one part of a state is unacceptable to the bureaucracy. Measurement thus focuses upon before-and-after and after-only models, attempting to ascertain some change. Cost-benefit analysis, cost-effective analysis, attitudinal measures, and quality of service indicators are often not feasible.

### INCOMPATIBILITY OF
### STATE HUMAN SERVICE PROGRAMS

Ideally, data from one state human service program where there was a policy change could be compared to data of a state where there was not a policy change. Assuming that the states are identified to approximate each other demographically, within the same human service program there are differences in policies, in who is eligible to receive services, in who is actually receiving services, in what services are provided, in what services are not provided, in definitions for data, in the way in which data are collected, and in the rendering of specific services. Needless to say, inter-state comparisons are often not feasible.

### THE NEED FOR CHANGE

Since human service programs lack definition of goals and specificity of the data necessary to conduct evaluative research, minimum changes required to remove the aforementioned obstacles to evaluation research include: definition of program goals; definition of quantitative and qualitative outcome measures; collection of data useful for evaluative research; standardization of all record-keeping practices; and emphasis upon the quality of human service delivery. These changes will not happen overnight. In the meantime, obstacles to evaluative research in state human service programs should be understood when analyzing existing data and considered in the development of future research designs.

# SECTION II
## IMPROVING EVALUATION DESIGNS

# 5

## EXPANDING OUR VIEW OF
## CONTROL GROUPS IN EVALUATIONS

### Leonard Saxe and Michelle Fine

A central issue in evaluation research has been the conduct of social programs as "true" experiments (e.g., Campbell, 1969, 1971). Much of the discussion of true experimental methods has dealt with the importance of this methodology and the ways to implement the necessary randomized control group procedures (e.g., Cook and Campbell, 1976; Riecken and Boruch, 1974). While some literature has advocated true experimental methods, other literature has been critical of using these methods for program evaluations (e.g., Guttentag, 1973, 1977). This debate over methodologies threatens to become more heated, causing a division among evaluators who are experimentalists and those who are not. Such an outcome seems unnecessary. Evaluation research should be able to accommodate multiple methodological approaches; in fact, it may only be through the use of multiple research strategies that program evaluation's role in social policy formation can be realized.

Although the use of experimental methods (i.e., of randomized control group procedures) to study social programs is not a totally new idea (see Chapin, 1947), their application has become increasingly important. Much of the recent impetus for the development of such experimental procedures in program evaluation has derived from the work of Donald Campbell (e.g., 1969) and his colleagues (e.g., Campbell and Boruch, 1975; Cook and Campbell, 1976; Conner, 1977). Campbell's well-known position that true experimental methods provide the most unequivocal assessments of program efficacy have been supported by a variety of conceptual and pragmatic arguments. At the conceptual level, the power of randomized control group designs in establishing causality between specific social programs and outcomes has been demonstrated through the development of validity criteria (see Cook and Campbell, 1976). At a pragmatic level, it has been shown that true experiments are not difficult to conduct—either in terms of time or resources—and often can take account of naturally occurring events, such as the scarcity of a treatment (see Boruch, 1976).

Criticism of randomized control group procedures in evaluation research has included both epistemological and pragmatic arguments (e.g., Guttentag, 1973, 1977; House, 1976; Sjoberg, 1975; Stufflebeam, 1969; Weiss and Rein, 1970). A principal objection is that the application of basic research methods (such as randomized control groups) does not facilitate decision making about evolving social programs, the raison d'être of evaluation research. Social programs, according to this view, cannot be conceptualized as simple independent variables, and experiments on such programs cannot be carried out in a timely or unobtrusive enough way to provide policy-relevant data. A variety of solutions are proposed, including the use of statistical decision models. Critics of social experimentation suggest—although it is not so bluntly stated—that the experimental and nonexperimental methodologies are basically incompatible with one another.

In contrast, our view is that the variety of methods available to evaluation researchers (see Anderson and Ball, 1978)—true experimental, quasi-experimental, survey, statistical, and so on—are fully compatible with one another. The choice of methodology should depend on the context of the program and the required decision needs. It should be possible to use methodologies either singly or together as part of the evaluation of a particular program. For some decision-making purposes, one type of methodology might be employed; and for other decision-making purposes, other methods might be used. For multiple decision purposes, multiple methods might be used within the same program evaluation.

# MULTIPLE METHOD APPROACH

**Overview**. Adopting such a heteromethodological approach is useful, as Boruch (1975) has noted, because it will lead to improvements in evaluation designs. It also moots the dispute between those who advocate experimental and those who advocate nonexperimental methodologies. Boruch, whose ideas were developed independently of our own, has presented a series of ways that true experimental methods can be used in conjunction with other procedures. The focus here is on what Boruch has called "component-wise experiments." In program evaluations using such designs, a quasi-experiment is conducted in conjunction with a series of true experiments to test program components.

We will use the term *macro evaluation* to refer to the use of nonrandomized control group techniques to assess the overall efficacy of a program. The term *micro evaluation* will refer to the use of randomized control group experiments developed to test hypotheses about central components of a program. When applied in conjunction with one another, macro and micro evaluation studies can provide a complete, yet practical, assessment of a program for multiple decision purposes.

**Integration of methods**. This approach to evaluation can be viewed as integrative. Its goal is to generate data both about the construct of the program (i.e., is the "idea" worth pursuing?) and about operational aspects of the program (i.e., is it well implemented?). The integration allows one to satisfy scientific demands for control (through the micro studies) without forfeiting the collection of nonexperimental data about the program (through macro studies). In practice, the macro study can assume the form of a time series design (in simple cases, a pre-post design) functioning to monitor the program from inception through termination. It provides decision makers with direct information about the operation of a program. The micro studies take the form of a series of highly controlled experiments which test the efficacy of particular components of the program. These data ultimately are generalizable both within and beyond the confines of the actual program being assessed. They help to establish its construct validity.

One basic assumption is that the macro-micro level assessments should be conducted in a formative rather than purely summative fashion (see Scriven, 1967), each feeding into the other. The goal of both types of studies is to understand the processes underlying the effectiveness (or ineffectiveness) of the program. Problems identified by the macro evaluation may be examined more scientifically in a micro study. Similarly, findings from the micro studies may reveal possible program problems, suggest the need for programmatic changes, or highlight a necessary shift in emphasis of the macro investigation. In such an action research model, data from the two levels feed into each other in a cyclical fashion in order to identify those program elements requiring revision or special attention.

The data developed from the macro and micro studies should not be viewed as orthogonal. They interact to identify those aspects of the program worthy of investigation by the alternative form of analysis. Macro results may stimulate a series of micro studies designed to examine, in greater detail, a particular component of the program. Micro-generated results may suggest a restructuring of the macro-level assessment to examine a more subtle feature of the program. The two levels are thus clearly interdependent modes of analysis.

**Using the approach.** A variety of evaluation problems can be dealt with using this multiple-method approach. For example, program developers often fall prey to the temptation to revise a program immediately upon noticing a fluctuation in programmatic performance (Riecken and Boruch, 1974). An acute fluctuation in performance, as might become apparent in a macro-level analysis, is all too often the instigation for a program modification. The multiple-method approach provides the opportunity for program developers to test experimentally the source of this problem before implementing a program change. The macro-micro model gives evaluators the option of exploring the basis of these fluctuations, under controlled conditions, to determine whether the problem is acute or chronic.

Consider also the difficulty of determining which factors are responsible for program ineffectiveness. The conduct of macro and micro studies should be very informative here, even when the results differ. Such incongruities may pinpoint the variables which are not functioning as hypothesized and lead to appropriate program redesign.

# A CASE EXAMPLE

As an example of the use of this multiple-method approach, consider the following problem. An interactive (two-way) telecommunications system (ITS) has been implemented at five hospitals located in a large rural area. The goal of the ITS is to facilitate communication between health professionals (physicians, nurses, and so on) who normally practice in isolation from their peers. It is hoped that two-way television will enable frequent, effective communication equivalent to that which results from face-to-face encounters. Case conferences and continuing education seminars as well as actual patient care can be facilitated by the system.

In order to generate information for implementing this system effectively and for developing generalizable knowledge about the use of interactive communication systems, an evaluation study has been planned. The evaluation will focus on the hardware of the system (i.e., the effectiveness of the cameras, transmission equipment, and the like) and the software developed for the ITS, as well as the implementation of the hardware and software. Lest the impression be given that evaluating ITS represents a trivial problem, such systems cost from $1 to $5 million. Of the twenty or so networks funded by the federal government, only a few can be characterized as even moderately successful (see Bashshur, Armstrong, and Youssef, 1975).

In terms of an evaluation of the ITS, it is impossible to use a fully randomized control group design. Neither hospital selection nor user participation can be randomly assigned. The hospitals have previously been selected (on the basis of location and internal resources), and in-hospital sampling of ITS participants is precluded because of the nature of the program. The multimethod approach was designed to accommodate these structural constraints on random assignment.

In the past, evaluation studies of interactive telecommunications systems have typified either macro or micro studies. The Practical Concepts (1973) study of the Dartmouth INTERACT system illustrates a macro evaluation of an interactive telecommunications system. Although there were a number of components to this study, the design was nonexperimental. It involved the collection of user satisfaction data during the several-year operation of the system. The important outcome of this study was a set of recommendations about how the system could be better managed.

Micro studies, far fewer in the evaluation literature, may be discussed in the context of a telecommunications experiment conducted by Zinser (1975). She studied a satellite-connected interactive telecommunications system designed to interconnect a number of health facilities. As part of this study, randomly selected groups either used the telecommunications system or met face-to-face to solve specific problems. Zinser's study indicated minimal differences, in terms of overt behaviors, between the telemediated and face-to-face interaction conditions. On one of the sets of variables which yielded differences (frequency of greetings, complimenting and reassuring), telemediated communications yielded a greater frequency than occurred in the face-to-face situation. While this study supports the idea that two-way television communication is as effective as face-to-face interaction, Zinser's findings are statistically problematic and are possibly dependent on the specific conditions of her experimental situation. Also, since they were not directly compared with the actual implementation of the interactive telecommunication system, their generalizability is difficult to ascertain.

Several important distinctions can be made between these examples of macro and micro study approaches. The two differ in sample and population parameters, level of control over extraneous variables, extensivity of research findings, generalizability and potential utilization of the results. The INTERACT evaluation, a macro study, assessed total program performance. The evaluators assumed a monitoring posture rather than the role of experimenter engaged in manipulating and controlling environmental variables. The results adequately describe the program, but fail to explain why the program did not have the desired effects. Such macro-generated data are somewhat "dirty" (i.e., low on internal validity). While they provide some useful program-specific feedback, their generalizability beyond the immediate context is not easy to ascertain.

A micro study, in contrast, concentrates on the assessment of specific components of the program. In Zinser's case, this had to do with the potential for communicating information and affect via two-way television. By assessing differences between randomly assigned groups of individuals under highly controlled experimental conditions, a central component of the program is tested. Whether program components (e.g., the software) work together is a question that can only be answered by further micro, as well as macro, evaluation.

The macro and micro studies, in an integrative model, complement one another by providing data distinct in their implications and applicability. In the present example, a macro evaluation design could be developed for assessment of the ITS impact: pre-, during-, and postimplementation measures, collected without imposition of control over, or limitation of, ITS use.

Although such a design could capture changes over time in physician and health care worker communications, it would be difficult to sort out the cause of these changes. The micro studies could be developed to test particular hypotheses about the efficacy of interactive television as a medium for communication between various users (e.g., physicians, patients, teams of health workers) and for various purposes (e.g., patient education, case diagnoses, conferences, bedside visits). The objective of these micro studies would be to determine the extent to which telemediated communications function in ways similar to or different from face-to-face and other communications. These studies would provide no direct data about the efficacy of the particular ITS program being evaluated. However, by determining the theoretical potential of the communication medium, the micro studies would provide an important basis of comparison for the macro studies. They would permit researchers to distinguish technological and behavioral issues from those based on how the system has been implemented.

There are several possibilities for interpreting the results of these multiple investigations. If the results of micro studies are "successful" (i.e., they show that telemediated communications are as effective as other modes) and the results of the macro study are not successful (i.e., users do not seem to utilize ITS effectively), then the problem probably involves how the system was implemented. If both the macro and micro studies indicate that the program is unsuccessful, then the technology probably is at fault and has to be improved before any further large scale testing is undertaken.

## CONCLUSION

The multiple-methodological approach advocated here should not be seen as inimical to evaluation practice. Many programs subjected to evaluation have been developed on the basis of small-scale experimental research, and evaluation research sometimes stimulates more basic research. Although our suggestion to conduct micro as well as macro evaluation studies may appear to be a thinly disguised call to return to the unidisciplinary basic research model (see Fine and Saxe, 1978), this is not the intent. What is suggested is that the typical basic-to-applied research process be modified so that basic research studies can be conducted as part of program evaluations. We are proposing a revitalization of the Lewinian (1951) ideal of research, where research is conceptualized as a cyclical process between the laboratory and the field, and between theory and action. If achieved, this type of evaluation research can only lead to better understanding of our social world and the prospect of better social policy.

# REFERENCES

ANDERSON, S. B. and S. BALL (1978) The Profession and Practice of Program Evaluation. San Francisco: Jossey-Bass.

BASHSHUR, R. L., P. A. ARMSTRONG, and Z. I. YOUSSEF [eds.] (1975) Telemedicine: Explorations in the Use of Telecommunications in Health Care. Springfield, IL: Charles C. Thomas.

BORUCH, R. F. (1976) "On common contentions about randomized field experiments," pp. 158-194 in G. V. Glass (ed.) Evaluation Studies Annual Review, Vol., 1.

——— (1975) "Coupling randomized experiments and approximations to experiments in social program evaluation." Sociological Methods & Research 4: 35-57.

CAMPBELL, D. T. (1971) "Methods for the experimenting society." Presented at the meetings of the American Psychological Association, September.

——— (1969) "Reforms as experiments." American Psychologist 24: 409-429.

——— and R. F. BORUCH (1975) "Making the case for randomized assignment to treatments by considering the alternatives: six ways in which quasi-experimental evaluations in compensatory education tend to underestimate effects," pp. 195-285 in C. A. Bennett and A. A. Lumsdaine (eds.) Evaluation and Experiment: Some Critical Issues in Assessing Social Programs. New York: Academic Press.

CHAPIN, F. S. (1947) Experimental Design in Sociological Research. New York: Harper.

CONNER, R. F. (1977) "Selecting a control group: an analysis of the randomization process in twelve social reform programs." Evaluation Quarterly 1: 195-244.

COOK, T. D., and D. T. CAMPBELL (1976) "The design and conduct of quasi-experiments and true experiments in field settings," pp. 223-326 in M. D. Dunnette (ed.) Handbook of Industrial and Organizational Psychology. Chicago: Rand McNally.

FINE, M. and L. SAXE (1978) "Evaluation research and psychology: towards synthesis. Presented at the meetings of the American Psychological Association, Toronto, August.

GUTTENTAG, M. (1977) "Evaluation and society." Personality and Social Psychology Bulletin 3: 31-40.

––– (1973) "Evaluation of social intervention programs." Annals of the New York Academy of Science 218: 3-13.

HOUSE, E. R. (1976) "Justice in evaluation." pp. 75-100 in G. V. Glass (ed.) Evaluation Studies Review Annual, Vol. I. Beverly Hills; Sage.

LEWIN, K. (1951) Field Theory in Social Science. New York: Harper & Row, 1951.

Practical Concepts (1973) Interactive television: A Study of Its Effectiveness as a Medical Education Resource in the Rural Northeast (NLM Contract N01-LM-3-4719). Washington, DC: Practical Concepts.

RIECKEN, H. W. and R. F. BORUCH [eds.] (1974) Social Experimentation: A Method for Planning and Evaluating Social Interventions. New York: Academic Press.

SCRIVEN, M. (1967) "The methodology of evaluation." in R. W. Tyler, R. M. Gagne and M. Scriven (eds.) Perspectives on Curriculum Evaluation. AERA Monograph Series on Curriculum Evaluation, No. 1. Chicago: Rand McNally.

SJOBERG, G. (1975) "Politics, ethics, and evaluation research." pp. 29-51 in M. Guttentag and E. L. Streuning (eds.) Handbook of Evaluation Research, Vol. 2. Beverly Hills; Sage.

STUFFLEBEAM, D. L. (1969) "Evaluation as enlightenment for decision-making," in Association for Supervision and Curriculum Development (eds.) Educational Assessment and an Inventory of Effective Behavior. Washington, DC: National Education Association.

WEISS, R. S. and M. REIN (1970) "The evaluation of broad-aim programs: experimental design, its difficulties, and an alternative." Administrative Science Quarterly 15: 97-109.

ZINSER, E. (1975) "The assessment of technical feasibility, studio direction, communication patterns and user acceptance at teleconsultation via satellite—a methodology and results." Presented at the Second Telemedicine Workshop, Tucson, December.

# 6

## NONEXPERIMENTAL EVALUATION RESEARCH: CONTRIBUTIONS OF CAUSAL MODELING

Peter M. Bentler and J. Arthur Woodward

Perhaps no research challenge currently facing the social sciences is more difficult than evaluating complex social programs. As noted many times (e.g., Cronbach, 1977), a source of this difficulty is that evaluation is not entirely a scientific activity. While it is true that evaluation research involves an important nonscientific interplay between social and political realities, the scientific method does constitute an essential link in the chain of activities leading to useful understanding of the social program. Therefore, the problem of matching research technologies to the unique problems posed by evaluation research must be solved as an integral part of the maturation of this new discipline of the social sciences.

A rapidly growing body of new research methodology appears to have great relevance to problems faced in evaluation research. Current writings in the field of evaluation yield hardly a hint of the existence of

AUTHORS' NOTE: This investigation was supported in part by a research grant (DA01070) from the U. S. Public Health Service. The assistance of Bonnie Barron, Byerly Woodward, and Janet Hetland is gratefully acknowledged.

the newly developing causal modeling technologies; indeed, even the technical psychometric literature is relatively devoid of these new developments (see Bentler and Weeks, 1979a). This chapter discusses the relevance of causal modeling research methodologies to evaluation research, reviews in a nontechnical manner a series of causal modeling techniques for both quantitative and qualitative measures, and concludes with an example applying structural equation models to data from a summer Head Start program. This nontechnical introduction is intended as only a first step toward assessing causal modeling in evaluation research. Ultimately, of course, the importance of these new methods must be demonstrated in convincing, large-scale applications to ongoing social program evaluations in the complicated political context facing the evaluator.


## CAUSAL MODELING AND EVALUATION RESEARCH

While conceptualizations, strategies, political orientations, and methodological philosophies abound in evaluation research (e.g., Bennett and Lumsdaine, 1975; Cook and Campbell, 1976; Guttentag and Struening, 1975; Riecken and Boruch, 1974; Rossi and Williams, 1972; Guttentag, 1977; Abt, 1976), two general views of evaluation have strong adherents (Ross and Cronbach, 1976). In the first, or "mainstream", view of evaluation, the evaluator acts somewhat like an impartial scientist and, within the constraints of the situation, provides a report based on objective data analysis. This mainstream view would seem to be consistent with the use of relatively standard methodological techniques growing out of a "statistical mill" that "grinds the Measures to a fineness the Gods of Methodology decree and produces a Conclusion if not a Causal Inference" (Ross and Cronbach, 1976: 17). In the "extended" view of evaluation research proposed by Ross and Cronbach, the interchanges among evaluator, program developer, politician, bureaucrat, and client are complex, with design, dependent variables, data collection, and analytic methods continually being modified in accord with the realities of the situation. Standard quantitative methods would seem to be less relevant to this latter view. Although the mainstream view itself faces difficult methodological issues, such as regression artifacts, the extended view is in particular danger of breaking loose from scientific moorings to drift in turbulent waters of subjectivity and politics. Almost certainly, the analysis of response-response relations will dominate over the analysis of stimulus-response relations (e.g., Bergmann and Spence, 1944; Cronbach, 1957, 1975), leaving objective conclusions and potential causal inferences beyond the reach of "extended view" evaluation research programs. In contrast to these views, a strong emphasis on construct validation (Cronbach and Meehl, 1955) of project-specific models or miniature theories, along with a relevant statistical methodology, could be an essential middle-course, maintaining a useful scientific approach in the face of the complex realities.

Cronbach and Meehl introduced construct validation to broaden conceptualizations of the validation process for psychological tests and measures. Since there might never be a single, universally agreed-upon criterion for a test, multiple sources of data have to be considered in arriving at a decision regarding the validity of a test. In a manner similar to Margenau (1950) and Torgerson (1958), they introduced the concept of a nomological network, suggesting that latent constructs, as postulated attributes of a measured object, would have to be evaluated with respect to their interconnection to other constructs as well as to overt measurement operations. This view of construct validity has remained controversial for two decades (e.g., Bechtold, 1959; Campbell, 1960; Cronbach, 1971; Loevinger, 1957) for a variety of reasons. Among such reasons lies the fact that construct-validation was not conceived and executed within a well-defined methodology. Campbell and Fiske (1959) attempted to specify a procedure that might allow triangulation upon constructs of interest, but their multitrait-multimethod approach was highly specific to a given problem and could not deal with influences of, and on, the latent constructs themselves.

In a beautiful mesh of two quite different research traditions, the evaluation research literature has mirrored some of the Cronbach-Meehl concerns. There exists a consensus among evaluators that the variables actually being assessed in a given study may not be scientifically optimal. Generally, they will not accurately mirror a latent construct that may represent the "real" target of intervention or process of change; at the very least, they will be error contaminated, if not misleading indicators of such constructs. Although the use of such imperfect variables is a necessary state of affairs in evaluation research, and some of the implications thereof have become apparent across the years (e.g., Campbell and Erlebacher, 1970; Cronbach and Furby, 1970;

Lord, 1960), the role of theory in understanding such latent constructs has been relatively ignored, and the relevance of newer methods for making correct inferences in realistic, evaluation-research-relevant situations has not been spelled out.

Current conceptions of evaluation have not seriously integrated the notion of construct validation into a methodology capable of meeting the challenge of the practical research situation. Actually, there now exist research methods that are capable of such an integration, although a perusal of recent publications on evaluation research would not suggest this. As pointed out in one recent review, for example, "the thinking (and rhetoric) of five years ago dominates the *Handbook [of Evaluation Research]*" (Ross and Cronbach, 1976: 10). Of course, there is an inevitable time lag involved in the publication of a compendium, so that such a source can rarely mirror fully the growth of new methodologies and technical concepts of relevance to evaluation research (e.g., Bentler, 1976; Hannan and Young, 1977; Hibbs, 1977; Kessler, 1977; Lin and Werts, 1977; Overall and Woodward, 1977; Pedhazur, 1977; Shaffer, 1977; Wheaton et al. 1977). Obviously, with such rapid technical development, a typical researcher could find keeping up with the field difficult. This is particularly true in the area of causal modeling, where, in spite of the first-time appearance of introductory texts on the topic (e.g., Duncan, 1975; Heise, 1975), the presentations have become completely overtaken by the developments of new models and methods (e.g., Jöreskog, 1977; Jöreskog and Sörbom, 1976; Keesling and Wiley, 1975; Sörbom, 1974, 1978; Weeks, 1978; Bentler and Weeks, 1979). Although one can debate about the merits of various quantitative techniques for evaluation research (e.g., Guttentag, 1977), causal modeling, when integrated into a conceptual scheme involving construct validation (cf. Bentler, 1978), represents a useful technique for this field.

A causal model can be defined as the representation of a substantive theory by a structural model and a measurement model. The structural model represents the interrelations among constructs through mathematical equations, whereas the measurement model represents the interrelations between constructs and manifest variables through mathematical equations. Not only are these definitions of structural and measurement models consistent with Cronbach and Meehl's "nomological network," but they represent integral aspects of the newer causal models. It is this coincidence of concept and method that holds some promise in evaluation research: the notion of construct validation being integrated into a statistical methodology in order to understand in a meaningful way the process and effects of a given social program. Such an approach need not consider a program as a fixed independent variable, but rather as a setting of social consequence within which to formulate and evaluate social science theory.

It is noted that, among the variety of causal modeling procedures, those able to reproduce observed means based on the structural and measurement models would seem to have the greatest relevance to evaluation research. They make available program impact assessment based on data that have been "purified" of many famous error-based measurement artifacts. Since one cannot predict the nature of latent mean differences by looking at the overt data in a covariance situation, there may be some hope that the newer causal modeling methods can find experimental versus comparison group effects where prior analyses have not been able to verify them. One major contribution of these methods may be the attribution of cause in nonexperimental settings; thus, our discussion of causal modeling begins here. While such causal explanation is most generally associated with classical experimental methods involving randomization, ethical, legal, and practical circumstances make classical methods difficult in some of the most important areas of evaluation research.

## NONEXPERIMENTAL RESEARCH AND CAUSATION

True experiments provide the most acceptable means to developing theory through confirmation and rejection of hypotheses, since potentially confounding extraneous variables through randomization will be uncorrelated with treatment outcome in large samples (e.g., Fisher, 1935). In the area of evaluation research, unfortunately, true experimentation cannot always be implemented. Consequently, moving from description to explanation remains difficult at best in this field.

Every researcher who has studied statistical methods has learned that correlation does not necessarily imply causation, yet there are ways to make causal attributions from correlational data since causation implies correlation. The idea of analyzing causation by analysis of correlations was introduced fifty years ago via path analysis (Wright, 1921), but the most well-known work on inference in nonexperimental research is the

Campbell and Stanley (1963) monograph, which discusses a variety of alternative quasi-experimental designs for data gathering as well as their associated strengths and weaknesses. Different research designs will yield results with different attributes with regard to causal inference, and none approaches the virtues of the true experiment. The possibilities for alternative explanations of given results are immense in naturalistic settings since confounding sources of variation cannot be unraveled through control variables when there is an absence of theory and knowledge of sampling conditions. Still, the literature on nonexperimental designs is growing rapidly (e.g., Cook and Campbell, 1976; Kenny, 1975; Linn and Werts, 1977).

Recently, methodologists have introduced mathematical models and methods of statistical analysis, such as causal modeling, which have made it possible to test relatively complex theories in nonexperimental data. For introductory discussions of causal modeling, see Duncan (1975) or Heise (1975). The most widely known hypothesis-testing model for quantitative data is the Jöreskog-Keesling-Wiley LISREL model (Jöreskog, 1977; Wiley, 1973), which is a special case of Bentler's (1976) general structural model (see Bentler and Woodward, 1978, for a proof as well as an illustration with Head Start data). Hypothesis-testing models of a quite different sort are being developed for qualitative data. Nonexperimental data can be inspected with these techniques to determine if the data are consistent with a given theory, or whether the theory must be inadequate, given the data. While there is no methodology for proving a theory to be correct, and while multiple theories may equally well describe the data, an incorrect theory can be rejected if the data logically (theoretically) provide a reasonable test of the theory. Ideally, correlational data as well as experimental data would be relevant to the development and testing of substantive theory. However, in spite of Cronbach's (1957) two-decade-old classic plea for the integration of these two "disciplines," their integration remains a task for the future (Cronbach, 1975). It seems that the methodology for integration finally may be developing as extensions of nonexperimental hypothesis-testing procedures about data structures.

In this context, the phrase *causal modeling* denotes hypothesis testing as part of the analysis of an entire system of nonexperimental data. The word *modeling* indicates that the data analysis will have to be guided by theoretical specification, and the word *causal,* that such a specification typically is intended to explain, rather than describe, the data. In its general form, a causal model can be represented as a path diagram displaying the essential variables, latent constructs, and their interrelations as specified by a substantive theory. Figure 1 schematically represents a hypothetical structural equation model as an illustration. The boxes on the left and right are the observed variables; the x's are the independent variables, and the y's are the dependent variables. The circles represent latent or postulated constructs that are "measured" by combinations of the observed variables. The single-headed arrows denote causal influences (e.g., $\xi_1 \to x_1$ is interpreted to mean "a change in $\xi_1$ produces a change in $x_1$"). In this example, the x's are postulated to be caused by two latent constructs (e.g., the $\xi$'s) and by measurement error variates (the $\delta$'s). Likewise, the y's are postulated to be caused by two latent constructs (the $\eta$'s) and by measurement error variates (the $\epsilon$'s). These constructs and their relations with observed variables specify the measurement models for the observed independent and dependent variables.

The structural model represents the relations among the latent constructs. On the independent variate side, the latent constructs ($\xi$'s) are correlated as represented by the double arrow, whereas on the

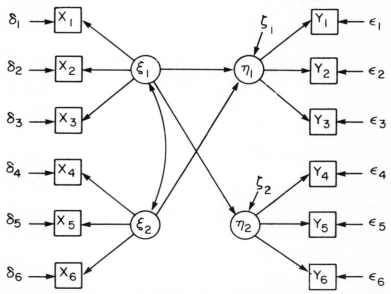

Figure 1 Illustration of a structural equation model with 12 observed variables (X's and Y's), 4 latent constructs (the $\xi$ and $\eta$'s), measurement error variates (the $\epsilon$ and $\delta$'s), and errors in equations (the $\xi$'s). The single arrows represent postulated causal influences; the double represent correlations.

dependent measure side the latent constructs ($\eta$'s) are independent of each other except for the influence of $\xi_2$ on the two $\eta$'s, which may induce a correlation between $\eta_1$ and $\eta_2$. In this example, it is postulated that $\eta_1$ is caused by $\xi_1$ and $\xi_2$, while $\eta_2$ is caused only by $\xi_1$. All measurement errors are independent of all other constructs. The errors in the structural model, labeled $\xi$, are referred to as errors in equations to distinguish them for the measurement errors $\delta$ and $\epsilon$. These variables of course also affect the $\eta$'s. Thus, a given construct is hypothesized to be caused by the various other constructs pointing at it.

It should be noted that the data of a study consist of the variances of the x's and y's, and all possible covariances. The two-headed arrows representing correlations among the variables are not drawn into the diagram, since they represent the data to be explained. A wide variety of different measurement models and structural relations among constructs can be represented as variations of this simple diagram; the substantive theory will specify, of course, the precise form. That is, the theory will specify arrows that are to be fixed at known values (e.g., at zero, in which case no arrow appears in the figure) and the arrows that represent relations whose magnitudes will be estimated from the observed data. Since these diagrams can be translated into a system of equations, standard statistical methods (e.g., least squares or maximum likelihood) can be used to determine the "best fitting" coefficients that represent the strength of postulated relations among variables and constructs, as well as the variances of all variates. The wide variety of forms possible with these models and their relevance to applied research have only now begun to be investigated.

## CAUSAL MODELING AND CONSTRUCT VALIDATION

The idea of construct validation, as introduced by Cronbach and Meehl (1955), represents an early attempt to broaden the conceptualization of the validation process for psychological tests and measures. Before Cronbach and Meehl, the major issues centered on content validity concerned with the adequacy of a universe of content for the purposes of the substantive researcher, and on criterion-oriented procedures concerned with describing relations of a test to externally chosen measures. Cronbach and Meehl expanded the notion of validation by proposing that measurement instruments must be validated in regard to correlational relationships, evidence about the internal structure of the measures, and studies of change over time. Since measures typically are designed to reflect a specific construct whose meaning ultimately must be determined from its relationships to other constructs and observable measures, construct validation was broadened to represent a continuing process that would tie down the given construct in a "nomological network." Thus, the concept of construct validation has stressed the importance of separating the notion of relationships among constructs from the notion of measurement operations. It is precisely this distinction that was picked up years later in the causal modeling literature with no reference to the construct validation origins of the idea.

In spite of the conceptual importance of construct validation, a major source of confusion and difficulty arose from the absence of an explicit operationalization of the procedure. If there were available adequate statistical methodology for construct validation, then perhaps the practical usefulness of the concepts would be enhanced.

The essence of the connection between construct validation and causal modeling is to be found in the following definitions:

(1) The construct validity of a theory refers to the empirical adequacy of a causal model, evaluated on relevant data by appropriate statistical methods;

(2) A causal model is the representation of a theory by a structural model and a measurement model;

(3) A structural model is a representation of the interrelations among constructs through mathematical equations;

(4) A measurement model is a representation of the interrelations between constructs and observed variables through mathematical equations;

(5) A construct is a postulated attribute of a measured object.

The above definitions were proposed (Bentler, 1978) because of their consistency with the writings on both construct validity and structural equation models in the social sciences. They represent a bridge between the traditional literature on construct validation and the rapidly growing causal modeling literature. Thus, the construct validity of a substantive theory refers to the adequacy of the mathematical model that interrelates various latent constructs to each other as well as to observed variables. In a given application, the researcher must be able to specify the causal model and to determine which aspects can be determined from theory (known parameters) and which aspects must be determined from the data (parameters to be estimated).

This view of construct validation extends the Cronbach-Meehl formation in one important respect; it focuses attention on the validation of a substantive theory, attending at once to the entire nomological network of relationships among constructs as well as among constructs and observed measures. The goal is to evaluate a theory. Cronbach and Meehl, on the other hand, focused greater attention on the more circumscribed goal of evaluating the construct validity of a test.

We now provide an overview of recently developed models that can be applied to the problem of making causal inferences in nonexperimental data, or to the more general problem of evaluating the construct validity of a substantative theory such as one developed in the evaluation of complex social programs. Two broad categories of models will be discussed: those appropriate for quantitative data and those designed for qualitative data. We will, of course, be highly selective, providing a review only of a few of the newer techniques.

## CAUSAL MODELS FOR QUANTITATIVE DATA

Although quantitative causal modeling is appropriate with nonlinear data as well as the simpler linear forms, the assumption of linearity has made the development of a variety of models and the relevant statistical theory much simpler. In the application of causal models to quantitative data, the researcher will have to evaluate whether the linearity assumption is reasonable in a given situation.

### CONFIRMATORY FACTOR ANALYSIS

Factor analysis seeks to resolve covariances or intercorrelations among variables into latent dimensions, or factors, that account for the intercorrelations. Consider the partial correlation of the formula $r_{12.3}$ . When $r_{12.3} = 0$, the formula produces the result $r_{12} = r_{13}r_{23}$. If this is true for some variable three in relation to variables one and two, variable three is said to explain or be consistent with the hypothesis that it "causes" variables one and two. Factor analysis generalizes this equation to $r_{ij.12\ldots m}$, sets it equal to zero, and solves for the correlation between any pair of variables i and j in terms of the latent common factors one through m. The variance not accounted for by these common factors is accounted for by the unique variances, each unique variance being composed of error variance and reliable variance unshared by other variables.

The factor analytic model utilizes a specific type of causal model. There is a measurement model, which relates the observed variables to the latent factors; its information is typically summarized in the factor loading matrix whose rank is determined by the number of factors. The structural model represents the interrelations among the latent constructs, or factors. These are symmetrical, with all factors having an equal causal status in the system. If these factors do not affect each other, the model is said to be orthogonal; if they do affect each other, reciprocally, with the direction of influence unspecified, it is said to be oblique, and the factors are correlated.

The problem posed by exploratory factor analysis, as traditionally developed, is to find a measurement structure that would be consistent with the observed data. Typically, the only hypothesis tested concerns the number of factors necessary for this task. After the number of factors is determined, the solution may be modified into an alternative, mathematically equivalent, orthogonal or oblique solution through rotation or transformation (cf. Bentler, 1977; Bentler and Wingard, 1977).

It has long been recognized that there are important hypotheses to test other than the number of factors (e.g., Anderson and Rubin, 1956); Bechtold (1958) suggested the name "confirmatory" factor analysis for this purpose. However, no statistical methodology for evaluating factor models that "restrict" parameters was available until Jöreskog (1969) published his classic paper on the topic and made a computer program available. In the confirmatory approach, one may have knowledge or hypotheses regarding a particular set of values for the factor loading parameters. Values of zero, for example, would specify that certain factors do not influence certain variables. The process of confirmatory factor analysis involves translating substantive theory into restrictions on parameters in the factor model, and then evaluating statistically whether the given causal model could account for the observed intercorrelations. If so, the model could be accepted; if not, it would be rejected, requiring modification as an appropriate mathematical description of the data. Confirmatory factor analysis represents more than an alternative way of fitting the factor model to data, since analyses that could never be represented with the exploratory model can be tested with the confirmatory approach. To illustrate, a larger number of factors with fewer numbers of parameters can be obtained than would be possible under the traditional model. Because of the wide range of possibilities, however, substantive theory must play a much greater role in guiding the analyses. If one is attempting to "discover" the factors that account for given data, the confirmatory approach is not the appropriate one; there are simply too many possibilities.

One of the most informative uses of confirmatory factor analysis lies in its ability to quantify and evaluate models for multitrait-multimethod matrices (Campbell and Fiske, 1959; Jöreskog, 1974); see Kenny (1976) for an example. It may be remembered that Campbell and Fiske proposed various rules for evaluating the role of method or trait variance in data that are obtained on similar variables measured under quite different circumstances, in order to determine the convergent and discriminant validity of the measures. With confirmatory factor analysis, a measurement model can be defined to reflect the presence of pure trait factors, pure method factors, or mixture factors. By judicious selection of fixed zeros in the factor loading matrix, various models can be tested for adequacy. Another interesting application involves testing the adequacy of various unidimensional measurement models, for example, a model involving equal error variances for the variables, leading to an appropriate model-based internal consistency coefficient (Jöreskog, 1971a). (Internal consistency based on no assumptions about dimensionality cannot be obtained by confirmatory factor analysis; see Bentler, 1972; Bentler and Woodward, 1979). A more general form of confirmatory factor analysis is to be found in models that allow the factors themselves to have a factor analytic structure. Such models are consequently higher-order factor analytic models. For example, general intelligence is often considered to be a higher-order factor, with verbal and quantitative intelligence representing first-order factors. Models and methods for such situations have been described by various authors (e.g., Bentler, 1976; Jöreskog, 1970, 1973a, 1974; Weeks, 1978).

## THREE-MODE FACTOR ANALYSIS

Tucker (1966) developed a generalization of principal components analysis to more than two modes of measurement. Typical factor analytic models deal with two-mode data, such as a matrix of data obtained by crossing a set of variables with a set of subjects. In the three-mode situation, data can be classified in three ways, such as by subjects, variables, and occasion of measurement. Consequently, a more complicated measurement structure can be postulated to account for the data. The Tucker (1966) model was developed primarily as an exploratory mode, but Bentler and Lee (1979) provided a statistical development of the model that allows it to be used as a hypothesis-testing causal model. Like other factor analytic models, the Bentler-Lee approach considers subjects to be random samples from a population of subjects, and the parameters of the model are those associated with the other two modes of measurement. These parameters can be placed into factor loading matrices and interpreted as in traditional factor analysis. In addition, however, there is a core box, which represents three-mode parameters; these are significantly fewer in number than would be found in the original three-way data. A more restricted three-mode model was also developed by Bentler and Lee (1978). It does not make use of the concept of a core box.

## FACTOR ANALYSIS WITH STRUCTURED MEANS

In the factor analytic model the variables' means are not of particular interest; they are not structured or explained by the constructs. Thus, estimation of population means is based on sample means, and the causal model deals primarily with the covariance structure. This approach is not entirely satisfactory, as in situations where there are several groups of subjects who may be drawn from populations with different means but possibly similar measurement or structural parameters. In the newer approaches, the mean and covariance structure for all groups are estimated simultaneously; consequently, estimation is somewhat more complicated. The basic work in this area is given by Jöreskog (1971b) and Sörbom (1974), with Bentler (1973) providing an alternative conceptualization of the problem as applied to longitudinal data. As noted by Bentler, in longitudinal data it might be desirable to determine whether the measurement and structural models are stationary across time, with only the means shifting.

## STRUCTURAL EQUATION MODELS

Although many disciplines have developed approaches to the simultaneous analysis of sets of interrelationships, econometrics has provided the most explicit development of causal models in which a given set of variables can be expressed as linear functions of another set of variables as well as a function of its own set. These simultaneous or structural equation models are appropriate to the analysis of data concerned with unidirectional causal influences, as well as with reciprocal causation in which each set of variables influences the others. As developed in econometrics, however, structural equation causal models were formulated at the level of overt variables, and consequently, errors in variables could introduce biasing effects leading to erroneous conclusions about the causal relations among latent constructs. Thus, the early work on structural equation models did not explicitly acknowledge the Cronbach-Meehl (1955) arguments regarding the important separation of the nomological net (i.e., the constructs' theoretical relationships) from the operational definition of manifest variables (i.e., the relation of the variables to latent constructs through measurement operations). In the context of longitudinal research, Corballis and Traub (1970) did realize that the measurement of change should be described at the level of the purified constructs, or factors, rather than at the level of overt variables, but their model is a specialized one not capable of dealing with a wide variety of causal influences. It was Jöreskog (1973b), Keesling and Wiley (1973), and Wiley (1973) who first recognized that structural equation models could be improved by distinguishing between the measurement and structural models, thus strengthening the idea that theoretical relations should be distinguished explicitly from empirical relations (e.g., Block, 1963; Rock et al., 1977). In these more general developments, the measurement model usually involves a confirmatory factor analytic model relating manifest variables to latent constructs. The latent constructs are related to each other, in turn, by linear structural equations of the econometric sort; basically, these are multivariate regression models among unobserved variables. Jöreskog, Keesling, and Wiley further realized that the entire structure consisting of both measurement and structural models represents a class of covariance structure models. Consequently, the principles and methods of estimation previously developed for covariance structure models (e.g., Jöreskog, 1970) could be applied to structural equations. Bielby and Hauser (1977) and Bentler (forthcoming) provide an overview of this class of models, which is becoming extremely popular in sociology and social psychology (cf. Bentler and Huba, 1979).

Currently, the best-known structural equation model is the Jöreskog-Keesling-Wiley (JKW) model, also known as the LISREL approach (Jöreskog, 1977). In this approach each of two sets of variables has a confirmatory factor analytic measurement structure in which a common factor of one set of variables represents a dependent variable in the linear regression on the common factors of the other set as well as on other factors in the same set. As a consequence, both sets of variables have a simple confirmatory factor structure, composed of factor loadings, factor intercorrelations, and uniquenesses, but the dependent set of variables has its factor intercorrelations represented by another, relatively complicated, structural model. The idea of such a model is that the common-factor constructs of one set of variables cause or lead to the common-factor constructs in the other set, and that reciprocal causation among factors in the dependent set is possible. Application of causal models to evaluation research can be found in Magidson (1977) and Bentler and Woodward (1978), where the cognitive effects of a summer Head Start program have been assessed within the context of a structural equation model. The application of causal modeling to the evaluation of social programs also has been carried out in the context of a desegregation study. McGarvey (1978) and Maruyama (1977) used confirmatory factor analysis and structural equation models to evaluate the effects of school integration across time. While the findings of their studies are too complex to summarize here, the attempt to use causal modeling proved useful but also showed some limitations of the currently programmed methods which cannot handle the large data sets typically found in real evaluation research settings.

This model also allows the indicators of constructs to be correlated across sets of variables, a useful feature in the longitudinal context where a test-retest correlation may consist in part of correlated errors. An example with longitudinal data can be found in the Olsson and Bergmann (1977) study of ability structure of individuals between the ages of ten and thirteen. A more comprehensive discussion of the value of the model in longitudinal contexts can be found in Jöreskog and Sörbom (1976, 1977) and Wheaton et al. (1977).

A very general structural equation model is that developed by Weeks (1978). This model, which is based on Bentler's (1976) multistructural model, includes LISREL as a special case (see Bentler and Weeks, 1979a). The measurement model allows for factors at various levels. In addition to allowing higher-order factors, the structural model is more complicated, allowing a choice of regression in the latent variables. Regressions can be carried out either for the factors themselves or for various orthogonalized, derived factors. This type of model would seem to be particularly appropriate for certain types of social program indicators, in which higher-order factors such as socioeconomic status frequently can be postulated. Weeks showed that the Olsson-Bergmann (1977) longitudinal ability model could be replaced by a conceptually simpler model involving the stability of general intelligence. A particularly simple, yet extremely general, model that allows all the features of LISREL and Weeks' model is given by Bentler and Weeks (1979b).

## ANALYSIS OF COVARIANCE WITH MEASUREMENT MODEL

Where data exist on several randomly assigned treatment groups, and one is interested in drawing inferences about group means after pre-existing differences between the groups have been removed statistically, one rather naturally turns to the analysis of covariance. However, analysis of covariance is inappropriate when the covariates are measured with error, the typical situation in the social sciences. Measurement error can have the effect of implying a treatment effect when in fact there is no such effect, or the analysis may fail to detect an actual treatment effect. This biasing effect of measurement error has been noted many times (e.g., Lord, 1960). The only simple correction would be to use a type of correction of attenuation (e.g., Cochran, 1968), but this would require knowledge of the variables' reliabilities in several groups.

Sörbom (1978) recently has proposed an interesting combination of the LISREL structural equation model and his method of factor analysis with structured means. A measurement model is constructed that relates the observed dependent and covariate measures to some latent factors, the latent factors in the dependent variables are regressed on the latent factors of the covariates, and the observed means are structured in terms of the latent factors. The result is a model whose parameters influence both the covariance matrices and the means in dependent variables and covariates. The parameters of the model first are estimated by maximum likelihood, and the adequacy of fit of the model to the data is evaluated by chi-square tests. If the model does not fit the data, no further inferences about means can be drawn. If the model does fit, a variety of covariance models can be tested, i.e., a model that might assume equal dependent-covariate slopes. The measurement and structural models must be modified if they do not adequately reproduce the observed data within sampling errors, since the goal of the enterprise is to evaluate the mean effects generated by the latent factors. The Bentler and Weeks (1979) model subsumes Sörbom's work, since it allows more general specifications of dependent and covariate constructs.

# CAUSAL MODELS FOR QUALITATIVE DATA

There is no agreed-upon classification of methods for the analysis of qualitative data. Because of the relative newness of the statistical methods involved, it is uncertain what specific methodologies will prove most useful for data analysis in evaluation research. These methods require computer assistance since the methods of estimation are so complicated that it is simply not practical to use these techniques without canned programs. In most cases, the sources cited in the references provide computer programs to perform the analyses, or indicate where such programs might be available.

## FACTOR ANALYSIS MODEL

Factor analysis models for dichotomous variables have been recently formulated by Christoffersson (1975) and Muthén (1977). The Christoffersson and Muthén models are essentially the same, but Muthén has developed a more efficient method of estimation of parameters of the model. In these models, it is assumed that each observed dichotomous variable is simply a manifestation of an underlying, latent continuous variable. The observed dichotomous variable is related to the latent continuous variable by a threshold parameter that maps the dichotomous response onto the latent continuum in a step fashion. If the response strength of the latent variable is above a given magnitude, a "correct" response is made by the subject; otherwise, an incorrect response is made. The latent continuous variable is assumed to have an ordinary factor analytic representation. That is, it represents a weighted combination of latent common factors and uniqueness. In this way, the ordinary factor analytic model is made relevant to the analysis of binary data. The model is fit to the data by a generalized least squares approach, using information in the first- and second-order proportions to fit the model to data. A chi-square test can assess the goodness of fit of the model to data.

Because of the attention to underlying multidimensional representations, the factor analysis model is applicable in a variety of circumstances. However, the model makes the strong assumption of multivariate normality of the underlying latent variables. This assumption poses a problem when the model fails to fit the data, since it is difficult to know whether the fault lies in the specific factor analysis model postulated or, rather, with the distribution assumed for the latent variables.

The factor model for dichotomous variables can be treated as other factor models, in both exploratory and confirmatory contexts. That is, it is possible simply to determine the dimensionality of the latent space; the number of factors is varied until the model fits a given set of data. The model can also be used in confirmatory contexts, in which one has a theory about the space. A theory could demand that certain parameters be equal to one another, or that some parameters be set at zero. In this way, more complicated measurement models could be entertained. The ability to evaluate competing models would seem to represent a necessary condition for the effective utilization of causal modeling.

In the qualitative model described above, the primary aim is to relate observed data to underlying continuous attributes that are presumably more important, since the manifest variables are simply considered to be realizations of the latent variables under the various specific models. There are important research circumstances, however, where the purpose is not understanding the latent structure generating the data, but rather prediction. In the context of quantitative continuous variables, the prediction problem can be stated in terms of multiple regression or canonical correlation, while the structural problem is stated in terms of factor analysis models. In the analysis of dichotomous variables, there is a potentially useful regression model for predicting a single dependent variable from a set of independent variables, as well as a more complicated model relating dichotomous dependent variables to quantitative and qualitative independent variables through a structural measurement model.

### DICHOTOMOUS REGRESSION MODEL

When the variables in regression are dichotomous, including the predictor and criterion variables, the ordinary linear least-squares model is not appropriate. When used in a statistical context, this traditional model requires that the criterion variable be normally distributed with equal variances in the predictors (i.e., homoscedasticity). These conditions are not met with binary variables, and predicted values under the model could fall outside the 0-1 range. Consequently, an alternative methodology is desirable. One such is the logit model, as developed by Grizzle et al. (1969), Theil (1970), Goodman (1972a, 1975) and others. This model can be written in a general form that allows the predictors and criterion variables to relate through higher-order interactions in addition to the simple main effects of predictor variables.

In the logit model, a multiplicative version of the log-linear model is written to represent the probability that a criterion response (such as "yes" or "correct") is associated with a particular pattern of responses on all other variables. This probability is a given entry in the multidimensional contingency table relating all variables to each other. The model written to express this probability, or frequency, is like a multiplicative version of an analysis of variance (ANOVA) model. It differs from the ANOVA model in that the logit model contains the products (rather than sums) of terms representing the marginal distributions (main effects) of all variables, as well as various levels of interactions, from two-way interactions to highest-order interactions. (In practice, as in very complex analysis of variance designs, only the lowest level interactions are required; but effects more complex than main effects are needed to fit most models). A second, multiplicative equation is written for the other response to the criterion variable (such as "no" or "wrong"). The ratio of the two criterion probabilities can then be expressed as ratios of only certain terms in the very complete multiplicative model previously written; the remaining terms simply cancel. This ratio of criterion probabilities thus itself is expressed as a product of terms that similarly can be interpreted as main effects and interactions. Now, taking logarithms of this ratio of probabilities, a logit is obtained. Since the logit equals the log of the product of various multiplicative parameters, the logit also equals the simple sum of the logs of those parameters. Thus, there results an additive model for the logit as a dependent variable. This dependent variable can be regressed on the various predictor terms. As might be expected, in many circumstances only several predictor terms or parameters are needed to account for the observed data within statistical accuracy, and various terms can be dropped. Goodman (1972a) suggests that the complete logit regression equation can be estimated for data (but not tested, since it has no remaining degrees of freedom), and the size of the parameters may provide a clue as to which terms seem to be insignificant and could be dropped from the analysis without significant loss of predictive accuracy. An overall test of significance of a logit model is based upon the chi-square test; various competing models, containing certain specified interaction terms but not other terms, can be compared for adequacy of fit.

Approaches vary to obtaining statistical estimates of the parameters of these models. Grizzle et al. (1969), for example, favor the method of weighted least squares, whereas Goodman (1972a) prefers a method based on maximum likelihood. Goodman suggests that his methods are asymptotically more efficient, but this is not a well-established result. His computerized implementation of the method, however, appears to be more rapid and, consequently, less expensive.

An alternative approach to regression with dichotomous variables was outlined by Goodman (1975). This involves writing an additive (rather than multiplicative) model for the probabilities of criterion class versus response pattern, and estimating the parameters in the additive model. It is not particularly recommended, although when all variables have marginal probabilities in the .25-.75 range, there appears to be little practical difference between the two approaches.

Because of the bewildering number of higher-order effects possible with a large number of variables (these effects grow exponentially with the number of variables), it is necessary in these models to deal with a relatively small number of variables and with relatively explicit causal models. The more explicit the various possible causal models, the greater the number of variables that can be accommodated. This is because only a certain set of models might be evaluated statistically. There is no simple way of using these regression models in exploratory ways to find the optimal regression model, with the fewest number of parameters, and with the most explanatory power. Nonetheless, such an exploratory methodology is possible when considering only three, four, or maybe five variables. Goodman provides some guidelines in such a situation.

## STRUCTURAL EQUATION MODEL

Earlier the dichotomous factor analysis model of Christoffersson (1975) and Muthén (1977) was discussed. In that model, binary manifest variables were related to latent continuous factors. Muthén (1976) has extended this general model by including a structural equation component, namely, an additional set of equations that considers the latent, quantitative variable to be a dependent variable in its regression on a set of known, manifest variables. These manifest independent variables can be qualitative or quantitative in nature. Thus, the ultimate effect of the combined model is to consider the dichotomous dependent variables related, as a set, to several independent predictor variables (through the latent variable as a mediator of the regression). The model represents an interesting generalization of a regression model with multiple dependent variables.

As was pointed out previously, the factor analytic model for dichotomous data allows for the existence of multiple, quantitative latent variables. The structural equation model does not single out *one* latent variable as an intermediary in the regression, but rather uses all the latent variables that might exist simultaneously. In addition, it is possible to investigate the causal effects of various latent variables on one another. It must be reiterated that it is extremely helpful to have a causal model to test, rather than to hope that the method will find the causal structure through exploration. At best, data can be considered to be consistent with a causal hypothesis, but not proof of it. Those hypotheses that must be implausible, given the data, can be rejected in accord with a statistical test.

## LOG-LINEAR MODEL

A popular approach to the analysis of unordered categorical data is the linear-logistic or the log-linear model. An entire class of data-analytic procedures has been developed as variations of this and similar models (e.g., Bishop et al. 1975; Davis, 1975; Goodman, 1972b; Haberman, 1974; Nerlove and Press, 1973; Plackett, 1974). One of the more relevant techniques involves fitting data to multiway contingency tables. Bock (1975) refers to the statistical problem involved as one of estimating multinomial response relations, based upon the sampling distribution that appears most relevant to such tables and to more general qualitative data situations.

With regard to prediction, in the analysis of general, cross-classified categorical data, the distinction between predictors and criterion variables does not make sense. It is still possible, however, to write the probability of frequency associated with a given cell in a multiway contingency table as a multiplicative function of various types of parameters. When natural logarithms of these frequencies are obtained, the model is decomposed into linearly additive components (hence, the name, log-linear model). The problem in the analysis of such data lies in obtaining a model accounting for the observed probabilities or frequencies within desired statistical accuracy. As an example, if the categorizations were completely independent, then knowing the marginal distributions on each nominal, unordered variable would make it possible to estimate the probability of being in a given joint cell of the table as a simple product of marginal probabilities, as is well-known from principles of statistical independence applied to the two-by-two contingency table. The hypothesis of independence can be tested by chi-square, which here represents an indication of closeness of the observed frequencies to those that would be obtained under the model of independence. The log-linear model takes the simple idea of hypothesis testing associated with the two-by-two table and generalizes it to multiway, larger tables.

When the probability of a variable's falling in a given joint cell of the multiway table cannot be predicted simply from the marginals of the table, the task of finding a model that can predict this probability for every cell of the table becomes complicated. An extremely large class of potential models grows exponentially with the number of variables and number of categories on a variable. Goodman (1972b) suggests that in small tables it is possible to fit a saturated model, which can be considered to be a nontestable model that includes all possible parameters from the lowest order to the highest order. The presence of apparently powerful and trivial effects in such an analysis can be a clue to the elimination of parameters associated with some given effects, and to a concentration on others. Typically, for example, very-highest-order interactions turn out to be quite small and can be discarded. It helps to have a causal model to test in these situations, since the number of potential exploratory models quickly becomes too large to consider as the number of variables increases. To provide a specific idea, the reader is no doubt familiar with two-by-two versus two-by-two-by-two factorial designs in analysis of variance. As the design increases from only two binary cross-classified variables to three, the number of analytic parameters and effects to be interpreted grows substantially. Consider the case of $2^{10}$ contingency table, however. Data associated with such a table quickly become incomprehensible to most researchers unless higher-order effects can be ignored; indeed the computations become prohibitively expensive as well.

# EVALUATION OF
# HEAD START EFFECTS WITH CAUSAL MODELS

The following example applies structural equation models to the problem of evaluating the effect of a summer Head Start program on white first graders' cognitive ability. The original analysis of these data (Cicirelli et al., 1969) and subsequent reanalysis (Barnow, 1973) employed analysis of covariance in an effort to control statistically for the possible biasing effects of differing levels of socioeconomic status (SES) that existed between the treatment and comparison groups. Since the covariance analysis used a single, fallible measure of SES, the results were considered statistically inadequate because of measurement error in the covariate (Campbell and Erlebacher, 1970).

Recently, these same Head Start data have been reanalyzed by Magidson (1977) and Bentler and Woodward (1978) in an effort to estimate the Head Start effect in the context of a causal model postulating measurement models for dependent measures and covariate and structural relations between latent constructs. An advantage of the causal modeling approach is that it permits the effects of the Head Start program to be estimated after statistical adjustment for differences on the latent SES construct as contrasted with adjustment based on the fallible SES measure. Although several different causal models were tested, the only examples discussed here postulate measurement models for both the dependent cognitive measures and the covariate.

The basic data, taken from Barnow (1973), include as dependent variables, posttest scores on the Illinois Test of Psycholinguistic Abilities ($Y_1$) and posttest scores on the Metropolitan Readiness Test ($Y_2$). Participation in the Head Start Program, (Z), was coded 1,0 for treatment and comparison groups, respectively. Finally, four indicators of socioeconomic status (SES) were mother's education ($X_1$), father's education ($X_2$), father's occupation ($X_3$) and income ($X_4$). The correlations among all measures computed in the sample of 303 6-year-old, white first-graders are presented in Table 1. As can be seen, the cognitive measures ($Y_1$ and $Y_2$) are correlated substantially with each

TABLE 1: Correlation Matrix for Head Start Data (N = 303)

|        | $Y_1$  | $Y_2$  | $X_1$  | $X_2$  | $X_3$  | $X_4$  | Z     |
|--------|--------|--------|--------|--------|--------|--------|-------|
| $Y_1$  | 1.000  |        |        |        |        |        |       |
| $Y_2$  | .652   | 1.000  |        |        |        |        |       |
| $X_1$  | .259   | .275   | 1.000  |        |        |        |       |
| $X_2$  | .246   | .215   | .468   | 1.000  |        |        |       |
| $X_3$  | .217   | .255   | .241   | .285   | 1.000  |        |       |
| $X_4$  | .116   | .190   | .297   | .209   | .407   | 1.000  |       |
| Z      | -.097  | -.094  | -.118  | -.084  | -.220  | -.179  | 1.000 |

NOTE:        $Y_1$ = Illinois Test of Psycholinguistic Abilities
             $Y_2$ = Metropolitan Readiness Test
             $X_1$ = Mother's Education
             $X_2$ = Father's Education
             $X_3$ = Father's Occupation
             $X_4$ = Income

other—evidently they measure something in common. The four SES indicators correlate negatively with program participation (Z), and the possibility arises that if the concomitant variables $X_1$ ... $X_4$ could be controlled statistically then unbiased estimates of the effect of program (Z) on the dependent measures (Y) could be obtained.

Figure 2 is a schematic representation of the structural equation model. The measurement model for the SES measures postulates three latent constructs ($\xi_1$ ... $\xi_3$). The first is a general SES construct that is common to all observed measures. The second and third constructs are specific to the education measures and the occupation/income measures, respectively. The Head Start treatment variable is considered to be measured without error; the variance of its error variate, $\delta_5$, is set to zero, and its relation to the latent variable, $\xi_4$, is set to 1.00, as indicated by the asterisks. This specifies the measurement model of the independent variates. On the dependent measure side, the two cognitive tests are hypothesized to measure a single underlying latent variable $\eta_1$. A parallel measurements model is hypothesized by constraining the relations of the true score ($\eta_1$) with the y's to be equal as well as by constraining the variances of the $\xi$'s to be equal.

The structural model specifies that the independent latent constructs are correlated with each other. The general SES construct is allowed to correlate with Z, the treatment variable, but not with the other SES constructs. The remaining constructs (e.g., $\xi_2$ and $\xi_3$) are correlated with themselves and with the treatment variable Z. Of greatest importance in the structural model are the connections between the independent latent variables and the latent outcome measure. It is hypothesized that only the general SES construct and the treatment variable are causes of the latent outcome measure $\eta_1$.

Several aspects of this representation should be stressed. First, the relations between treatment, outcome, and concomitant variables are stated at the level of the latent constructs. Second, this hypothesis (i.e., measurement models and structural model) represents a particular pattern of relations whose magnitudes are to be estimated from the data, while certain relations are fixed at zero (e.g., between $\xi_2$ and $\eta_1$, $\xi_3$ and $\eta_1$). For the present example, the magnitudes of the relations not fixed at zero or at some other value were estimated using the method of

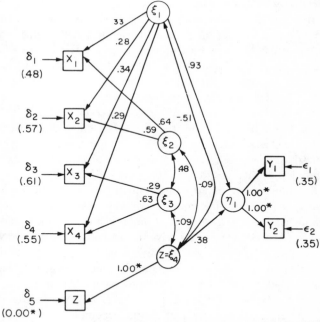

Figure 2 Schematic representation of a structural equation model for evaluating Head Start effects on cognitive development. $Y_1$ = Illinois Test of Psycholinguistic Abilities; $Y_2$ = Metropolitan Readiness Test; $X_1$ and $X_2$ = mother's and father's education; $X_3$ and $X_4$ = father's occupation and income. Values in parentheses below the $\delta$'s and $\epsilon$'s are maximum likelihood estimates of the variances of those error variates.

maximum likelihood as implemented by the LISREL III computer program of Jöreskog and Sörbom (1976). The obtained estimates appear in the figure beside the appropriate arrows. The estimated variances of the errors appear in parentheses below the appropriate $\delta$ and $\epsilon$. The variances of all other constructs were fixed at 1.00.

In addition to the parameter estimates that appear in the figure, a chi-squared goodness-of-fit test statistic is computed that permits a statistical test of the plausibility of the hypothesized model. In the current example, the chi-squared test statistic is 8.38 on 9 degrees of freedom; the model is accepted as a plausible explanation of the observed data.

Here the summer Head Start effect is estimated as a positive result opposite to that yielded by the covariance reanalysis of Barnow (1973). However, the significance of this single parameter must be investigated statistically by evaluating the model of Figure 2 with the Head Start effect fixed at zero. The difference in chi-squared test statistics for models with and without the parameters can be tested on one degree of freedom in order to assess the importance of the Head Start effect. In our second model the Head Start effect was fixed at zero. The LISREL III program yielded a chi-squared value of 8.18 on 9 degrees of freedom. The difference in chi-squared variates is 1.70 on 1 degree of freedom, a result that is not significant. It is concluded that the model of Figure 1 is a plausible one, but that plausibility does not depend upon the Head Start effect on the cognitive outcome measures, because a diametrically opposed model also is plausible. For an alternative interpretation of these results, see Magidson (1978).

In this application of structural equation models the total-group correlation matrix resulting from the combined treatment and comparison groups was analyzed. A method more analogous to the analysis of covariance (ANCOVA) would involve fitting a model to the two within-group covariance matrices and the two sets of means, and evaluating such effects as a possible treatment-covariate interaction. Such an extension of the ANCOVA that focuses on the latent covariate was developed by Sorbom (1978) and Weeks (1978; Weeks and Bentler (1979). A computer program that can accomplish this analysis of covariance with a specified measurement model soon will be available.

The analysis of covariance with measurement model as well as the application of structural equation models presented in this paper are based on the assumption that the treatment is a *fixed* independent variable in the classical sense. As has been pointed out forcefully by Guttentag (1977), this assumption frequently is not acceptable in evaluation research. A more realistic characterization of the program recognizes that it is neither simple (i.e., all or none) nor fixed, but rather a very complex set of separate "treatments" that vary in intensity across participants and across time. The effects of the program, therefore, are hypothesized to result from some underlying continuous combination of the overt experiences of participants.

Using structural equation models, it is possible to postulate the treatment represented by the program as a latent continuum (or several continua) on which participants vary because of the realities of program administration and program change. Some participants receiving all separate aspects of the program will be high on this latent treatment continuum, while at the other extreme there will be those who have been involved to a much lesser extent. This quantified continuous treatment construct could be used as a possible cause of treatment outcome in precisely the way the binary Head Start versus comparison group was used in our example. Since such a model fits the practical realities of evaluation research, we believe that our proposal for considering treatment as a latent construct has great promise in applied social research.

# REFERENCES

ABT, C. C. (1976) The Evaluation of Social Programs. Beverly Hills: Sage.
ANDERSON, T. W. and H. RUBIN (1956) Statistical inference in factor analysis. Proceedings, Third Berkeley Symposium of Mathematical Statistics and Probability 5: 111-150.
BARNOW, B. S. (1973) "The effects of Head Start and socioeconomic status on cognitive development of disadvantaged children." Ph.D. dissertation, University of Wisconsin–Madison.
BECHTOLD, H. P. (1959) "Construct validity: a critique." American Psychologist 14: 619-629.
――― (1958) "Statistical tests of hypotheses in confirmatory factor analysis." American Psychologist 13: 380. (abstract)
BENNETT, C. A. and A. A. LUMSDAINE [eds.] (1975) Evaluation and Experiment. San Francisco: Academic Press.
BENTLER, P. M. (forthcoming) "Multivariate analysis with latent variables: Causal modeling," in Mark R. Rosenzweig and Lyman W. Porter (eds.) Annual Review of Psychology. Palo Alto, CA: Annual Reviews.

――― (1978) "The interdependence of theory, methodology, and empirical data: causal modeling as an approach to construct validation," pp. 267-302 in D. Kandel (ed.) Longitudinal Research on Drug Use: Empirical Findings and Methodological Issues. New York: Hemisphere.

――― (1977) "Factor simplicity index and transformations." Psychometrika 42: 277-295.

――― (1976) "Multistructure statistical model applied to factor analysis." Multivariate Behavioral Research 11: 3-25.

――― (1973) "Assessment of developmental factor change at the individual and group level," pp. 145-174 in J. R. Nesselroade and H. W. Reese (eds.) Life-span Developmental Psychology: Methodological Issues. New York: Academic Press.

――― (1972) "A lower-bound method for the dimension-free measurement of internal consistency." Social Science Research 1: 343-357.

――― and D. G. WEEKS (1979a) "Interrelations among models for the analysis of moment structures." Multivariate Behavioral Research 14: 169-185.

――― (1979b) "Linear simultaneous equations with latent variables." (unpublished)

BENTLER, P. M. and G. J. HUBA (1979) "Simple minitheories of love." Journal of Personality and Social Psychology 37: 124-130.

BENTLER, P. M. and J. A. WINGARD (1977) "Function invariant and parameter scale-free transformation methods." Psychometrika 42: 221-240.

BENTLER, P. M. and J. A. WOODWARD (forthcoming) "Inequalities among lower-bounds to reliability: with applications to test construction and factor analysis." Psychometrika.

――― (1978) "A Head Start reevaluation: positive effects are not yet demonstrable." Evaluation Quarterly 3: 493-510.

BENTLER, P. M. and S. Y. LEE (1979) "A statistical development of three-mode factor analysis." British Journal of Mathematical and Statistical Psychology 32: 89-104.

――― (1978) "Statistical aspects of a three-mode factor analysis model." Psychometrika 43: 343-352.

BERGMANN, G. and K. W. SPENCE (1944) "The logic of psychophysical measurement." Psychological Review 51: 1-24.

BIELBY, W. T. and R. M. HAUSER (1977) "Structural equation models." Annual Review of Sociology 3: 137-161.

BISHOP, Y.M.M., S. E. FIENBERG, and P. W. HOLLAND (1975) Discrete Multivariate Analysis: Theory and Practice. Cambridge, MA: MIT Press.

BLOCK, J. (1963) "The equivalence of measures and the correction for attenuation." Psychological Bulletin 60: 152-156.

BOCK, R. D. (1975) Multivariate Statistical Methods in Behavioral Research. New York: McGraw-Hill.

CAMPBELL, D. T. (1960) "Recommendations for APA test standards regarding construct, trait, or discriminant validity." American Psychologist 15: 546-553.

――― and A. ERLEBACHER (1970) "How regression artifacts in quasi-experimental evaluations can mistakenly make compensatory education look harmful," pp. 185-210 in J. Helmuth (ed.) Compensatory Education: A National Debate. Volume III of The Disadvantaged Child. New York: Brunner/Mozel.

CAMPBELL, D. T. and D. W. FISKE (1959) "Convergent and discriminant validation by the multitrait-multimethod matrix." Psychological Bulletin 56: 81-105.

CAMPBELL, D. T. and J. C. STANLEY (1963) "Experimental and quasi-experimental designs for research on teaching," pp. 171-246 in N. L. Gage (ed.) Handbook of Research on Teaching. Chicago: Rand McNally.

CHRISTOFFERSSON, A. (1975) "Factor analysis of dichotomized variables." Psychometrika 40: 5-32.

CICIRELLI, V. G. et al. (1969) The Impact of Head Start: An Evaluation of the Effects of Head Start on Children's Cognitive and Affective Development, Volumes 1 and 2. A report presented to the Office of Economic Opportunity pursuant to contract B89-4536. Athens: Ohio University and Westinghouse Learning Corporation.

COCHRAN, W. G. (1968) "Errors of measurement in statistics." Technometrics 10: 637-666.

COOK, T. D. and D. T. CAMPBELL (1976) "The design and conduct of quasi-experiments and true experiments in field settings," pp. 223-336 in M. D. Dunnette (ed.) Handbook of Industrial and Organizational Psychology. Chicago: Rand McNally.

CORBALLIS, M. C. and R. E. TRAUB (1970) "Longitudinal factor analysis." Psychometrika 35: 79-93.

CRONBACH, L. J. (1977) "Remarks to the New Society." Evaluation Research Society Newsletter 1: 1-3.

――― (1975) "Beyond the two disciplines of scientific psychology." American Psychologist 30: 116-127.

――― (1971) "Test validation," pp. 443-507 in R. L. Thorndike (ed.) Educational Measurement. Washington, DC: American Council on Education.

――― (1957) "The two disciplines of scientific psychology." American Psychologist 12: 671-684.

――― and L. FURBY (1970) "How should we measure 'change' . . . or should we?" Psychological Bulletin 74: 68-80.

CRONBACH, L. J. and P. E. MEEHL (1955) "Construct validity in psychological tests." Psychological Bulletin 52: 281-302.

DAVIS, J. A. (1975) "Analyzing contingency tables with linear flow graphs: D Systems," pp. 111-145 in D. R. Heise (ed.) Sociological Methodology. San Francisco: Jossey-Bass.

DUNCAN, O. D. (1975) Introduction to Structural Equation Models. New York: Academic Press.

FISHER, R. A. (1935) The Design of Experiments. Edinburgh: Oliver and Boyd.

GOODMAN, L. A. (1975) "The relationship between modified and usual multiple-regression approaches to the analysis of dichotomous variables," pp. 83-110 in D. R. Heise (ed.) Sociological Methodology, 1976. San Francisco: Jossey-Bass.

——— (1972a) "A modified multiple regression approach to the analysis of dichotomous variables." American Sociological Review 37: 28-46.

——— (1972b) "A general model for the analysis of surveys." American Journal of Sociology 77: 1035-1086.

GRIZZLE, J. E., C. F. STARMER, and G. G. KOCH (1969) "Analysis of categorical data by linear models." Biometrics 25: 489-504.

GUTTENTAG, M. (1977) "Evaluation and society." Personality and Social Psychology Bulletin 3: 31-40.

——— and E. L. STRUENING [eds.] (1975) Handbook of Evaluation Research, Volume 2. Beverly Hills: Sage.

HABERMAN, S. J. (1974) The Analysis of Frequency Data. Chicago: University of Chicago Press.

HANNAN, M. T. and A. A. YOUNG (1977) "Estimation in panel models: results on pooling cross-section and time series," pp. 52-83 in D. R. Heise (ed.) Sociological Methodology. San Francisco: Jossey-Bass.

HEISE, D. R. (1975) Causal Analysis. New York: John Wiley.

HIBBS, D. A. (1977) "On analyzing the effects of policy interventions: Box-Jenkins and Box-Tiao versus structural equation models," pp. 137-179 in D. R. Heise (ed.) Sociological Methodology. San Francisco: Jossey-Bass.

JORESKOG, K. G. (1977) "Structural equation models in the social sciences: specification, estimation and testing," pp. 265-286 in P. R. Krishnaiah (ed.) Applications of Statistics. Amsterdam: North Holland.

——— (1974) "Analyzing psychological data by structural analysis of covariance matrix," pp. 1-56 in R. C. Atkinson, D. H. Krantz, R. D. Luce, and P. Suppes (eds.) Contemporary Developments in Mathematical Psychology, Volume II. San Francisco: Freeman.

——— (1973a) "Analysis of covariance structures," pp. 263-285 in P. R. Krishnaiah (ed.) Multivariate Analysis III. New York: Academic Press.

——— (1973b) "A general method for estimating a linear structural equation system," pp. 85-112 in A. S. Goldberger and O. D. Duncan (eds.) Structural Equation Models in the Social Sciences. New York: Seminar Press.

——— (1971a) "Statistical analysis of sets of congeneric tests." Psychometrika 36: 109-133.

——— (1971b) "Simultaneous factor analysis in several populations." Psychometrika 36: 409-426.

——— (1970) "A general method for analysis of covariance structures." Biometrika 57: 239-251.

——— (1969) "A general approach to confirmatory maximum likelihood factor analysis." Psychometrika 34: 183-202.

——— and D. SORBOM (1976) "Statistical models and method for test-retest situations," pp. 135-157 in D.N.M. Gruijter and L.J.T. VanderKamp (eds.) Advances in Psychological and Educational Measurement. New York: John Wiley.

——— (1977) "Some models and estimation methods for analysis of longitudinal data," pp. 285-325 in D. J. Aigner and A. S. Goldberger (eds.) Latent Variables in Socioeconomic Models. Amsterdam: North Holland.

KEESLING, J. W. and D. E. WILEY (1975) "Measurement error and the analysis of quasi-experimental data." Chicago: University of Chicago. (mimeo)

KENNY, D. A. (1976) "An empirical application of confirmatory factor analysis to the multitrait-multimethod matrix." Journal of Experimental Social Psychology 12: 247-252.

——— (1975) "A quasi-experimental approach to assessing treatment effects in the nonequivalent control group design." Psychological Bulletin 82: 345-362.

KESSLER, R. C. (1977) "Rethinking the 16-fold table problem." Social Science Research 6: 84-107.

LINN, R. L. and C. E. WERTS (1977) "Analysis implications of the choice of a structural model in the nonequivalent control group design." Psychological Bulletin 84: 229-234.

LOEVINGER, J. (1957) "Objective tests as instruments of psychological theory." Psychological Reports 3: 635-694.

LORD, F. M. (1960) "Large sample covariance analysis when the control variable is fallible." Journal of the American Statistical Association 55: 307-321.

MAGIDSON, J. (1978) "Reply to Bentler and Woodward: the .05 significance level is not all-powerful." Evaluation Quarterly 2: 511-520.

——— (1977) "Toward a causal model approach for adjusting for preexisting differences in the nonequivalent control group situation: a general alternative to ANCOVA." Evaluation Quarterly 1: 399-419.

MARGENAU, H. (1950) The Nature of Physical Reality. New York: McGraw-Hill.

MARUYAMA, G. M. (1976) "A causal model analysis of variables related to primary school achievement." Ph.D. dissertation, University of Southern California.

McGARVEY, W. E. (1977) Longitudinal factors in school desegregation. Ph. D. dissertation, University of Southern California.

MUTHEN, B. (1976) "Structural equation models with dichotomous dependent variables." Uppsala: University of Uppsala. (mimeo)

——— (1977) "Contributions to factor analysis of dichotomous variables." Psychometrika 43: 551-560.

NERLOVE, M. and S. J. PRESS (1973) Univariate and multivariate log linear and logistic models. Santa Monica: RAND.

OLSSON, U. and L. R. BERGMANN (1977) "A longitudinal factor model for studying change in ability structure." Multivariate Behavioral Research 12: 221-241.

OVERALL, J. E. and J. A. WOODWARD (1977) "Nonrandom assignment and the analysis of covariance." Psychological Bulletin 84: 588-594.

PEDHAZUR, E. J. (1977) "Coding subjects in repeated measures designs." Psychological Bulletin 84: 298-305.

PLACKETT, R. L. (1974) The analysis of Categorical Data. London: Griffin.

RIECKEN, H. W. and R. F. BORUCH (1974) Social Experimentation. New York: Academic Press.

ROCK, D. A., C. E. WERTS, R. E. LINN, and K. G. JORESKOG (1977) "A maximum likelihood solution to the errors in variables and errors in equations model." Multivariate Behavioral Research 12: 187-197.

ROSS, L. and L. J. CRONBACH (1976) "Handbook of evaluation research: essay review by a task force of the Stanford Evaluation Consortium." Evaluation Researcher 12: 9-19.

ROSSI, P. H. and W. WILLIAMS [eds.] (1972) Evaluating Social Programs. New York: Seminar Press.

SHAFFER, J. P. (1977) "Reorganization of variables in analysis of variance and multi-dimensional contingency tables." Psychological Bulletin 84: 220-228.

SORBOM, D. (1978) "An alternative to the methodology for analysis of covariance." Psychometrika 43: 381-396.

––– (1974) "A general method for studying differences in factor means and factor structure between groups." British Journal of Mathematical and Statistical Psychology 27: 229-239.

THEIL, H. (1970) "On the estimation of relationships involving qualitative variables." American Journal of Sociology 76: 103-154.

TORGERSON, W. S. (1958) Theory and Methods of Scaling. New York: John Wiley.

TUCKER, L. R. (1966) "Some mathematical notes on three-mode factor analysis." Psychometrika 31: 279-311.

WEEKS, D. G. (1978) "Structural equation systems on latent variables within a second-order measurement model." Ph.D. dissertation, University of California, Los Angeles.

WHEATON, B., B. MUTHEN, D. F. ALWIN, and G. F. SUMMERS (1977) "Assessing reliability and stability in panel models," pp. 84-136 in D. R. Heise (ed.) Sociological Methodology. San Francisco: Jossey-Bass.

WILEY, D. E. (1973) "The identification problem for structural equation models with unmeasured variables," pp. 69-83 in A. S. Goldberger and O. D. Duncan (eds.) Structural Equation Models in the Social Sciences. New York: Seminar Press.

WRIGHT, S. (1921) "Correlation and causation." Journal of Agricultural Research 20: 557-585.

# 7

## SOME APPROACHES TO ASSESSING CHANGE

Barry S. Tuchfeld

## SOME APPROACHES TO ASSESSING CHANGE

A persistent concern with the phenomenon of change over time has been characteristic of the social sciences. Assessing change has been troublesome in program evaluations, since experimentation, which provides the methodological foundation for assessing causal influence, has been difficult to achieve.

Problems in assessing change become pronounced in nonexperimental research when subjects cannot be controlled through randomization. Techniques which attempt to take such differences into account have become increasingly sophisticated as a result of evolution in technique and thinking. As will be discussed, three general strategies for assessing change in nonexperimental research have emerged. Problems which still confound the issue are examined, and implications for the attribution of programmatic effectiveness when using nonexperimental data are noted.

## THE QUESTION OF CHANGE

Change studies, unlike cross-sectional comparative studies, may involve the same units at different points in time and space. Hence, the concerns of change studies involve the analysis of differences that may occur, and the relationship of such differences to interventions between the initiation of the research and the conclusion. The issue is relevant particularly when some intentional manipulation has been made.

Glock (1955) has summarized the central questions relevant to the study of change. These include:

(1) What is the effect of a stimulus in producing change?
(2) What are the conditions which produce differential changes in attitudes or behavior among various groups in a population?
(3) What is the mutual interaction between attitudes or behavior patterns which occur simultaneously?

To address these issues methodologists have developed analytic approaches that may be utilized with various nonexperimental or quasi-experimental designs (see Campbell and Stanley, 1962, and Nunnally, 1975, for discussions of design issues). These can be classified as: (1) Simple Change Scores, (2) Covariance Strategies, and (3) Effect Models.

### SIMPLE CHANGE SCORES

When one measures some variable $(X_1)$ prior to the occurrence of some event or process and measures the same variable (now $X_2$) after an occurrence, it is intuitively appealing to compute a simple change score

$$C = X_2 - X_1.$$

"C" is then a single variable that can be correlated with measures presumed to be related to C. These correlates might be different treatment conditions, programmatic manipulations, or variables otherwise assumed extraneous to the causal effect.

The simplicity of computation for change scores is attractive. However, their use in technical analyses has been in disrepute for quite some time and some argue that group trends can be analyzed without having to deal with individual changes (Nunnally, 1975). A problem with simple change scores occurs when they are used as correlates of some independent variable (IV). In a sense the problem is related to regression to the mean as, in most cases, there is some correlation between $X_1$ and $X_2$. The result is that subjects (or elements) with initially low scores may have a greater opportunity to "gain" (toward the mean of "C") than those originally high on $X_1$ values. Likewise, those with the highest post-scores on $X_2$ have gains, i.e., large "C" scores.

Related to the issue is the problem of reliability (Bohrnstedt, 1969). Among others, Lord (1963) has demonstrated that measures of "C" are highly unreliable. Bereiter (1963) terms this the "unreliability-invalidity dilemma." If test-retest correlations are low, then one must ask if the same concept is being measured.

To counter these problems, numerous suggestions have been made to modify change scores. Some researchers have thought it more important to try to adjust postscores for initial differences than to ignore them altogether. However, the general conclusion is that such adjustments (e.g., correcting for unreliability in pretest scores) are appropriate only under certain highly specified conditions (Cronbach and Furby, 1970). The utility of such approaches for most evaluations is moot since those conditions generally entail random assignment.

## COVARIANCE STRATEGIES

Analysis of Covariance (ANCOVA) was first introduced by R. A. Fisher. ANCOVA is a technique for comparing group means on a dependent variable after adjusting groups for observed differences on some relevant covariate (concomitant) variable. Thus, data on treatment effectiveness could be statistically compared after adjusting for age differences in nonrandom groups. Theoretically, numerous covariates can be used to adjust group means so long as there is a low correlation between each pair of covariates.

As when using any linear model, the failure to satisfy its assumptions results in suspect analyses and in findings which are impossible to cross-validate (Schussler, 1969). In evaluation research, where the examination of programmatic effectiveness is prominent, failing to satisfy assumptions can have embarrassing consequences.

The problem with covariance is pronounced for evaluators using nonexperimental data. In such cases the researcher is compelled to investigate any potentially salient, nonprogrammatic correlates about which information is available. Covariates thought to have some relationship with the dependent variable $(X_2)$ must necessarily be included in analyses. If, for example, age is associated with $X_2$ (outcome), then it is also reasonable in nonexperimental research to anticipate it being related to $X_1$ (pretest). If so related, and covariance is being used to control for pretest differences in $X_1$, then the researcher is forced to input variables $(X_1$ and age) that will likely fail the assumption of homogeneity of regression. The results: analyses of questionable utility as such correlations will confound interpretation. A similar problem occurs when preexisting groups are compared after exposure to some treatment episode, since it is unlikely that within-group regression slopes are equivalent (Nunnally, 1975).

Cohen and Cohen (1975) offer a solution to the problem in the case where the prescore $(X_1)$ is related to any or all of the covariates. The technique is an extension of the general linear model and is referred to as the analysis of partial variance. In simple terms, the effect of premeasures are removed from the variance of $X_2$, the postmeasures. The analysis of the remaining variance is thus free of contamination by this or any set of covariates which may be partialled out. Further, they suggest a way of adjusting unreliable covariates by using estimates of the standard deviation of true scores to offset over- or underestimation.

This "residualization" technique is not without controversy. Bohrnstedt (1969) concludes that the use of residualized scores is preferable to simple change scores. Yet, even Cohen and Cohen (1975: 373) are quick to warn "that [their] method has not been proved mathematically nor even tested by extensive computer trials on data of known characteristics." Cronbach and Furby (1970) further argue that thinking in these terms is not generally necessary. Thus, while the analysis of partial variance appears to be an improvement over simple gain scores or ANCOVA, it is not a panacea to the problems of assessing change.

Finally, it is important to recognize that adjustment procedures are attempts to reconcile nonrandom differences by statistical manipulations. They are oriented to treating groups of subjects "as if" they were equal prior to the occurrence of some event or process and are attempts to approximate random assignment when it is not feasible or ethical. Substantive interpretations must not neglect the statistical nature of such adjustments; and, evaluative researchers should recall that, controlling for atmospheric pressure, the Himalayan and the Catskill ranges are equal in average heights.

## EFFECTS MODELS

The orientation of the above approaches is to predict change scores or adjusted outcomes as a function of some independent variable(s). More recently, some methodologists have begun focusing on the development of structural equation models which may contain multiple indicators, estimates of unobserved variables, and estimates of measurement error (Long, 1976). Though also dependent on the general linear model, the perspective underlying the analysis of effects via multivariate structural models suggests a shift from prediction per se to the formulation of a series of causal models which are tested for adequacy against data collected for the problem at hand. As Jöreskog (1969: 201) explains, "From this point of view the statistical problem is not one of testing a given hypothesis but rather one of fitting models with different numbers of parameters and of deciding [conceptually as well statistically] when to stop fitting."

The use of multiple indicators assumes that some underlying factor (F) may be represented by a common set of interrelated indicators. Though not measurable directly, F may be estimated through these indicators. For example, income and prestige may be common to socioeconomic status.

Magidson (1977) gives an example of the utility of reducing SES indicators to a common factor. Unlike ANCOVA, the single-factor model (1) allows for an estimate of the direct and indirect effects of covariates on the test and outcome variables and (2) admits the presence of measurement error into the analysis of its effects. Moreover, the use of multiple indicators does not make ANCOVA's implicit (and often questionable) assumption that pretreatment differences are measured exhaustively by a linear combination of covariates.

Effects models give special attention to statistical estimation and hypothesis testing. These efforts reflect an increasing concern that greater realism about the dynamics of social reality be considered and assessed in our analyses (Nambodiri et al., 1975: 440). The goals of assessing and explaining unmeasured variables suggest a shift in focus for the analysis of change. Effects models emphasize the estimation of measurement error, an emphasis that is critical in evaluative research efforts that include abstract concepts which have concrete implications.

The introduction of structural models to the analysis of change does not solve the technical issues with measurement. The worth of the approach is substantive as well as statistical. It forces the researcher to develop more carefully causal hypotheses and to consider more extensively the common factors which the numerous covariates in nonexperimental research may share (Blalock, 1964).

Theoretically, an infinite number of causal models are possible. Consequently, researchers have to be prepared to propose and justify alternative models which may be subjected to empirical testing. The assessment of change in nonexperimental research, particularly in field situations, requires that researchers construct explanations of the causal mechanisms by which change is proposed to operate. The incorporation of effects models will significantly enhance the specificity of this process. And, in those situations where the final model is empirical and the explanatory scheme post hoc, researchers should be prepared to cross-validate the empirically based model against a similar set of empirical circumstances.

## IMPLICATIONS FOR ASSESSING PROGRAMMATIC EFFECTIVENESS

When nonrandom assignment to treatment and comparison groups is present, one can never be certain that all nonrandom covariates have been measured. In this sense, Lord (1963: 38) was farsightedly correct that "there is often no way to determine what is the appropriate adjustment to be made for initial differences between groups." The statistical approaches for attempting such adjustments have evolved from simple difference scores to adjustments to covariates of the criterion variable to effects modeling which allows for estimating and assessing the consequences of measurement error.

This evolution in strategy reflects an increasing emphasis on explanation and accurate estimation. Incorporating causal models in nonexperimental evaluations encourages parsimonious explanations, adds specificity, and reinforces the cautions to which one must adhere when analyzing nonexperimental data. The use of such strategies does not relieve the researcher of the responsibility to investigate rival hypotheses which may threaten internal or external validity. Statistical advances are worthwhile when they can be used to increase our understanding; they are not ends in themselves.

# REFERENCES

BEREITER, C. (1963) "Some persisting dilemmas in the measurement of change," pp. 3-20 in C. W. Harris (ed.) Problems in Measuring Change. Madison: University of Wisconsin Press.

BLALOCK, H. M. (1964) Causal Inferences in Non-experimental Research. Chapel Hill: University of North Carolina Press.

BOHRNSTEDT, G. W. (1969) "Observations on the measurement of change." pp. 113-136 in E. F. Borgatta (ed.) Sociological Methodology. San Francisco: Jossey-Bass.

CAMPBELL, D. T. and J. C. STANLEY (1962) Experimental and Quasi-Experimental Designs for Research. Chicago: Rand McNally.

COHEN, J. and P. COHEN (1975) Applied Multiple Regression/Correlation Analysis for the Behavioral Science. New York: Lawrence Erlbaum.

CRONBACH, L. and L. FURBY (1970) "How we should measure change—or should we?" Psychological Bulletin 74: 68-80.

GLOCK, C. (1955) "Some applications of the panel method to the study of change," pp. 242-250 in P. F. Lazersfeld and M. Rosenberg (eds.) The Language of Social Research. New York: Free Press.

JÖRESKOG, K. G. (1969) "A general approach to maximum likelihood factor analysis." Psychometrika 34 (June): 183-202.

LONG, J. S. (1976) "Estimation and hypothesis testing in linear models containing measurement error." Sociological Methods and Research 5: 157-206.

LORD, F. M. (1963) "Elementary models for measuring change," pp. 21-38 in C. W. Harris (ed.) Problems in Measuring Change. Madison: University of Wisconsin Press.

MAGIDSON, J. (1977) "Toward a causal model approach for adjusting for pre-existing differences in the non-equivalent control group situation: a general alternative to ANCOVA." Evaluation Quarterly 8: 399-420.

NAMBODIRI, N. K., L. F. CARTER and H. M. BLALOCK, Jr. [eds.] (1975) Applied Multivariate Analysis and Experimental Designs. New York: McGraw-Hill.

NUNNALLY, J. C. (1975) "The study of change in evaluation research: principles concerning measurement, experimental design, and analysis," pp. 101-137 in E. Struening and M. Guttentag (eds.) Handbook of Evaluation Research, Vol. 1. Beverly Hills: Sage.

SCHUSSLER, K. (1969) "Covariance analysis in sociological research." pp. 219-244 in E. F. Borgatta (ed.) Sociological Methodology. San Francisco: Jossey-Bass.

# 8

## APPLYING TIME SERIES STRATEGIES:
## AN UNDERUTILIZED SOLUTION

Michael S. Knapp

Many social program evaluations have involved control group studies assessing the extent to which prespecified objectives were reached. The research strategy tends to be quantitative, focused on outcomes, and analyzed by statistics based on parametric assumptions. Program effects typically are estimated by comparing mean performance of those exposed to the program with the mean performance of a comparable group not so exposed.

There are, however, calls for alternatives. In the context of large-scale broad-aim programs, Weiss and Rein (1972) argued for a model combining process-oriented qualitative data, historical narratives of program events, and case-study comparisons. With open-education programs in mind, Patton (1975) pointed to the potential contribution of more subjective, holistic approaches to evaluation, which imply that the researcher be closer to the data, attend more to the uniqueness of each evaluation situation, and focus on the deeper issues of the meaningfulness of the data gathered.

The increased interest in applying time series models to social science research represents a step toward a third alternative, one which combines elements of both the dominant experimental paradigm and the qualitative, context-sensitive alternatives. Time series strategies use quantitative data, build carefully controlled—often comparative—research designs, and increasingly involve sophisticated forms of data analysis. The designs also imply a focus on process over time rather than on discrete outcomes measured at one or at the most two points. In addition, time series strategies direct attention to the evolving historical narrative of the phenomenon in question and to the unique characteristics of the individual case. The elements at work in time series research seem applicable in many program evaluation situations. But increased use of such program evaluation strategies requires recognition of the limitations of time series methods and efforts to offset these limitations.

## TIME SERIES RESEARCH TRADITIONS

Time series research approaches have been used in the social sciences in two nearly opposite research traditions, behavioral psychology and econometrics. The operant tradition in psychology has investigated patterns of change over time in the behavior of individual subjects or animals. In the past decade or two, the same basic techniques have been used for more clinically oriented research, for example, in studies of psychotherapy (Gottman, 1973) or behavioral counseling (Thoresen and Anton, 1974). Here time series designs form the basis on which the effects of treatment programs on individual clients have been evaluated. Such studies have not confined themselves to investigating individual behavior patterns: in an increasing number of reports, repeated measurements are made over time of the behavior of client groups or of communities. In these cases the group or the setting is regarded as the single unit subjected to some treatment.

Econometric research has been concerned with the investigation of change in economic systems over time. Mathematical models have been developed to describe fluctuations in company profits, the wholesale price of a given product, or the activity of the stock market. In contrast to the behavioral psychology focus on individuals and small groups, econometric time series typically have been developed with more macro-level phenomena in mind. Building to a great extent on the economic model, advocates of the social indicators movement have urged a time series based method of social accounting, with regularly gathered statistics on specific social problems and conditions. Proponents have advocated the development of such indicators to establish priorities and evaluate social welfare programs. Problematic as this enterprise may be (see Sheldon and Freeman, 1972), it represents one extension of economic time series thinking into the realm of social programs and their assessment.

Glass et al. (1975) were among the first to synthesize these diverse types of research in their discussion of time series experiments. Their focus was on developing the capacity of time series designs and analytic techniques for testing causal claims. Applying time series research strategies to evaluation has been recommended by Campbell (1969). In his view, time series designs are categorized most appropriately as quasi-experiments, that is, second-best approximations to the randomized true experiments, which he believes provide the soundest basis for causal inferences regarding an intervention effect (see Campbell and Stanley, 1966; Cook and Campbell, 1976). Other writers on evaluation methodology tend to follow Campbell's lead, recognizing the usefulness of time-series designs as quasi-experiments but not elaborating much on their application (e.g., Weiss, 1972: 68-69). Later work points to the unique contributions of time series approaches to specific kinds of program evaluation problems (e.g., Popham, 1975; Wortman, 1975).

# BASIC ELEMENTS OF
# A TIME SERIES RESEARCH APPROACH

A time series research approach includes at least the following elements: (a) quantitative measures (b) taken of a single unit (c) repeated at regular intervals over an extended period of time, along with (d) some concurrent record of historical events. The individual unit acts as its own experimental control; the unit's performance during, and subsequent to, an experimental treatment or program intervention is compared with prior baseline performance patterns.

An experimental effect is said to occur when a noticeable fluctuation in the series, detected either visually or statistically, appears after the onset of an intervention, over and above fluctuations attributable to previous trends, seasonal cycles, or chance instability in the series. The attributed effect becomes believable as a true effect after plausible alternative interpretations are ruled out logically through design variations or empirically through supplementary sources of data. Replication of patterns across units, across conceptually related measures on the unit, or the persistence of patterns over time offers evidence of generalizability.

Time series can be analyzed in ways ranging from visual inspection to statistical procedures such as those involving integrated moving averages (see Kazdin, 1976). All techniques aim at answering the same questions: Did a noticeable change take place in the series other than that attributable to chance, cyclical fluctuations, or previous trends? Can the changed pattern in the series be attributed to the intervention? What is the form of the pattern over time? Typically, three characteristics are examined: the level of the series (i.e., its position on the vertical axis), its slope, and its degree of variability.

Time series designs have made use of individuals, programs, states, and even countries as units. Small clinical or behavioral programs are evaluated very frequently by time series designs. One example is the investigation by Bornstein and Quevillon (1976) into the effects of a self-instructional package on the classroom behavior of overactive preschool boys, in which three boys were given the treatment at staggered intervals with a separate series of observations made of each one. Smith et al. (1976) used small groups of Outward Bound participants as the single unit measured over time. Self-esteem, self-awareness, self-assertion, and acceptance of others were measured at repeated intervals over a six-month period in the midst of which the participants attended a summer Outward Bound course.

The unit was a larger aggregated entity in the case reported by Simon and Smith (1973) concerning the effects of relocating a university health center on utilization patterns by the university community. A comparable, but somewhat larger, unit was involved in the evaluation by Schnelle et al. (1975) of the effects on city crime rates of a stepped-up antiburglary effort by police. The aggregate unit may be larger still, as in the investigation of the effects of legislation at the state level (see Campbell, 1969, on the Connecticut speeding crackdown), the studies of the impact of Federal Gun Control legislation (Zimring, 1976), and of stiff drinking-and-driving laws in Scandinavian countries (Ross, 1976).

In process-oriented evaluations, the unit on which time series measurements are made may well be the program itself, or some component of it, in addition to measurements made of individuals, groups, or aggregates on which the program has impact. For example, part of a time series study of the 1968 Gun Control Act (Zimring, 1976) determined the extent to which a government agency implemented the legislated program by documenting change in the numbers of cases recommended for prosecution by the agency.

# ADVANTAGES OF EVALUATING PROGRAMS BY TIME SERIES METHODS

**Looking for a pattern of change over time: a different notion of "effect."** Most experimental designs demonstrate change by comparing an experimental group with a control group on measurements made at one or two points in time. But what if the outcome of interest does not reveal itself so readily at one point in time? A mental ability may be detectable at a single point in time; a learning curve by definition cannot. As Gottman (1973: 95) puts it, time series approaches

> "offer a unique perspective on the assessment of interventions. Experimental designs in the Fisherian tradition obfuscate important observations about the *form* of intervention effects across time. . . . Fisherian methodology was most appropriate for comparing agricultural treatments with respect to relative yields. The yields were crops which were harvested when ripe; it was irrelevant whether the crops grew slowly or rapidly. . . . Interventions with clients, institutions, communities, and societies do not merely have an "effect" but an "effect pattern" across time. The value of an intervention is not judged by whether the effect is observable at the fall harvest but whether it increases or decays, whether it is temporarily or constantly superior to the effects of an alternative intervention evaluated in a cost/benefit sense."

Chapman and Risley's (1974) study assessing the effects of several types of antilitter campaign on litter levels in a low-income housing project provides one example of an effect pattern. These time series data demonstrated rapid decay over time in participation levels for certain kinds of antilitter strategies, a finding which would have been missed by evaluations relying on a single post-treatment measurement. Similarly, the abrupt decrease in prison disruption levels following a policy shift towards stricter punishment (Schnelle and Lee, 1974) could appear in any short time-span pre-post measurement as a great success. But the abrupt downward movement of the series was followed by a gradual return in the ensuing two-year period to the original level of disruption. Again, the effect pattern told more than any single point estimate of effect.

**Looking for change within the individual unit.** Comparative research designs tend to look for a group effect common to all people exposed to an experimental treatment above any aggregate change in a control group. But often the goal of evaluation is to determine whether a particular program brought about desired changes within individual clients, or within a single aggregated unit or system. In clinical programs, to take one example, the unique variations of individual patients usually are of great interest. Time series designs encourage investigation of patterns of individual change. Individualized learning casework efforts and therapeutic programs of many kinds all would seem to be prime candidates for time series treatment, as would the implementation and impact of legislation or policy within a single state, region, or municipality.

**Where no meaningful control group exists.** For a variety of reasons, no meaningful control population may exist (see Cook and Campbell, 1976). For example, in voluntary programs, where self-selection may be an important determinant of potential program effectiveness, it is unlikely that a truly equivalent control can be located. Where the focal population represents the extreme of some distribution, as in the case of many compensatory or therapeutic programs, it often is difficult to locate an equivalent, equally extreme population against which experimental gains may be assessed. Finally, in the largest aggregated units, such as governmental jurisdictions, it is unlikely that functionally equivalent units exist.

In each of these cases, approximations to the true control group may be arranged; that is, after all, what group-comparative quasi-experiments attempt to do. But in many instances, it seems more powerful to build a research scheme in which the experimental unit acts as its own control, with some additional comparisons to aid in interpreting the resulting patterns of effect. Many time series designs do exactly that. The extremely overactive boys in the Bornstein and Quevillon (1976) evaluation act as their own controls, and additionally provide a point of comparison with each other since the treatment was introduced at different times to each one. The self-selected participants in the Outward Bound Program (Smith et al., 1976) represent a group with unique motivational characteristics, suggested by their applying for and anticipating the rugged experience of outdoor survival and self-discovery; it made sense to compare them with themselves at an earlier point in time. Finally, it was clear that each Scandinavian country reported in the Ross (1976) study differed enough from the others that it was most appropriate to analyze its drinking-and-driving pattern with reference to its own earlier history, though some rough comparisons with the other countries were possible and did aid in interpretation.

**Where "the program" is not really a fixed or definable treatment.** Charters and Jones (1975) note that program evaluators too often have behaved as if the independent variable in their research designs—the program—were a relatively fixed or definable treatment. These writers argue that all social programs must be thought of as existing at several independent levels of reality simultaneously—the levels of institutional commitment, resource allocation, staff role performance, and client participation.

Time series strategies are useful in such situations because they encourage relation of a continual record of measures to whatever record of program evolution can be assembled. One example is Zimring's (1976) analyses of the effects of legislative reform. At the other end of the unit size continuum, assessment of clinical counseling by time-series measures allows for considerable change over time in treatment strategy, as the clients' needs change and as ongoing feedback from the series indicates more or less promising results (Thoresen and Anton, 1973).

**Where causal processes are poorly understood.** Even if the treatment were relatively definable, the causal mechanisms by which program efforts affect the behavior of clients or the characteristics of a target setting may be understood only dimly. The power of a time series approach for generating hypotheses about a phenomenon is mentioned frequently (see, e.g., Kiesler, 1971; Gottman, McFall, and Barnett, 1969). This would appear to be particularly useful in programs directed at stubborn social problems, poorly understood mental phenomena, or the like. Test-score decline in America might be explored by time series techniques, even though this is not strictly speaking a program evaluation situation.

The preceding advantages concern the logical structure of an evaluation design where time series based strategies frequently may provide more relevant information than group comparative designs and accommodate conditions which restrict true experiments. Time series designs also may be more practical and useful.

**Evaluation after the fact.** Often the problem confronting the evaluator is to provide some answers to questions concerning program effectiveness asked well after project initiation. If some reliable measurement record exists for the period of time leading up to and after the start of the program, a time series approach suggests itself. One example is Schnelle and Lee's (1974) retrospective evaluation of a prison policy change, based on existing records of disruptive behavior of inmates. Although numerous logical problems exist in drawing inferences from such data, post hoc experiments are often the only way to look at a program's past performance without relying solely on participants' memories. But one is limited, of course, to those aspects of program performance on which reliable and relevant records are kept. Evaluations of this type typically will be directed at programs taking place within established institutional or governmental settings—schools, hospitals, prisons, or the bureaucratic settings in which legislative reforms are implemented.

**Interpretability and usefulness to practitioners.** The evaluator-practitioner gap is a commonly noted feature of many program evaluation situations (Caro, 1971). In an almost literal sense the two parties do not speak the same language, to say nothing of the organizational and administrative strains inherent in the relationship. Practitioners tend to disbelieve—or else to put blind faith in—the increasingly technical presentations of evaluative findings. Time series strategies offer the potential for a readily interpretable, intuitively meaningful display of information through graphic presentation. Schnelle et al. (1975) provide a good example of intuitively obvious patterns in a graphic display of data regarding the effects of installing a police walking patrol in several housing developments. Not all those involved in time series research would agree that visual inspection or simple analytic methods such as split-middle trend analysis are wholly satisfactory, but at least they offer the possibility of data presentations which can be grasped readily by those who must make use of evaluative information in assessing decision alternatives (see Parsonson and Baer, 1978).

**The timing of evaluation reporting.** Numerous writers have commented on the lack of fit between the decision makers' need for information, which often arises at unpredictable moments, and the necessity under most conventional evaluation designs to wait until the data are all in and analyzed before providing information (e.g., Guba, 1972). Time series designs can provide some information to decision makers at almost any time. If decision makers ask for data before a program has been in operation long enough for an interpretable series of measurements, then there are obviously serious risks that the data will be thought to mean something other than what later turns out to be the case. But the important point is this: there is no one time at which the time series data collection is over. A series can be inspected at various points along its development, and new things can be learned from it each time, thus permitting a form of evaluation more akin to monitoring than to formal experiment. From the decision makers' point of view, this flexibility may be important, though the strength of causal inference may be compromised.

**Cost.** Time series strategies may provide a cheaper alternative for evaluation in a number of instances: where the relevant data are collected routinely over time and some method of estimating reliability is possible; where the number of individual units is relatively small; where the measurements to be repeated over time are not elaborate and can be made regularly without complicated preparations. The Outward Bound evaluation previously cited (Smith et al., 1976) is a provocative example of a time series evaluation in which a more elaborate measuring instrument was used (a 47-item questionnaire), presumably for the same cost as one large cross-sectional survey. In that evaluation the overall target population (N = 620) was divided into randomly equivalent subgroups of approximately 20 each, which received mailed questionnaires sequentially over time so that no subgroup responded to the questionnaire more than once. Each data point in the series consisted of the mean responses of one subgroup.

## PREDICTABLE PROBLEMS ENCOUNTERED WHEN USING TIME SERIES APPROACHES IN PROGRAM EVALUATION

The special characteristics of time series research approaches create some problems. These difficulties arise as matters both of intrinsic design logic and of practicality. Five problems stand out as particularly serious.

**Ruling out historical interpretations.** As underscored by Cook and Campbell (1976), a major logical problem facing the interpretation of any single time series is that concurrent historical or external events rather than the programmatic intervention may be responsible for changes in the series. Studies covering a long span of time are especially vulnerable to this alternative interpretation. Various techniques developed to deal with this problem include comparing a unit's series with other units exposed at different points in time to the same intervention, with other units not exposed to the intervention, and with simultaneous measures on the same unit which are independent conceptually (the multiple baseline design).

Thus, for example, in their evaluation of the effects of introducing a police walking patrol in low-income housing projects, Schnelle et al. (1975) took advantage of the fact that the intervention was scheduled by the police to start at different times in each of two similar neighborhoods. External causal factors most likely would have affected both neighborhoods simultaneously, but a marked change in the series was observed only immediately following the intervention in each case. Note that there is still room for alternative interpretations: external factors might have affected each unit at different times, what Cook and Campbell (1976: 229) refer to as the threat of local history.

Other means of ruling out extraneous concurrent events as a cause are found in reported evaluations. The traffic fatalities pattern for the state of Connecticut was compared with those of neighboring states which did not adopt a strong antispeeding policy at the same time as Connecticut (Campbell, 1969). In their evaluation of several antilitter strategies, Chapman and Risley (1974) returned to baseline (removed the intervention altogether) for three different periods during their study. It was unlikely, though not impossible, that external factors repeatedly would have brought about noticeable shifts in the series three different times in a row.

Still, ruling out the plausible history interpretations with time series designs often involves a rather extended analysis, particularly with large aggregated units. This may create a problem in reporting data to evaluation sponsors. The more successful time-series evaluations may be those which focus on the most salient, plausible alternative historical interpretations rather than trying to exhaust every reasonable possibility.

**Finding nonreactive and unobtrusive measures.** Because measurements in time-series strategies are repeated over and over again, it is essential that nonreactive measures be found. Observational measures of behavior and archival data typically will be useful. Many standard measurement techniques, such as elaborate tests, questionnaires, or interviews, will not (see Edgar and Billingsley, 1974). Most examples of time series evaluations have used institutional records. The long questionnaire in the Outward Bound evaluation previously cited is one interesting exception. Counting behaviors in the classroom (Bornstein and Quevillon, 1974) provides another example, fairly typical of applied behavioral studies. A third exception is the unobtrusive measurement device of the bus turnstile, which counted daily ridership in an evaluation of an experimental intracampus bus (Everett et al., 1974).

Lack of nonreactive measures is clearly a severe limitation. Where the variables of interest can only be detected by some means which itself becomes an intervention over time, the time series design probably is not appropriate.

**Developing sufficiently long baselines.** It often is difficult to gather a meaningful pattern of observations during the period leading up to the start of a new program, so that it becomes impossible to establish any firm sense of prior trends, cyclic movements, or characteristic irregularities in the data of the series, unless retrospective records are used. Thus, a whole category of direct measurements is ruled out.

The appropriate length of the baseline measurement phase varies considerably, from a matter of weeks in classroom observation studies to a matter of years in studies of legislative reform. The less control evaluators have over the timing of the intervention's introduction, the less likely they are to establish an adequate baseline. Ross (1976) acknowledges this kind of deficiency in his data on the effects of Scandinavian drinking-and-driving laws. The Chapman and Risley (1974) investigation of antilitter campaign effects suffers from a lack of prior baseline, though baseline periods are interspersed within the time series design between intervention periods.

When the evaluation examines a single person, the baseline problem may be less severe, particularly if the individual is in an established institutional setting. For voluntary programs, however, there is often no way of gathering data on individuals who will volunteer before they have in fact done so. After they have volunteered, one faces the possibility that whatever motivated them to join the program influences their subsequent behavior as strongly as any effect of the program.

**It takes a long time.** Carrying out a time series evaluation study without baseline data in records of past performance may require a long time, longer than many alternative evaluation strategies. Decision makers become restive, and with good reason, given the political and administrative realities of keeping programs alive. However, the possibility of building ongoing time series measuring processes to provide long-range feedback into decision-making systems, as suggested by Wortman (1975: 573), still exists, and may become a reality in certain situations.

**How generalizable are the findings?** The degree to which evaluation results can be generalized to larger populations is a prominent concern of program planners and decision makers. Time series strategies on the whole do not provide this kind of generalizability, but then even a well-randomized, well-executed group comparative study only allows one to say, "These results, within certain limits of confidence, are equally likely for any similar random sample from the specified population at this point in time." Time series strategies do offer a somewhat different conception of generalizability, allowing more confident estimates of probable change over time and of the persistence of effects over time. They also permit cautious estimates of generalized effects through the replication of patterns across units, across settings, or across different measures of the same unit.

In some time-series evaluations, such as that of Simon and Smith (1973), apologies are made for the fact that the findings from one unit do not seem particularly applicable to a variety of other settings because of the special characteristics of the unit being studied. These evaluators had hoped to conclude something of a more general nature about the relationship of health center location to utilization. However, it may be sufficient, particularly where the unit involved is a large aggregate, to look primarily at change within the unit, and to seek generalizability to other periods of time within this unit.

Other problems of time series evaluations are not as limiting as the five already discussed. Briefly, they include the following:

**Changes in instrumentation.** As discussed by both Glass et al. (1975) and by Cook and Campbell (1976), the possibility of changes in the manner of keeping records part way through a time series study creates an alternative interpretation of shifts found in the series. Crime statistics are the classic example of this difficulty. Large-scale reforms of police practice often are attended by considerable changes in the manner and extent to which crimes are reported. As another example, before the institution of a harsher penalty for disruptive behavior in the prison, as reported in the Schnelle and Lee (1974) evaluation, guards were less likely to report infractions so as to stay on the good side of the inmates.

**Changes in unit composition.** As Glass et al. (1975) have observed, in unit replicative designs repeated measures are made of similar or even randomly equated units, but the exact composition of the unit is different for different measurement points. Almost all of the evaluations cited in this paper involving an aggregated unit fall into this category. In such cases, subtle changes in unit composition may be responsible for changes in the time series. Equating units through randomized assignment, as in the Outward Bound evaluation (Smith et al., 1976), helps rule out this interpretation. Or if the exact nature of the unit changes are known, as in the Schnelle and Lee study in which certain individuals were removed from the prison population, the time series can be analyzed excluding the data from those who were part of the unit only during the baseline phase. Evaluations based on time series of individuals do not face this interpretation nor do studies of client groups whose membership does not change over the course of the study.

**Masking treatment effects in larger aggregated units.** Data from large and complex social units raise the issue of appropriate levels of analysis for detecting effects. A large jurisdictional unit may be simply too large and too poorly understood to allow a reasonable time series analysis. The solution usually consists of searching for smaller, more bounded subunits in which the effects will be demonstrated more clearly, if they exist at all. This general strategy underlies Zimring's analysis of Gun Control Law effects by a time series of several comparable cities' crime rates. Even here, it is not clear that he has isolated a unit which is sufficiently manageable and interpretable.

**Masking treatment effects in cyclical patterns and chance instability.** Seasonal or cyclic fluctuations in a measurement series (Cook and Campbell, 1976: 277) or the chance instability of measures due to statistical error or unexplainable variation (Glass et al., 1975: 61-62) may be confused with the effect of an intervention.

Dealing with these problems requires a firm grasp of the nature of the problem and its setting. For example, an evaluation involving classroom observation must attend to the weekly rhythm in the behavior and performance of students. Good baselines and adequate statistical tools also are important, but statistical findings still may run counter to the visual intuitive sense of the data. This limits the believability of time series data to many laypersons. A further limitation occurs where statistical procedures require more data points for reliable results than are available.

Cost. For certain kinds of time series studies, the costs of gathering repeated measures on a number of subjects within an aggregated unit may be fairly expensive in comparison with the costs of other ways of conducting an evaluation. Where elaborate or expensive measuring procedures are called for, it is unlikely that time-series strategies will meet sponsors' needs.

Legitimacy. Underlying the success of any evaluation scheme is the degree to which it is seen as legitimate by those who commission it. Time series designs to date have been used less widely in program evaluations than more conventional group comparative designs. Evaluators and decision makers alike are less familiar with them as a tool of formal program evaluation. But only by increasing use and better understanding of their characteristics will time series strategies achieve the place among approaches to evaluation which they probably deserve.


## SUMMING UP

In summary, the time series research framework brings to program evaluation situations some special advantages over more conventionally accepted evaluation strategies. It focuses directly on the individual unit, whatever that unit may be. It allows investigation of effect patterns in addition to effects measurable at any one point in time. In a situation of uncertainty about casual mechanisms or the nature of program implementation, it is an evocative mechanism whereby hypotheses can be generated systematically. Finally, it offers a somewhat different notion of the generalizability of effects by demonstrating the persistence of effects over time and the replicability of effects across individual units.

In addition to these conceptual contributions, time-series strategies bring to certain types of evaluation situations advantages of a more practical kind. Unstable treatments can be accommodated more flexibly by designs looking for changing patterns over time. Time-referenced evaluations can be mounted after the fact, if reliable records exist, on a more solid basis than the selective memories of participants. The data emerging from an evaluation study may be understood more intuitively by the practitioner, and more flexibility exists in data report timing. Finally, given the existence of records or a small number of units with simple measures, time series evaluations can be implemented cheaply.

Time-series evaluation strategies also have special limitations. Alternative interpretations of history must be ruled out, necessitating design complexities which may be difficult to implement. Easily repeatable measures for the most part are behavioral and archival indicators; variables assessed by complex tests or interviews are excluded from time series treatment. Time series studies mounted as planned experiments often take a longer time to complete than policy makers want. Establishing a long enough baseline to allow solid interpretations of changes in the data series is frequently a problem. Results are generalizable to large populations only in a special sense. Changes in record-keeping, shifts in the composition of an aggregated unit over time, and missing data can complicate interpretation of a time series. Treatment effects may be masked in measures of large, complex social units, or may be mistaken for chance instability or cyclical fluctuations in the series.

Still, time series approaches seem to offer a powerful potential to allow those who wish to form an evaluative judgment of an ongoing programmatic effort to combine systematic arrays of precise measurement at regular intervals with the unfolding narrative of events which includes a knowledge of the start and duration of the program. By using time series approaches, a quantitative picture of program effects over time can be brought together with a more qualitative understanding of the program as a phenomenon taking place within a specific time context. The potential for a fuller understanding of program effects deserves to be further developed and more widely utilized in the often complex task of evaluation.

## REFERENCES

BORNSTEIN, P. H. and R. P. QUEVILLON (1976) "The effects of a self-instructional package on overactive preschool boys." Journal of Applied Behavioral Analysis 9, 2: 179-188.

CAMPBELL, D. T. (1969) "Reforms as experiments." American Psychologist 24: 409-429.

CAMPBELL, D. T. and J. C. STANLEY (1966) Experimental and Quasi-Experimental Designs for Research. Chicago: Rand-McNally.

CARO, F. G. (1971) "Evaluation research: an overview," pp. 1-34 in F. G. Caro (ed.) Readings in Evaluation Research. New York: Russell Sage.

CHAPMAN, C. and T. RISLEY (1974) "Anti-litter procedures in an urban high density area." Journal of Applied Behavioral Analysis 7, 3: 377-383.

CHARTERS, W. W. and J. E. JONES (1975) "On neglect of the independent variable in program evaluation," pp. 341-353 in T. Baldridge and N. Deal (eds.) Managing Change in Educational Organizations. Berkeley: McCutchan.

COOK, T. D. and D. T. CAMPBELL (1976) "The design and conduct of quasi-experiments and true experiments in field settings," pp. 223-325 in R. Dunnette (ed.) Handbook of Industrial and Organizational Psychology. Chicago: Rand-McNally.

EDGAR, E. and F. BILLINGSLEY (1974) "Believability when N = 1." Psychological Record 24, 2: 147-160.

EVERETT, P. B., S. C. HAYWARD, and A. W. MEYERS (1974) "The effects of token reinforcement on bus ridership." Journal of Applied Behavioral Analysis 7, 1: 1-9.

GLASS, G. V., W. L. WILLSON, and J. M. GOTTMAN (1975) The Design and Analysis of Time-Series Experiments. Boulder: Colorado Associated University Press.

GOTTMAN, J. M. (1973) "N of one and N of two research in psychotherapy." Psychological Bulletin 80, 2: 93-105.

———, R. McFALL, and J. T. BARNETT (1969) "Design and analysis of research using time-series." Psychological Bulletin 72, 4: 299-306.

GUBA, E. G. (1972) "The failure of educational evaluation," pp. 250-266 in C. Weiss (ed.) Evaluating Action Programs. Boston: Allyn and Bacon.

KAZDIN, A. E. (1976) "Statistical analyses for single case experimental designs," pp. 265-316 in B. Hersen and R. Barlow (eds.) Single-Case Experimental Designs: Strategies for Studying Behavior Change. Oxford: Pergamon.

KIESLER, D. J. (1971) "Experimental designs in psychotherapy research," pp. 36-74 in A. E. Bergin and S. Garfield (eds.) Handbook for Psychotherapy and Behavior Change. New York: Wiley.

PARSONSON, B. S. and D. S. BAER (1978) "The analysis and presentation of graphic data," pp. 101-166 in T. R. Kratochwill (ed.) Strategies to Evaluate Change in Single Subject Research. New York: Academic Press.

PATTON, M. Q. (1975) Alternative Evaluation Research Paradigm. Grand Forks: University of North Dakota Press.

POPHAM, W. J. (1975) Educational Evaluation. Englewood Cliffs, NJ: Prentice-Hall.

ROSS, H. L. (1976) "The Scandinavian myth: the effectiveness of drinking-and-driving legislation in Sweden and Norway." pp. 578-604 in G. V. Glass (ed.) Evaluation Studies Review Annual. Beverly Hills: Sage.

SCHNELLE, J. F. and J. F. LEE (1974) "Quasi-experimental retrospective evaluation of a prison policy change." Journal of Applied Behavioral Analysis 7, 3: 483-496.

SCHNELLE, J. F., R. E. KIRCHNER, M. P. McNESS, and J. M. LAWLER (1975) "Soial evaluation research: the evaluation of two police patrolling strategies." Journal of Applied Behavioral Analysis 8, 4: 353-365.

SHELDON, E. B. and H. B. FREEMAN (1972) "Notes on social indicators: promises and potential," pp. 166-173 in C. Weiss (ed.) Evaluating Action Programs. Boston: Allyn and Bacon.

SIMON, J. L. and D. B. SMITH (1973) "Change in location of a student health service." Medical Care (January-February): 59-67.

SMITH, M. L., R. GABRIEL, J. SCHOTT, and W. L. PADIA (1976) "Evaluation of the effects of Outward Bound," pp. 400-421 in G. V. Glass (ed.) Evaluation Studies Review Annual. Beverly Hills: Sage.

THORESEN, C. E. and J. L. ANTON (1974) "Intensive experimental research in counseling." Journal of Counseling Psychology 21, 6: 553-559.

--- (1973) "Intensive Counselling." Focus on Guidance 6, 2: 1-12.

WEISS, C. H. (1972) Program Evaluation: Methods of Assessing Program Effectiveness. Englewood Cliffs, NJ: Prentice-Hall.

WEISS, R. S. and M. REIN (1972) "Evaluation of broad-aim programs: difficulties in experimental design and an alternative," pp. 236-249 in C. Weiss (ed.) Evaluating Action Programs. Boston: Allyn and Bacon.

WORTMAN, P. M. (1975) "Evaluation research: a psychological perspective." American Psychologist 30: 562-575.

ZIMRING, F. E. (1976) "Firearms and federal law: the Gun Control Act of 1968." pp. 511-577 in G. V. Glass (ed.) Evaluation Studies Review Annual. Beverly Hills: Sage.

# SECTION III
# IMPROVING MEASUREMENT

# 9

## SEARCHING FOR THE JND
## IN MENTAL HEALTH

Charles Windle

## INTRODUCING THE SCD

The key part of the title is the *n* in "just noticeable difference." This term draws attention to the importance of subjectivity in assessing the usefulness of program evaluation results. In addition to magnitude of differences, drama, human interest, and style of presentation influence what is noticed. However, this title perpetuates a common misconception: that use of program evaluation results is based largely on rational, economic decisions and therefore one needs only to get the attention of potential utilizers.

A behavioral model seems more applicable than an economic model. Organizational and personal interests often differ greatly from formal goals or job assignments. Program policies and practices are shaped by many influences, of which study results are only a small part. Thus, for study results to play an appreciable role, results must be more than "noticeable." They must be compelling, motivating to action.

To understate what seems a consensus, program evaluation does not have a good record for improving programs by use of results. Thus, rather than a jnd, we need to search for an scd, or "socially compelling difference." The term scd also focuses on social factors in the use of results. Many organizations are structured loosely with multiple, competing components. Roos (1974) described these organizations as relatively unable to use information to pursue overall goals, and more likely to change by accommodating to external pressures. A hierarchical organization seems necessary for information to shape decisions maximizing the organization's goals. Thus, external pressure frequently may be necessary to impel use of program evaluation results.

Primack and von Hippel (1974) found that scientists' advice to the federal government had little impact except when it became a part of the public discourse. This potentiating of evaluation results can apply also in local agencies, if it is likely that study results will become public. Some legislation already encourages such disclosure. For example, the Community Mental Health Centers (CMHC) Act requires that federally supported CMHCs disclose the results of program evaluation to residents of the catchment area and review these results with them (Windle and Ochberg, 1975). This potential for public attention makes the results of evaluations more likely to be attended to also by program managers. For these reasons, the concept of the socially compelling difference may be useful for program evaluation.

The concept of scd implies a change in the usual model for program evaluation. Guttentag (1977) has made a carefully reasoned argument for expecting moderately large changes in paradigms for program evaluations. She notes that the nature of science is changing in the shift from an industrial to a postindustrial society, the latter being oriented to decisions rather than the laws of nature. She urges a corresponding change in evaluations to incorporate such a decision orientation in evaluation studies. I want to make a more radical suggestion: that we model program evaluations not on procedures to gather information, but on procedures to impel change.

## PROGRAM EVALUATION IN
## MENTAL HEALTH SERVICES

This argument is based less on a grand view of social change and more on experiences in mandated evaluations at federal and local mental health facility levels. This limited perspective may restrict the generality of these suggestions, as will the fact that although this experience was gained at the National Institute of Mental Health, these views do not necessarily represent those of the NIMH.

I am concerned about the gap between social expectations for evaluation and actual accomplishments. Some have asserted that program evaluation is failing to contribute directly to social decisions. This harsh judgment may be unfair, since there has not been adequate time or support conditions for useful program evaluation to develop. Yet convincing evidence that program evaluation is worth its costs remains wanting.

This seems true at both federal and local levels. Buchanan and Wholey (1972) observed that evaluation of federal programs is supported on the basis of the recognized need for evaluative information, rather than on evidence of accomplishments. This is true at NIMH, where the earmarked 1% for program evaluation has been used for studies to help local CMHCs evaluate their own programs and to influence Congress more than to help the agency's own decisions (Stockdill, 1977). At the CMHC level, evaluations seem supported because of concern with three serious problems in service delivery: rising costs, structural difficulties leading to inequities and inefficiencies, and a still primitive treatment technology (Windle, 1976).

Program evaluation is unlikely to solve these problems. It is seldom oriented towards costs, and it lacks techniques to relate costs to outcomes. Many service system structural problems stem from providers' having greater power than consumers, an imbalance reflected throughout the country in many social conditions, and an imbalance which evaluation within-agencies can't challenge. Improving treatment technology requires applying the careful controls of basic research to new treatments, not rapid study of entire programs. What happens, in fact, from much evaluation is advocacy of specific programs to funding sources. It is doubtful that this is of great overall societal benefit. Therefore, some disappointments from evaluations, however improved, seem likely.

Given this likelihood of the failure of program evaluation to remedy the most serious problems in the service systems, we should consider using a new model. The current model remains based on assumptions of managers' rationality and desire for accurate information. These assumptions are consistent with the expertise and vested interests of scientists, whose power and legitimacy are based on the importance of information and sophisticated study methods. But evaluation is vulnerable to what Fuchs (1968) called a technological imperative, the pressures to use available techniques. Evaluation may be distracted into elegant, but irrelevant, methodologies.

A rival model to basing program evaluation on careful research methods is to base it on characteristics needed for program change and use of information. Usually we do a study and then look to see if anyone can use it. We could instead start with determining what forms and content of information and what procedures for information gathering would have a practical impact, and then consider how to obtain this information in a way to make it meaningful. Use of information requires focus on dramatic, attention-catching features and public dissemination of the evaluation results. And it often focuses on current bad conditions needing remedy. Three examples may make this suggestion clearer.

## CENTERS' EMERGENCY SERVICES

The NIMH recently undertook a collaborative survey of CMHCs' emergency services. This collaboration was between two interest group organizations, the National Council of Community Mental Health Centers and the Mental Health Association, and the Institute and Regional Offices responsible for monitoring CMHCs. The collaboration was more accidental, based on similar views, than conspiratorial. There is wide concern about the quality of the centers' services. Some arises from difficulties in managing the program (U.S. General Accounting Office, 1974). Monitoring for compliance with the law is not a popular duty for federal employees (Abt, 1976), contrary to popular impressions of the bureaucracy. Bureaucrats want to be loved, too. And those monitored are not without power to cause trouble if they feel the monitoring is too demanding. There is also concern about the future of the CMHC Program as financing shifts toward national health insurance. The NIMH and the interest groups want CMHCs' services to qualify for third-party coverage, and to be seen as of value for public funding.

A 24-hour emergency service is required of all centers. A simple, dramatic means to test this service was readily at hand. After conversations about a potential test among interested parties, the National

Council of CMHCs and the Mental Health Association telephoned a random sample of 99 centers on a Sunday. This survey found that a third of the centers did not answer the number called.

Now this is dramatic program evaluation, compelling action. The drama springs not so much from the size of the gap between observed and expected, the 33%, as from the clear importance of the criterion of answering the phone. The agency had irresistible justification for management efforts to improve the centers.

The Institute asked all regional offices to (1) survey all their centers' compliance with the required 24-hour emergency service and (2) conduct a stratified random sample survey on another Sunday, using the centers' emergency telephone numbers, since these might be more appropriate if publicized locally. Many of the regional offices' surveys were change oriented, designed to use the study process to improve adequacy of services at the centers (Windle, Albert, and Scharfstein, 1978).

This involved first advising centers of the impending survey and the importance of emergency services. Next, the surveys were conducted, using a variety of approaches. At least one region incorporated corrective action into the survey process. A center which did not answer because staff did not know how to use the new telephone equipment was given time for retraining and retested, as one example. The regions found various centers out of compliance, using criteria broader than simply answering the telephone at all times. With these centers, the regions are encouraging change more forcefully, investigating thoroughly to determine that findings are accurate, and insisting that centers correct deficiencies to retain funding. The agency's survey verified the meaningfulness of the interest groups' survey, even though fewer problems were found.

The last stage in this action research is assembling information and disseminating it to help centers. Analysis of the correlates of center deficiencies showed little relationship between area demography and adequacy of emergency services (Windle and Goodstein, 1978). However, in-compliance centers had higher utilization rates and a higher percentage of patient care staff hours by volunteers than did out-of-compliance centers. These trends suggest a greater outreach effort, and volunteers have been found useful and economical in providing emergency services. As a capstone to this monitoring effort, the agency conducted a workshop in connection with the National Council of CMHCs to produce a guide to future technical assistance to the centers.

This collaborative style of program evaluation has special relevance in reducing care provider isolation. The experience of being in the position of the client, as consumer advocate DeVito (1977) says, allows one to "evaluate without numbers." Studies which simulate what being a client is like or report convincingly on the experience also qualify as effective program evaluations.

## EQUITY IN SERVICES TO NONWHITES

The second example is an attempt to improve the equity of CMHCs' services. Centers are supposed to be responsive to the needs for services within designated service areas. A crude measure of whether centers are responsive may be derived from utilization rates by race. In general, if only because they usually are poorer, nonwhites seem to have more mental health problems for which they cannot get service privately than do whites. Therefore, one would usually expect a responsive CMHC to serve nonwhites at higher rates than whites. This pattern does apply for the CMHC Program as a whole (Redick, 1976) but not for all centers. We felt this expectation could be used, at least for screening purposes, in monitoring CMHCs in areas with appreciable numbers of nonwhites.

We examined the 211 centers which had over 2,000 nonwhites in the catchment area, reported over 500 admissions in 1974 by white and nonwhite status, and reported that over half the persons served lived in the catchment area. Feedback sheets were produced for each center comparing the racial composition of the catchment area, the clients served, and the professional and nonprofessional staff. Ratios were calculated of the nonwhite client and staffing rates as a percentage of white rates. Our major concern was the clients served. We used equality in rates of service as the critical level for screening, since this was a natural, easily understood distinction, with face validity as a criterion of adequacy. The data for 79 centers indicated lower rates of service to nonwhites than to whites (Windle, 1977).

The agency effort to cause change required working with the regional offices to inform centers of apparent inadequacies, and to ask centers to take corrective actions. Most centers agreed that lower rates of service for nonwhites was inappropriate. All those responding to queries claimed that they had already taken remedial actions and planned future ones. The most frequently claimed action was to recruit minority staff and have educational and outreach efforts. Seldom were changes in types of service proposed. We do not yet know what impact this monitoring type of program evaluation had, but plan to look next year. The point here relates to the common sense appeal and drama of the criterion used, namely, equality in rates.

# EXPOSES

The third example also applies to the National Institute of Mental Health, but in a somewhat different way. This is an evaluation which has been done in and by the media on the inadequacies of St. Elizabeth's Hospital, formally a part of the agency. The TV and newspaper reports are dramatic and emotional exposes, descriptions of conditions which are patently inappropriate.

According to one article,

The finances of Saint Elizabeths Hospital approach Alice in Wonderland in quality. One of the wealthiest public hospitals in the United States, its budget almost tripled (to $90 million annually) over the past 10 years at the same time patients were *decreasing* from 6,000 to 2,500 and its accreditation was being lost. Last year, for example, almost $2 million was wasted in overtime pay alone through poor management. Maryland cares for twice as many admissions with the same number of personnel at four state hospitals, all accredited, for a total cost $30 million less than Saint Elizabeths [Torrey, 1977].

Exposés in mental hospitals sometimes use shocking pictures of patients' living conditions with great effect. The muckraking type of program evaluation is likely to be strongly motivating. The rules of evidence may leave something to be desired, and the thrust of these evaluations may be negative, personalized, and oversimplified, but they are usually relevant, timely, and productive of action, unlike much evaluation. The comparison illustrates that we must be concerned lest the technological imperative of our research techniques leads us, with precision, into irrelevance.

When the criterion for our work is action, the product should be motivating, not merely convincing.

# REFERENCES

Abt Associates (1976) "Study and evaluation of the impact of regional office technical assistance and monitoring activities." Report to the Department of Health, Education and Welfare, Contract No. 292-76-0002.

BUCHANAN, G. N. and J. S. WHOLEY (1972) "Federal level evaluation." Evaluation 1: 17-22.

DeVITO, P. J. (1977) "Evaluating without numbers: one consumer's view on the evaluation of mental health facilities." *Ripple* (New York State Department of Mental Hygiene Newsletter). May, 5-6.

FUCHS, V. (1968) "The growing demand for medical care." New England Journal of Medicine 279: 190-195.

GUTTENTAG, M. (1977). "Evaluation and society." Personality and Social Psychology Bulletin 3: 31-40.

PRIMACK, J. and F. Von HIPPEL (1974) Advice and Dissent: Scientists in the Political Arena. New York: Basic Books.

REDICK, R. W. (1976) "Addition rates to federally funded community mental health centers in the United States." National Institute of Mental Health Statistical Note No. 126, DHEW Publ. No. (ADM) 76-158.

ROOS, N. P. (1974) "Influencing the health care system: policy alternatives." Public Policy 22: 139-167.

STOCKDILL, J. W. (1977) "Mental health," pp. 13-15 in E. Chelimsky (ed.) Proceedings of a Symposium on the Use of Evaluation by Federal Agencies. McLean, VA: Mitre.

TORREY, E. F. (1977) "A cure for D.C. psychiatry" Washington Post (September 4): C-8.

U.S. General Accounting Office (1974) Need for More Effective Management of Community Health Centers Program.

WINDLE, C. (1977) Statistics on community mental health center services to non-whites and use of these statistics to improve services. Presentation at conference on centers services to minorities. Washington, DC.

––– (1976) "A crisis for program evaluation: an embarrassment of opportunity." Rhode Island Medical Journal 59: 503-516.

––– and F. M. OCHBERG (1975) "Enhancing program evaluation in the community mental health centers program." Evaluation 2, 2: 31-36.

WINDLE, C. and J. GOODSTEIN (1978) Correlates of the Adequacy of Centers' Telephone Emergency Services. (unpublished)

WINDLE, C., M. ALBERT, and S. SCHARFSTEIN (1978) "Collaborative program evaluation to improve emergency services in Community Mental Health Centers." Hospital and Community Psychiatry 29: 708-710.

# 10

## MEASURING IMPACT: POWER THEORY
## IN SOCIAL PROGRAM EVALUATION

### Robert F. Boruch and Hernando Gomez

This article's aim is to present some theory and technique for improving our ability to understand the effects of a new social program. Our special interest lies in the measurement of treatment and response so that we may better establish the statistical power of an evaluation design, enhance power, and understand the evaluation results. We confine attention to *outcome evaluation,* that is, estimating in the least equivocal and least biased way possible the relative effect of a program on its target group. The estimate may be made with respect to a control group, to a competing treatment group, or to some other standard. Goal-free evaluation and other approaches with different aims fall outside the scope of this article.

One of the motives for exploring the topic is sheer frustration. Evaluations often yield "no significant differences," and that finding is often a matter of weak evaluation design. Poor design is partly a

**AUTHORS' NOTE:** This chapter was prepared with support from the National Institute of Education (C-74-0115). It is reprinted with permission: Copyright (1977) by the American Psychological Association.

function of measurement. Another motive is developing a more informative theory of statistical power for evaluations. The theory, as it is usually presented in textbooks, is arid, and partly for that reason, it is underutilized. We believe it should be embellished to reflect better the realities of social experimentation, and so we present an outline for augmenting the theory. The third motive is to lend more substance to the theory of field testing innovative social programs. The approach taken here constitutes a rude but reasonable theory for describing how observable effects of a new program, conscientiously estimated, are degraded in the field. Its merit lies partly in its relation to statistical power theory and partly in its accommodation of a few realities of field testing.

The first section below illustrates briefly the problem of ensuring power in evaluation design, links the problem to measurement issues, then offers a modest theory to guide its reconnaissance. The second major section discusses the response variable in evaluations, and the third section discusses the treatment program in more detail. The illustrations come from a variety of social sciences because the problems addressed here are general.

## THE PROBLEM OF ENSURING POWER

Consider the following scenario. A theorist invents a novel compensatory education program, tests it fairly in a laboratory experiment, and finds that the effect on children's achievement is notable. The effect size is a half standard deviation difference between the experimental group's mean and some standard. A foundation then decides that the program is promising, supports a half dozen field versions of the program, and submits each to evaluation. Each field experiment shows no evidence of a notable effect; that is, treated and untreated groups exhibit no major difference.

Our interest lies in the reasons for the failure to detect effects in the field. We assume, as will sometimes be the case, that the field evaluator has exploited standard tactics for enhancing the power of experimental tests, e.g., blocking or covariance, or both (Cohen, 1969; and Riecken et al., 1974). We make the more tenuous assumption that in evaluations based on quasi-experimental designs, newer tactics for avoiding statistical biases have been used (Campbell and Boruch, 1975).

Our small theory posits that partial irrelevance of the response variable and degradation of the treatment variable in the field will often be major causes of the failure to detect effects. To carry this idea beyond simpleminded speculation, consider the same example made more concrete. With a program effect of a half standard deviation in the laboratory, a sample of size 40, and a conventional significance level such as .01, the power of the laboratory test will be about .92; that is, the chances are 9 out of 10 that an effect will be detected in such tests when the standard is specified.

The algebraic version of our theory suggests that this power cannot be reasonably expected in the field. In particular, the response variables chosen by evaluation contractors or program staff are often only partly relevant to the program content. A standardized achievement test chosen for convenience in the field, for instance, may only be 75% relevant to the program content. And because of natural random variation in quality of measurement, the test's reliability may dip to .80. Further, it will usually be the case that the treatment delivered in the laboratory will not be the treatment delivered in the field. Simple indifference among field staff may reduce the treatment's fidelity to 75% of its design value, and natural random variation in staff delivery and in student receipt will reduce the uniformity of treatment as well. It is easy to show that under such conditions the power drops to about .30. That is, the chances of discovering the effect in the field are small.

This, we believe, is a dreadful but realistic state of affairs. The phenomenon is roughly analogous to voltage drops in the transmission of electrical power from a generating station to a customer. The precipitous drop in statistical power occurs because invalidity of response and infidelity of treatment have a multiplicative, rather than an additive, effect. The following remarks present the theory and evidence in a bit more detail.

## AUGMENTING STANDARD THEORY

We first posit a treatment variable as ideal or theorized and a response variable as ideal or theorized; each is potentially measurable. We suppose that in the laboratory test both the response and treatment variables are ideal. *Treatment variable* here means *both* novel program and normal conditions, i.e., both treatment and control or two competing treatments. The normal theoretical assumption is that the response and treatment variables are functionally related. The simplest form of the assumption is that the response is an additive function of treatment effects and some unknowable random variables. This little model, of course, underlies any orthodox analysis of variance. We regard the model as adequate in the laboratory and less adequate in the field.

Consider first how the notion of *response variable* might be augmented to better reflect reality. The example of compensatory education implies that problems of measurement must be divided into two categories. The first concerns the choice or construction of a measurement device that, under good conditions, is valid with respect to the treatment variable. That is, elements of response are nicely linked in theory to elements of treatment. The second issue involves degradation of this nice measure in field settings. To represent generic validity of the response variable, we rely on a simple statistical model which expresses the observable response as an imperfect function of response as theorized; reliable but irrelevant variation in response accounts for the imperfection. To recognize the fact that the generically good response measure is further degraded randomly in the field, we add to the model some random error, called unreliability.

Consider next the variable labeled *treatment*. It is reasonable to propose, based on the evidence at hand, that classical statistical conceptions of treatment be augmented in two ways. First, admit that gross structural differences between the treatment as theorized and the treatment as it is actually imposed in the field will normally appear. The simplest way to represent this idea is to posit an index of structural integrity or fidelity of treatment that, like a proportion, varies between 0 and 1. In the simplest case, this might be the percentage of overlap between the staff behaviors prescribed for inducing client change in an experimental program and the staff behaviors actually exhibited in the field. Second, recognize that in social programs the actual level of treatment imposition and reception will vary on a continuum for each client. Even if that variation cannot be measured, it does affect sensitivity and so ought to be recognized in design. The idea of a macrolevel bias, induced by structural infidelity of treatment, and a microlevel variation at the recipient level can be simplified by using a regression model. That is, describe treatment in the field as a function of its structural integrity and as a function of individual variation in imposition and receipt.

The response and treatment variables in the field are represented here then by simple regression models that recognize variation in fidelity. By augmenting the usual analysis of variance model with these and computing the power for both the simple and the augmented models, it is easy to show the drop in power. In the following remarks we add literal flesh to this theoretical bone.

# THE RESPONSE VARIABLE

Ensuring that the response variables adequately reflect treatment effects is a cyclical dilemma in *exploratory* research. We do not know if a response variable is relevant until we detect effects, but to detect effects, we need to know if the variable is indeed relevant. Any arguments about relevance in this instance are primarily theoretical. For *confirmatory* field research, and especially for policy-related evaluations, however, we believe there ought to be both sound theory and data to support the contention that the response variable proposed for the evaluation is indeed relevant to the treatment variable. The distinction between exploratory and confirmatory research is consistent with Kempthorne's (1975) use of the terms and is the case considered here.

Our aim is to identify a measure of the response variable that is relevant to treatment, relevance being determined by some clear criteria. Having said this ever so piously, it is difficult to say more because the criteria for determining relevance are not often simple. They include substantive theory, prior data, and pilot tests. And they include side theories for understanding how the response variable is related to the actual status of the individual and to the program content.

## SUBSTANTIVE THEORY

Few substantive theories of human behavior specify how relevance of a response variable with respect to a treatment program ought to be established. More important for field evaluations, the theoretical linkages between response and treatment ought to be laid out beforehand, but rarely are. At least one group of evaluators, Wholey, Nay, Scanlon, and Schmidt (1975), have built a notable reputation partly by trying to specify such linkages in ongoing programs.

Their general approach focuses on determining the extent to which a program can be evaluated. Their strategy is to lay out the *assumed* linkages between program activity and program objectives in a rhetorical program model. This literally describes, for example, how components of a community mental health center program are expected to affect inappropriate use of state mental hospitals, maintenance of economically viable community programs, quality of service, and so on. By eliminating untestable assumptions about linkage between program elements and objectives and by eliminating unmeasurable objectives, the analysts produce an evaluatable program model. The product is a rudimentary and truncated theory of why treatment and response variables may be related. It is a simple strategy in the sense that it seeks only to establish plausible and testable linkages. It is sophisticated in the sense that it can help the researcher avoid choosing gratuitous response variables for an evaluation. That is, it helps to eliminate naive reliance on those variables as indicators of program quality.

The approach, as proposed by Wholey and his colleagues, is distinctive but not new. Its origins lie in good advice offered in the past—that whether one can invent an effective ameliorative program depends heavily on understanding the processes underlying deficiency, e.g., on a theory of why criminals repeat crimes. That theory, in elaborate form, specifies how the response variable, recidivism, for example, might be altered by manipulating conditions (Rossi, 1977). The theory may be wrong, but that is the reason for the field test; the point is that theory should be quite explicit.

To be concrete about what appears to be good practice for *new* theory-based programs, we cite both good and bad examples and confess our inability to do much more. George Fairweather, Louis Tornatsky, and others built community mental health programs whose content, activity, and target group are dedicated in theory to patients' social adjustment, so their use of multiple indicators of social adjustment, behavioral and otherwise, makes sense. In education, the Heber, Garber, Harrington, Hoffman, and Falender (1972) work was designed on the basis of a theory that links infant IQ to stimulation in early infancy, so their use of standard measures of IQ as a response variable has a special place in their program evaluation, and that emphasis is laudable regardless of other features of the research. Waldo and Chiricos (1977) justified their use of over a dozen measures of recidivism as a response variable in evaluations of work release programs on the basis of five different theories of the way such programs are supposed to affect the ex-offender's behavior. At the level of individual interaction in the classroom, Brophy (1977) and his colleagues rationalize the linkage between microlevel student behaviors and microlevel teacher behaviors toward the student.

These examples illustrate the painstaking effort that is sometimes required to establish a linkage, and sometimes they are dead wrong. They do stand as a bit of an embarrassment to the less careful researcher. The latter category includes researchers who believe a program developer's announcement that the program objective is "social adjustment" of its clients only to find out later that the staff who have direct contact with the clients not only reject the idea that social adjustment is a primary goal but cannot agree on specific objectives. It includes the researcher who, with touching optimism and slender rationalization, measures children's IQs after six months of a busing program to discover that busing has no effect on IQ. And so on.

Relying on weak substantive theory appears to be more risky than relying on available data, and so we consider that evidence next.

PRIOR DATA

The data available prior to an evaluation can be used to argue that a particular response measure is indeed sensitive to the program as designed and so should be measured in the field test. The data can be used to help decide *which* measures of an attribute are most likely to reflect differences in the field, some measures being more robust against deliberate or accidental corruption than others. And the data can be used to guess the likely size of the program's effect under formal evaluation, that is, to establish the power of the experimental design. This last function represents a higher consciousness level, so it is the main focus of the following remarks.

The nature of the available data varies enormously, of course. Most often the evidence on a response measure will be complicated to interpret, if simple to collect. Multiple regression of a response variable on treatment-related variables in surveys and other nonrandomized studies can be informative *provided* we recognize the shortcomings of estimated regression coefficients. The little brutes can be inflated *or* deflated by measurement error in the variables (Cochran, 1968). And if the substantive theory, and therefore the regression equation, fails to include some variables that nature says are important, then the bias in estimates of the coefficients may be unknowable (Campbell and Boruch, 1975). Perhaps more commonly, the evidence is very difficult to interpret, being based on simple correlations or cross-tabulations that are unencumbered by any information about reliability of measures, the nature of the sample on which the statistic is based, or the sampling process. It is at this point that weak theory and weak data force rather more vigorous approaches to establishing the relevance of response measures, notably the pilot studies considered later.

Regardless of the data's nature, access to pertinent information is growing. Archives such as the DOPE (Databank of Program Evaluations) file at the University of California, Los Angeles, MEDLARS (Medical Literature Analysis and Retrieval System) in medical research, ERIC (Educational Resources Information Center) in education, though imperfect in many respects, can be helpful in building dossiers on response variable use in evaluation. At the very least, they report whether a given response variable was affected by a treatment program. And at best, they also provide information on the variable's reliability or validity with respect to other standards. They beg for better organization for this purpose and better exploitation. These resources are augmented periodically by the release of raw data from completed program evaluations. The secondary analyses of these data can yield better understanding of the size of program effect under various conditions and some feeling for the degree to which a response variable is relevant to the program (e.g., Cook et al., 1975). Finally, meta-analyses of the sort constructed by Glass (1976) are also useful in this enterprise. They consolidate information about the size of effect of roughly similar programs from field studies regardless of the specific response variables, and the information can be used to anticipate the size of effect for the response variable and program at hand. The *specific* response variables used in the studies used as a sample in meta-analysis are, however, usually not examined closely.

The crude statistics on reliability and validity that are usually published for standardized measures are also pertinent. These constitute indirect rather than direct evidence: measures may be internally consistent, quite reliable in conventional test-retest settings, and valid with respect to the standards chosen by the developer of the inventory, but still unrelated in theory or in practice to the program under evaluation or to the target group to which it is directed. This does suggest that reviews published by Buros and others in education, by Anderson and his colleagues in health services, and by others ought to include references to experiments in which the measure has been used as a response measure. The absence of statistics on the sensitivity of a measure with respect to a treatment variable makes these reviews much less useful than they could be. Similarly, reports on evaluations published in scientific journals often include no explicit description of homemade tests or of relevant item content on the standardized tests actually used (Porter et al., 1978). Journal policies which require the simultaneous submission of instrumentation reports with articles, and the maintenance and dissemination of such reports through the documentation centers such as ERIC and others, do not seem unreasonable.

## ADOPTION, ADAPTION, AND CONSTRUCTION

The problem of deciding whether to adopt a standardized measure of response rather than to build one from scratch is not new. But it has become a bit more crucial, since the quality of program evaluations depends partly on the decision. The argument for the adoption of a standardized measure in a program evaluation is usually based on the measure's convenience and properties. That is, the measure is readily available and easily employed, and it is known to discriminate reliably among individuals in a standardization sample. Two important problems are implicit in the practice, however. First, the measure's relevance to the social program's target group is often unclear. Despite its reliability and validity with respect to a standardization sample, it may not be a valid indicator of the pertinent attribute in the idiosyncratic sample at hand. The second, more nearly unique problem concerns the measure's relevance to the program at hand.

In health services research, for instance, health status indicators that weight mortality heavily have been standard. Yet they are not particularly good indicators of the health status of many groups to which health services are targeted, notably economically deprived families (International Journal of Health Services Research 1976). And they are insensitive to many of the health program's activities (e.g., venereal disease control). In criminal justice research, recidivism is a standard indicator of the impact of new rehabilitation programs. It too is imperfect because many programs, recognizing a natural ceiling on what can be accomplished, direct their attention to reducing the severity of the recidivist's crime, controlling cost, or establishing equitable restitution for the victim.

Bianchini's (1978) research on the problem in evaluating compensatory education programs is among the most informative. He has examined California Achievement Test data within grade groups for both standardization samples and schools eligible for Emergency School Assistance Act (ESAA) funds. Although he found that the achievement test had good properties in the standardization sample, it was notably less valid an indicator of ability in the ESAA sample. In particular, the test floor for the latter sample puts 10%-25% of the students (depending on grade) at or below chance level scores, in contrast to a 3%-7% rate in the standardization sample. And though the range of scores was the same for the two samples, the pile-up at the lower extreme of the test for the ESAA sample raised the mean difficulty level of the test for that sample and lowered the measure's validity as an indicator of ability. This in turn made it a less valid gauge of the program's effects, if indeed the program was effective. To establish crudely how relevant the standard tests are to curriculum, he simply counted vocabulary common to tests and instruction. Doing so for the Stanford Reading Test, used in response to state legislative requirements for standardized testing, he found students performing well below national norms; but overlap in vocabulary content was only 20%. The Cooperative Reading Tests, used more recently by the state, placed California students closer to the national average; but test-curriculum content overlap was closer to 60%. Bianchini has suggested that the discrepancy in test results was due to the unique chracteristics of the standardization samples and the differences in curriculum content associated with each.

The approach can be elaborated in the interest of understanding comparability of standardized achievement tests, health status indicators, and other conventional inventories. Porter et al. (1978), for example, have constructed taxonomies to organize the types of items found typically in achievement tests. The work will facilitate systematic comparison of the contents of different tests, and comparison of test content with textbooks or other curriculum materials.

The point is that standard measures may be used to place people validly on a broad continuum of health or ability, but their quality in this respect implies virtually nothing about their validity in the extreme ranges. And indeed many new social programs are targeted to people in those ranges. Even when valid there, the indicator may be only partly relevant to program objectives—the overlap in indicator content and program content may be low. As Bianchini (1978) suggests, the first problem is the ordinary one of ensuring that the test has good properties in the sample at hand. The problem of determining that the measure chosen can register treatment effects is secondary but fundamental in evaluative research.

The construction of new response measures presents no less difficult a problem. In principle, it is possible to develop indicators of ability, say, that do not depend for their validity on the standardization sample and that can be used to estimate ability accurately in extreme ranges. Item parameters need to be independent of the standardization sample to avoid ceiling and floor effects, for instance. In practice, this is supposed to be one of the benefits of using such models as those discussed in Bock (1975) and proposed by Rasch, Samejima, and Bock to scale items in a test or inventory. The use of the models in major education and nutrition experiments and elsewhere has been promising (Gomez, 1977). Without the technical support and large samples that these methods demand, however, some less elaborate tactics are justified.

Strategies for the construction of response variables that suit the setting vary considerably. They are based on common sense or what passes for common sense occasionally embellished by good statistical sense. For Tyler (1978), the problem has been to avoid naive adoption of standardized achievement tests for assessing novel education programs. He has focused instead on the construction of tests that are obviously relevant to the program content. In particular, he espouses the notion that test items ought to be constructed and compiled on the basis of what teachers are teaching. For Fairweather and Tornatsky (1977) in mental health and for Katz and Akpom (1976) in health services research, the problem was similarly framed: examine the content of a program, and build instruments that overlap in an obvious way with program content. In each case, the effort was coupled with side study to ensure that the responses were reliable in the simplest sense and valid with respect to at least one standard—program objectives and content.

For Brickell (1976), merely having established a linkage between content of a test and content of a program was insufficient. He found, in evaluating career education programs, that response variables constructed on the basis of program objectives, content, and teacher behaviors do not differentiate between program participants and nonparticipants. He regarded this failure to detect program effects as contrary to the impressionistic opinions of his classroom observers. So, in a new cycle of test construction, Brickell and company developed a test based on children's behavior in the career education classroom, especially those behaviors and skills that are likely to differentiate such children from nonparticipants. The tactic is not unreasonable; its mathematical analogue, a discriminant analysis, is over fifty years old. And it does yield results—participants and nonparticipants do differ notably on the response variable. Unfortunately, Brickell's entertaining story line was not supported by any information about the properties of resulting tests, or with any analysis of the way participants and nonparticipants differ prior to the program evaluation. The tactic is promising and open to debate and investigation.

The arguments over adoption versus construction of new response variables are not likely to go away in the near future. We see no option when novel programs are tested on small and idiosyncratic target populations but to tailor the measures. We see no option but to adopt or adapt standard measures for global programs run over longer periods if the program under evaluation is directed to populations used as a basis for developing the standardized measure. The use of both tailored and standard measures seems natural for research falling between the two extremes and for tests of novel programs. In the latter case, the use of both new and standard indicators is warranted to establish relations between the two.

### SIDE THEORIES

Social theories fail to attend at all to the idea that validity of the response variable will be degraded in field evaluations of theory-based programs. That disability is being corrected in a few quarters. Total survey design theory, for example, is a formal effort to couple classical sampling theory to more realistic assumptions about how people respond—fallibly (Reeder, 1976). Credibility approaches to marketing research involve theory to recognize that some people will not always do what they say they will do (Brown, 1969). Still other theories are auxiliary, tied more closely to the use of evaluative data.

In broadening his thesis on social experimentation, for example, Campbell (1975) espoused a side theory on corruption of social indicators. The idea is that as soon as it becomes well known that a measure is being used in making policy decisions, notably in program evaluations, the measure will be corrupted in some degree. To get beyond the statement, one must identify the main influences on corruption. For Knightly (1975), in what must stand as a model of crude theory in war reporting, this meant tracing the quality of battle statistics as a function of incompetent journalists, self-interested generals, self-serving politicians, and as a function of what appears to have been a minority, the virtuous members of each camp. For program evaluations, the magnitude of corruption ought to be anticipated at least approximately. The task is less difficult with methodological studies on how response bias depends on the training and attitudes of interviewers, level of threat to the respondent, and so on (Reeder, 1976; Sudman and Bradburn 1974). The task of controlling some forms of distortion has become less formidable with the advent of specialized methods for eliciting sensitive information in surveys. So-called randomized response techniques and other methods can sometimes be effective alternatives to pious assurances of confidentiality (Boruch and Cecil, 1979).

The perspective reflected in each of these activities is distinctive and fundamental, but not new. It may be found, for example, in James Madison's remarkable theories of social enterprise, including small theory of degradation in social statistics. He suggested that inter alia if representation was to be governed by census alone, states "would have an interest in exaggerating their inhabitants. Were the rule to decide their share of taxation alone, a contrary temptation would prevail. . . . extending the rule to both objectives, the states. . . . will produce the requisite impartiality" (Cooke, 1961; Cassedy, 1969).

The more general side theories of validity of the response variable in contemporary research depend on changes in the target population and social system, as well as on the use of the indicator. Mortality statistics are a less informative indicator of health status than they once were, at least in the United States, partly because age-specific mortality is now so low for many age categories. And so they are not especially relevant to many health services programs (Elinson, 1977). Unemployment statistics are regarded by some contemporary theorists as a less informative indicator of economic hardship than they were when the unemployment statistics program started, because income transfer payments and other factors noticeably dilute the economic hardship dimension of those data (Levitan and Taggart, 1976). Self-reported victimization rates may supplement ordinary crime statistics partly because the latter's relevance can be affected by changes in the social definition of *reportable crimes* and the political and institutional influences on the accuracy of crime statistics.

All of this points up the fact that the special theory of response can be constructed to guide the understanding of validity of response. For evaluations, the theory is crucial: the failure to anticipate the degraded quality of response will degrade the quality of an outcome evaluation. The simple statistical model used in our appendix to represent degradation is adapted from Cleary, Linn, and Walster (1970) and illustrates the point. It is possible to anticipate the degradation in power and perhaps even to control it, provided that validity of the response variable with respect to treatment can be guessed.

## PILOT FEASIBILITY TESTS AND SIDE STUDIES

Mark Twain, according to Mark Twain, was not terribly bright. But even he had the wit to collect test-retest reliabilities and validity data on phrenologists' readings of his bumps and palmists' readings of his paw. (The most reliable palmister vouchsafed that Twain had no sense of humor; Clemens, 1917/1959). Some researchers exhibit a sturdier indifference to common sense.

Projects without a trace of concern for the matter include the Philadelphia Federal Reserve Bank's evaluation of the Philadelphia School District, the Federal Aviation Administration's evaluation of the Concorde's impact on communities in the airport's vicinity, and many of the recent studies of the impact of desegregation. For these and other cases, establishing the validity of a response measure in the field is essential for obtaining decent estimates of program effect. Regardless of these cases, it is reasonable to argue that the theoretical relevance of a proposed measure of response to treatment is not a sufficient guarantee of the variable's relevance for the program under field conditions.

To make matters concrete, we reiterate two recommendations that often fall on deaf ears. First, mount pilot feasibility tests prior to the main evaluation to establish properties of response measures and to determine the feasibility of evaluation design. Second, mount side studies during the main evaluation to ensure that the properties of measures are knowable and to ensure that when they warrant adjustment they can be adjusted. The idea is to anticipate problems using a pilot, understand and control problems using side study, and to use data obtained in both at the analysis stage of the evaluation.

*Pilot feasibility study* here means a small-scale evaluation mounted *primarily* to troubleshoot the evaluation design and measurement system. The approach is especially feasible in multisite evaluations: sins committed at pilot sites are transformed to virtues at later sites. Examples here include the Diet-Heart Feasibility Study (1968), the Negative Income Tax Experiment, and others. At a minimum, the pilots provide estimates of variance in response, reliability, and validity. Those statistics can be used to modify the design of subsequent evaluations, when statistical power is crucial, and in a pinch may be used to adjust bias in estimates of program effect produced by the design or by the measurement system.

The purpose of side studies adjoined to main evaluations is observation and control of variations in validity of response. Simple changes in reliability, for example, can often be expected in repeated measures designs for evaluating educational programs, complex clinical programs in mental health and health services, and elsewhere. The failure even to recognize changes in reliability means biased estimates of effect at worst and complicated analytic problems at best (Campbell and Boruch, 1975). Failing to estimate the magnitude of change in reliability means that no post facto correction is possible even if the algebra for correction can be developed. Side studies can be cheap, with subsamples of people and subsamples of their behavior. Mounting side studies as an afterthought is tempting partly because there is no formal theory on the topic. That formal theory needs to be developed.

Finally, we do not mean to imply here that these efforts are primarily quantitative in character. There is absolutely no reason to ignore the participant-observer, informant, and other tactics in monitoring and controlling response measurement. In fact, any quantitative effort must begin with the qualitative idea that the observation is fallible. There have been only a few interesting efforts to combine the two traditions better in evaluative research (Fisher and Berliner, 1977).

## CORRUPTIBILITY OF THE THEME

If the idea of choosing response variables which are relevant to programs has virtue, then, like all virtue, it can and will be corrupted by a few. That is, the claim that response variables in a particular evaluation are irrelevant may be entirely honorific, dedicated less to understanding program effects than to defending earlier advertisements. The virtue can be exploited deliberately to do no more than "teach the test" as in some Performance Contracting demonstrations. It can be diluted incidentally to guarantee that curriculum innovation is successful (Walker and Schaffarzick, 1974).

## THE TREATMENT VARIABLE

Classical theory in fixed effects experimental design assumes that the prescribed level of treatment is either present or absent. Our contention is that this assumption needs to be augmented routinely for field experimentation; otherwise, it may hinder the development of better theory of evaluation. Classical measurement theory is no less parochial. Its traditional focus on individual attributes, such as a person's achievement level, extroversion, and so on, is crucial. We maintain that its grave imperfection lies in not expanding theory to contracts like "treatment." The management sciences address neither theory though ideas about program dimensions and degree of program implementation seem to fit neatly in this territory as well. There are exceptions, to be sure, and they are discussed below. The focus is on fidelity of treatment and its implications for measurement and power of evaluations.

### STEREOTYPICAL PROBLEMS

In 1820, Accum wrote one of the earliest guides on typical forms of adulteration of foods—beer, mustard, and an assortment of other prandial delights. The precedent he set in Britain was matched considerably later by routine government oversight of some food industries. But until recently there was very little analogous effort to identify ways in which new social policy or social program can be naturally diluted or deliberately corrupted, and virtually no rich academic research on the topic.

For simplicity's sake, we begin here with three stereotypical problems in identifying and measuring treatment implementation in field studies: (a) policy packaged as program, (b) the structurally incomplete programs, and (c) incomplete program reception or delivery at the individual level. The message is simple. In the social and behavioral sciences and in education, the treatment labels may be meaningless or misleading, or they may be accurate but imprecise. To the extent that these problems are ignored, evaluations will be less informative and evaluation designs will be less powerful than they ought to be.

**Policy packaged as program.** Social policy at any level of goverance is often labeled as program and tested as such, when in fact the operational features of the policy are unknown and perhaps unknowable. A formal test of the impact of the policy under this condition is likely to be an empty exercise.

Early desegregation policy is a case in point. It is interpreted as a program by some researchers, but its nature goes unexplored, its existence goes unverified, except in the grossest possible sense. For example, the Riverside California desegregation study (Moskowitz and Wortman, 1977: n. 5) reported no operational indicators of desegregation more sophisticated than a bichromatic body count. What makes the matter more invidious is that the program in this instance is not clear with respect to commonsense concepts of integration—physical busing is not racial integration. Nor is racial contact indexed by the proportion of minority members in a geographic region or by proximity, despite sophisticated statistical analysis (Jackson, 1975). Nor can it be assumed that in smaller social enterprise, policy of Type A can be distinguished from policy of Type B. Blind expert ratings of recorded therapy sessions, for instance, sometimes show no differences between therapy types that are advertised as being different.

More commonly, the policy of program plan is specified so vaguely that almost any novel activity could be labeled as consistent with the program and the translation of the plan into action could be quite variable. The poor specification implies that we cannot know whether the program put into the field is actually the one implied by the plan. For example, the Executive High School Internship Program is a national project dedicated, under its written policy, to encouraging leadership training by experience among bright high school students. There is some good evidence that despite the national headquarters' emphasis, the programs generated at the local level are career education programs and are not particularly well tied to leadership (Crowe, Rice, and Walker, 1977). So an evaluation design that attempts to estimate the program's impact on leadership is more likely to be a test of its headquarters' pronouncements than a test of its actual effects. Similarly, an evaluation design based on the presumption that all community mental health centers supported by the state of Illinois are dedicated to improving personal adjustment, as they are advertised to do, is also bound to be specious. For under their mandate, the organization, operation, and clients of the centers vary greatly, and their local policies may deviate considerably from state policy.

**Structural Imperfections in Program Implementation.** That a new social program will be implemented imperfectly is obvious once said. It is even more reasonable to expect the level of program implementation to influence the size of the program's effect on its target population. Yet the problem of identifying imperfection and of measuring it has until recently not received much formal attention from the behavioral or social scientists in academia. Especially in evaluation studies, this buck gets passed to the program manager. There is, however, a developing fund of knowledge that can be used for more sophisticated work. It ranges from case studies on the one hand to efforts to quantify the observations on the other.

The acuteness of the problem and the evolutionary character of the solutions are most evident from the case studies, post mortems really. For instance, Weikart and Banet's (1975) attempts to introduce Piagetian ideas into regular classroom teaching led, in the early stages, to confusion and some loss of confidence among teachers (i.e., program implementors). The later efforts involved not only far more specific instruction and actual choice of curriculum materials, and a more collaborative style of research, but the development of tactics to accommodate scheduling difficulties engendered by the open classrooms and to alleviate the pressures exercised by excluded colleagues and unenthusiastic supervisors on the participating teachers. Gramlich and Koshel's (1975) surprisingly candid study of the performance contracting experiments put greater emphasis on the mismatch between the contractors' claims about their personnel, flexibility, and speed and the contractor's actual abilities. Both studies recognized that despite teachers' initial enthusiasm and agreement to participate, their adherence to an unfamiliar regimen cannot be taken for granted. That analogous problems occur in other sectors is also clear, judging by Fairweather and Tornatsky (1977) in mental health, Williams (1976) in poverty research, McLaughlin (1975) in financing compensatory education, Rossi (1977) in social service programs, and others. As case studies, these are precious but insufficient reading. They help us speculate about the factors that may produce incomplete programs, and so may help to explain the evaluator's finding that the program had only a small effect. But they are not especially helpful in understanding how to systematize observation of the problem and how to tie the observation to formal analysis.

To be sure, there are fragments of methodology that may be helpful here. For the program manager, it is reasonable to develop checklists (measurement of a crude sort) to reflect the gross administrative state of a program. The U.S. Agency for International Development's (1974) inventory for monitoring programs typifies the genre. Mead's (1977) work is a considerable elaboration of the same theme but under the rubric of institutional analysis. He focused on administrative, political, and economic factors that affect program implementation, and provided some guides, but he presented no concrete methodology for their measurement. Rossi (1977) presents an interesting catalogue of typical ways in which structural imperfections in program implementation appear and pins his observations to a rudimentary theory that imperfections will persist in any program which relies heavily on individual interaction rather than on material exchange. Although useful for crude control, these approaches are not often well tied to response variables, except rhetorically, and are not linked at all to experimental or quasi-experimental design technology or to measurement theory.

Examples of the next step along the measurement-control continuum are not hard to find. In field testing innovative teacher training programs, Crawford, Gage, and Stallings (1977) capitalized on structured classroom observations, measuring rates and consistency of teacher behaviors to determine the extent to which the prescribed teaching strategy was met. They designed their system of observation to establish whether teachers in control conditions have adopted the novel program also, to establish the presence of John Henry effects, and the like. That work runs parallel to Fairweather and Tornatsky's (1977) efforts in mental health to ensure, through systematic observation, that adoption level in the introduction of new therapeutic regimen matches plans. In research, it is reflected by Walberg (1974) and Brophy (1977) in education, by Sloane et al. (1975) in therapy evaluation, and others. That is, one builds inventories to systematically assay the level of major program elements and the level of competing elements in the program.

The final cluster of pertinent activities involves settings in which control is impossible but partially relevant data plentiful. Factor analysts and most users of structural equations try to find surrogate measures of treatment, for instance, in measuring amount of "schooling" by grade level, measuring quality of schooling by the number of books in a library, and so on. Some of the more thoughtful efforts are illustrated by Orlinsky and Howard (1975), for example, who factor analyzed process variables in therapeutic settings to better understand what that is about, and by Wiley (1976), who has made a remarkable case for measuring instruction time and absences to understand the effects of schooling. Activities like these evolve naturally from the use of treatment-related variables in more mundane regression analyses. In the latter cases, however, measures of the treatment variables are usually devoid of validity estimates, so we may find, as Jencks (1972) did in reanalyzing the survey of equality of educational opportunity (Coleman et al., 1966) that the information on treatment process is of doubtful worth if it comes from poorly informed sources.

Although methodological developments here are fragmentary, sub-stantive theory is in far worse condition. It is nearly impossible, for example, to find a social or behavioral science theory that specifies the probable ceiling on implementation of the theory-based program or explains how one might anticipate or predict a ceiling. Nor do substantive theories often specify which components of the program need to be adopted in the field for the program to be effective. That failure means the analyst cannot determine whether the program is in place, much less whether the intensity is sufficient to say that the program exists. Theories that specify the target population well are few, and those that specify how to contact members of the target group are fewer still. Yet the process of identification and selection of program participants does seem to be a natural part of the theory-based program and of the theory itself.

**Variation in Program Delivery and Receipt at the Individual Level.** This topic, like the preceding one, is not new, but it is understated in the design, measurement, and analysis literature. Some examples may help to illustrate its character.

The Kaiser Permanente Studies (Cutler et al., 1973) of the impact of free multiphasic screening on health status were designed as a rand-omized test with very large samples. The regimen for the treatment group, annual multiphasic screening, was *not* followed by the majority of individuals during the first year. In response to wholesale deviations detected by the simplest of measurement systems, body counts, telephone operators were employed to regularly remind individuals of their checkups, which brought cooperation rates to 65%. Roughly the same problems occur in drug studies, diet studies, and other investigations in which the members of the target group have some discretion in adhering to treatment. Similar feedback and encouragement strategies were adopted in the experimental tests of the impact of television show *Sesame Street,* in which encouragement constitutes a major treatment component. Crude information on level of social program receipt in such research is still sparse, but some order of magnitude estimates may be possible with contemporary data.

The absence of early warning systems which index receipt has led to the termination of tests on parent effectiveness training (Weaver, 1975), on judicial procedures for assignment of offenders to special treatment programs (Conner, 1977), and on others. The problem requires not only construction of real time-monitoring and feedback systems but designs which recognize that natural variation in simple adherence to treatment will degrade power of an experiment.

The more interesting and relevant problem involves the idea that the imposition of treatment, its receipt by the individual, or both can be regarded as a continuum. That is, underlying the labeled fixed treatment is a continuum of treatment imposition which is potentially measurable but which normally goes unobserved. The clinician trying out a new approach does vary in using it with each patient; the patient's reception may vary as a consequence, or independently. Tutors hired under grants to teach young children do not spend the same time with each, nor are they uniformly enthusiastic, energetic, and perceptive with each child. The level and nature of activity in work release programs, prison contracts, and the like in prison rehabilitation vary greatly, for the labeled treatment is only shorthand for a variety of activities.

Intuition suggests that latent variation in the reception of a program should affect the sensitivity of an evaluation. And indeed a thirty-year-old paper by Berkson (1950) verifies the intuition algebraically (also see Boruch, 1975). To capitalize on the notion, however, requires a good deal more work, notably systematically observing the variation even if one cannot control it.

That is where a major gap in the literature of psychometrics seems to lie. Principles of reliability and validity are there, to be sure, but there is no coherent theory or practice for dealing with the idea. Instead, there are fragments. In randomized tests of *Sesame Street,* Ball and Bogatz (1973) measured children's viewing time; the results formed an important basis for primary and secondary analysis (Cook et al., 1975). In some tests of compensatory education programs, personnel training programs, and the like, absence from class is a crude indicator of reception at the individual level. In some medical research, fixed dosage is divided by weight of the subject to get at the latent reception. Beyond these simple tactics, we have virtually nothing in the way of cheap but effective measurement schemes. Although the problem is second in importance to structural imperfection in treatments, it too warrants investigation.

## THE PROBLEM IN OTHER DISCIPLINES

The problem of measuring the treatment variable is not confined to the social sciences, of course. The controversy appears in the physical sciences, where, for example, allegations that there are 20% margins on reliability of measurement and control of variables in nuclear reactor cooling systems have been a grave concern (Primack and von Hippel, 1974). Flaws in the implementation of randomized cloud seeding in weather modification experiments have justifiably led to abandonment of some expensive data sets and rather more attention to verifying implementation in more recent research (Neyman, 1977). Bureaucracies have simply forgotten to implement program plans for pesticide control (U.S. General Accounting Office, 1968) and have overlooked delivery of vasectomy kits in fertility control efforts (Sullivan, 1976). They have denied the existence of treatments and mislabeled them. Recall U.S. Defense Department denial of the use of poison gasses at the Dugway Proving Grounds. Confirmatory tests of polio vaccine were disrupted briefly by vaccine that induced poliomyelitis rather than preventing it, a problem of quality control over batch production that affects any test of a new pharmaceutical. Roughly the same problem extends to the surgical arena where, for example, the integrity of an ostensibly uniform treatment such as coronary bypass is often imperfect judging by indices such as perioperative heart attacks, graft patency, and crude hospital mortality rates (Proudfit, 1978). Finally, the problem is implicit in early agricultural experimentation as well, if we judge correctly Yates' (1952) concerns about the "elimination, correction, and reduction of bias" in systematic movement from assessing the laboratory treatment to field studies.

These are extreme cases to be sure, but the less extreme are just as easy to identify. We mention them for the sake of context. The problems of identifying and measuring the treatment are severe enough in the social sciences to produce the idea that the social researcher could not find the way to the bathroom without help. The fact of the matter is that if this orientation difficulty is true, we have lots of company.

## PILOT FEASIBILITY TESTS

Pilot tests or side studies, mounted prior to a full-scale evaluation, seem well justified here. Neither social theory nor available data are usually sufficient to specify how one ought to measure dimensions of treatment, much less what the likely degree of program implementation is. Pilot tests, even demonstration projects, can provide early information on probable level of program implementation or adoption in the larger field tests. They may also be used to try out new methods for gauging variations in reception of treatment by members of the target sample and variation in delivery by members of the program staff.

Some large-scale efforts to adhere to this strategy have already been mentioned. The 1962 Diet-Heart Feasibility Studies (National Heart Institute, 1969) were mounted to see if diet regimens could be imposed and to assay the level of adherence to the diet by volunteers, *rather* than to test the diet's effects. As the first of several sites in the Negative Income Tax Experiments, the New Jersey program disclosed some embarrassing and unexpected difficulties in income transfer arrangements, problems avoided at later sites (Riecken et al., 1974). In education, the strategy undertaken by Crawford et al. (1977) was similar: their prior research on training teachers for novel programs provided a good deal of advance information on how to ensure adherence to the prescribed teaching regimen and how to observe adherence rate economically. Other examples are given in Riecken et al. (1974).

The product of pilot tests ought not to be simply the identification of treatment-related variables and the statistics that reflect the quality of their measurement. We know so little about how long it takes to mount social programs in complex bureaucratic settings that time itself becomes a measure of interest. In this instance, the pilot may provide better evidence for scheduling outcome measures in the actual field trial, thereby anticipating the chronic complaint of the program manager: you measured too soon, we weren't ready, the program's not fully operational yet, and so on.

## STATISTICAL MODELS FOR ANALYSIS

To predict the influence of problems like these on the power of an evaluation design and to gauge the impact of prophylactic action, the problem must be characterized algebraically as well as literally. That is, we need to model the problem to understand its influence. In fact, some work on the topic has been done, though far less than is necessary.

In his early work in biomedical research, Berkson (1950) posited a model in which mean level of treatment was fixed and delivered as advertised, but there is some latent variability about that mean. Estimates of treatment effect from randomized experiments under this condition are unbiased, but power is lower than it would otherwise be. In elaborations on the theme, Fedorov (1974) derived the consequence of latent variation for factorial experiments and for cases in which the latent variation is systematic (e.g., cyclic) rather than random. The same idea can be generalized in simpler form by measuring at least some of the latent variability within treatment and control conditions. That is, in addition to observing who is a member of the nominal treatment and nominal control groups, we measure observable variation in intensity of treatment and of the control group's incidental access to similar or identical treatment. The regression of response on the fixed (dummy) treatment variable constitutes a conventional between-groups regression (i.e., an analysis of variance) and provides an unbiased estimate of effect in a randomized test. The simultaneous regression of response on both the dummy variables and the measured latent variables gives us some additional information about the within-groups regression (i.e., how self-selection and variation within treatment predict variation in response). The model and estimation process is simple (Boruch, 1975), but testing hypotheses can be statistically complicated (Proctor, 1976).

A parallel but not independent schema for understanding sources of variation in observations of the treatment variable can be based on analysis of variance components. The generalizability theory presented by Cronbach et al. (1972), for example, is a framework for doing so. The components may include temporal variation (e.g., test-retest reliability) and interrater variation, as well as variation of more direct interest, such as adherence to the treatment regimen. The approach has been tried in educational research to untangle complex teaching processes (Cronbach et al., 1972), in therapy research (Howard, Orlinsky, and Perilstein, 1976), in research on the quality of census surveys, and elsewhere.

The model for treatment specified in the appendix is simple but differs from those described. It says that in the field, treatment deviates from structural plan or laboratory program and that the discrepancy can be recognized by describing actual treatment as a simple linear function of planned treatment and latent random variation. This model is only an approximation, but it is better than nothing, which is what we had at the start of this article. There are more realistic alternatives, but they are very complicated and must wait for another time.

## CONCLUSIONS AND RECOMMENDATIONS

We have tried to deliver four messages here. The first is that orthodox experimental design and the quasi-experimental approaches need to be augmented for evaluating social programs. The reader may already have guessed that. The embellishments we suggested are not all original and certainly not simple. But they can enhance the sensitivity of field tests of social programs and give us a better understanding of why notable effects fail to turn up when they are supposed to.

The second message is an exhortation to be catholic. There is little excuse (aside from time, money, and our own parochial reading habits) for failing to recognize that these problems cut across all the social and behavioral sciences, including our jaded sister, economics. They are not even unique there, for we can find similar dilemmas in the early history of agricultural statistics and medical research.

This applies also to specialties within the discipline. That is, the program manager with intuition about "degree of program implementation" ought to be accommodated by the evaluation designer responsible for predicting the power of the field experiment. Both will have something valuable to say to the measurement specialist, who must determine the extent to which degree of program implementation is measurable and who must choose or construct response variables that are relevant to treatment. And finally, the academic theorist or the theorist in mufti (i.e., the program developer) must be brought into the circle at the evaluation design level if at no other. For if he or she cannot provide literal guidance, none of the others will be able to manage their responsibilities terribly well.

Finally, social programs often produce small effects. If those are valued by society, under the presumption that progress is typically incremental rather than dramatic and episodic, or that despite small effect size the number of people so affected is large, then statistical power in field tests is crucial. Regardless of whether one accepts the theory or ideas tendered here, the power of designs ought to be routinely assayed *and* published with the evaluation results.

The work presented here suggests that at least two arenas of research need to be enlarged. The first involves mathematical and statistical augmentation of orthodox theory of statistical power, and parallel development of statistical models to represent the character of treatment implementation (e.g., fidelity). The second arena overlaps the first and concerns: development of substantive theory to understand how power and its ingredients are degraded in moving from the laboratory to the field; the development of side theory on level of implementation of treatment and degradation of response variables; and the acquisition of data bearing on each.

# REFERENCES

ACCUM, F. (1820) A Treatise on Adulterations of Food, and Culinary Poisons. Exhibiting the Fraudulent Sophistications of Bread, Beer, Wine, Spiritous Liquors, Tea, Coffee, Cream, Confectionery, Vinegar, Mustard, Pepper, Cheese, Olive Oil, Pickles, and other Articles Employed in Domestic Economy, and Methods of Detecting Them. Philadelphia: Abr'm Small (Mallinkrodt collection).

BALL, S. and G. A. BOGATZ (1973) Reading with Television: An Evaluation of the "Electric Company." Vols. 1 and 2. Princeton, NJ: Educational Testing Service.

BERKSON, J. (1950) "Are there two regressions?" Journal of the American Statistical Association 45: 164-180.

BIANCHINI, J. C. (1978) "Achievement tests and differential norms," pp. 157-181 in M. J. Wargo and D. R. Green (eds.) Achievement Testing of Disadvantaged and Minority Students for Educational Program Evaluation. Monterey, CA: CTB/McGraw-Hill.

BOCK, R. D. (1975) Multivariate Statistical Methods in Behavioral Research. New York: McGraw-Hill.

BORUCH, R. F. (1976) "On common contentions about randomized field experiments," pp. 158-194 in G. V. Glass (ed.) Evaluation Studies Review Annual. Beverly Hills: Sage.

––– (1975) "Coupling randomized experiments and approximations to experiments in social program evaluation." Sociological Methods & Research, 4: 31-53.

––– and J. S. CECIL (forthcoming) Assuring Privacy and Confidentiality in Social Research. Philadelphia: University of Pennsylvania Press.

BORUCH, R. F. and P. M. WORTMAN (forthcoming) "Evaluation research policy." Review of Research in Education.

BREWER, J. K. (1977) "Effect size and power." Florida State University Psychology Department.

BRICKELL, H. M. (1976) "Needed: instruments as good as our eyes." Journal of Career Education 2: 56-66.

BROPHY, J. (1977) "Training teachers in experiments." East Lansing: Michigan State University Department of Education.

BROWN, R. V. (1969) Research and the Credibility of Estimates. Boston: Harvard University Press.

CAMPBELL, D. T. (1975) "Assessing the impact of planned social change," pp. 3-45 in G. M. Lyons (ed.) Social Research and Public Policies. Hanover, NH: Dartmouth.

––– and R. F. BORUCH (1975) "Making the case for randomized experiments: six ways in which quasi-experimental evaluations in compensatory education tend to underestimate effects," pp. 195-296 in A. Lumsdaine and C. Bennett (eds.) Evaluation and Measurement. New York: Academic Press.

CASSEDY, J. H. (1969) Demography in Early America. Cambridge: Harvard University Press.

CLEARY, T. A., R. L. LINN, and G. W. WALSTER (1970) "The effect of reliability and validity on power of statistical tests," pp. 130-138 in E. F. Borgotta and G. W. Bornstedt (eds.) Sociological Methodology. San Francisco: Jossey-Bass.

CLEMENS, S. L. (1959) The Autobiography of Mark Twain. New York: Harper. (originally published, 1917)

COCHRAN, W. C. (1968) "Errors of measurement in statistics." Technometrics 10: 637-666.

COCHRAN, W. G., P. DIACONIS, A. P. DONNER, D. C. HOAGLIN, N. E. O'CONNER, O. L. PETERSON, and V. M. ROSENOER (1977) "Experiments in surgical treatment of duodenal ulcer," pp. 176-197 in J. P. Bunker, B. A. Barnes, and F. Mosteller (eds.) Costs, Risks, and Benefits of Surgery. New York: Oxford University Press.

COHEN, J. (1969) Statistical Power Analysis for the Behavioral Sciences. New York: Academic Press.

COLEMAN, J. S., E. Q. CAMPBELL, C. J. HOBSON, J. McPARTLAND, A. M. MOOD, F. D. WEINFIELD, and R. L. YORK (1966) Equality of Educational Opportunity. Washington, DC: U.S. Government Printing Office.

CONNER (1977) "Selecting a control group: an analysis of the randomization process in twelve social reform programs." Evaluation Quarterly 1: 195-244.

COOK, T. D., H. APPLETON, R. CONNER, A. SCHAFFER, G. TAMKIN, and S. J. WEBER (1975) Sesame Street Revisited. New York: Russell Sage.

COOKE, J. E. [ed.] (1961) The Federalist (No. 54, February 12, 1788). Middletown, CT: Wesleyan University Press.

CRAWFORD, J., N. L. GAGE, J. A. STALLINGS (1977) "Methods for maximizing the validity of experiments on teaching." Presented at the annual meeting of the American Educational Research Association, New York, April.

CRONBACH, L. J., G. C. GLESER, H. NANDA, and N. RAJARATNAM (1972) The Dependability of Behavioral Measurements: The Theory of Generalizability for Scores and Profiles. New York: John Wiley.

CROWE, M. R., J. RICE, and J. P. WALKER (1977) "Evaluation of the Executive High School Internship Program, final report." Columbus: Ohio State University Center for Vocational Education.

CUTLER, J. L., S. RAMCHARAN, R. FELDMAN, A. B. SIEGLAUB, B. CAMPBELL, G. D. FRIEDMAN, L. G. DALES, and M. F. COLLEN (1973) "Multiphasic checkup evaluation study: I. methods and population." Preventive Medicine 2: 197-206.

Diet-Heart Feasibility Study Group (1968) "The Diet-Heart Feasibility Study," Circulation (Supplement 1): 1-428.

ELINSON, J. (1977) "Insensitive health statistics and the dilemma of the HSA's," American Journal of Public Health, 67: 417-418.

FAIRWEATHER, G. and L. TORNATSKY (1977) Experimental methods for social policy research. New York: Pergamon.

FEDOROV, V. V. (1974) "Regression problems with controllable variables subject to error." Biometrika 61: 49-56.

FISHER, C. W. and D. C. BERLINER (1977) "Quasi-clinical inquiry in research on classroom teaching and learning." San Francisco: Far West Regional Laboratories.

FREIMAN, J. A., T. C. CHALMERS, H. SMITH, and R. R. KUEBLER (1978) "The importance of beta, the Type II error and sample size in the design and interpretation of the randomized control trial: survey of 71 negative trials." New England Journal of Medicine 299: 690-694.

GLASS, G. V. (1976) "Primary, secondary, and meta-analysis of research," Educational Researcher 5: 3-8.

GOMEZ, H. (1977) "Applications of the Rasch model for estimating abilities in the Cali experiment on nutrition and education." Evanston: Northwestern University Department of Psychology.

GRAMLICH, E. M. and P. P. KOSHEL (1975) "Is real world experimentation possible? the case of educational performance contracting." Policy Analysis 1: 511-530.

HALL, G. E. and S. F. LOUCKS (1977) "A developmental model for determining whether treatment is actually implemented." American Educational Research Journal 14: 263-276.

HEBER, R., H. GARBER, S. HARRINGTON, C. HOFFMAN, and C. FALENDER (1972) Rehabilitation of Families at Risk for Mental Retardation. Madison: University of Wisconsin Rehabilitation Research and Training Center.

HOWARD, K. I., D. E. ORLINSKY, and J. PERILSTEIN (1976) "Contribution of therapists to patients' experiences in psychotherapy: a components of variance model for analyzing process data." Consulting and Clinical Psychology 44: 520-6.

International Journal of Health Services Research (1976): 6: 3.

JACKSON, G. B. (1975) "Reanalysis of Coleman's Recent Trends in School Integration." Educational Researcher 9: 21-25.

JENCKS, C. S. (1972) "The quality of the data collected by the Equality of Opportunity Survey," pp. 446-512 in F. Mosteller and D. P. Moynihan (eds.) On Equality of Educational Opportunity. New York: Vintage.

KATZ, S. and C. A. AKPOM (1976) "A measure of primary sociobiological functions." International Journal of Health Services 6: 493-508.

KEMPTHORNE, O. (1975) "Inference from experiments and randomization," pp. 303-392 in J. N. Srivistava (ed.) A Survey of Statistical Design and Linear Models. Amsterdam: North-Holland Elsevier.

KNIGHTLY, P. (1975) The First Casualty. New York: Harcourt Brace Jovanovich.

LEVITAN, S. A. and R. TAGGART (1976) "Do our statistics measure the real labor market hardships?" Proceedings of the American Statistical Association: Social Statistics Section. Washington, DC: ASA.

LUMSDEN, J. (1976) "Test theory." Annual Review of Psychology 27: 251-280.

LUKAS, C. V. (1975) "Problems in implementing Head Start Planned Variations models," pp. 113-126 in A. M. Rivlin and P. M. Timpane (eds.) Planned Variation in Education, Washington, DC: Brookings Institution.

McLAUGHLIN, M.M.W. (1975) Evaluation and Reform: The Elementary and Secondary Education Act of 1965/Title I. Cambridge, MA: Ballinger.

MEAD, L. M. (1977) "Institutional analysis." Washington, DC: Urban Institute.

MIAO, L. L. (1977) "Gastric freezing: an example of the evaluation of medical therapy by randomized clinical trials," pp. 176-197 in J. P. Bunker, B. A. Barnes, and F. Mosteller (eds.) Costs, Risks, and Benefits of Surgery. New York: Oxford University Press.

MINOR, M. J. (1977) "Estimating treatment effects in social experimentation." Ph.D. Dissertation, University of Chicago.

MOSKOWITZ, J. and P. M. WORTMAN (1977) "Reanalysis of the Riverside Desegregation Study," Evanston: Northwestern University Psychology Department.

National Heart Institute, Diet-Heart Panel (1969) Mass field trials of the diet heart question. American Heart Association Monograph No. 38. New York: American Heart Association.

NEYMAN, J. (1977) "Experimentation with weather control and statistical problems generated by it," pp. 1-25 in P. R. Krishnaiah (ed.) Applications of Statistics. Amsterdam: North-Holland.

ORLINSKY, D. E. and K. I. HOWARD (1975) Varieties of Psycho-therapeutic Experience. New York: Columbia Teachers College Press.

PORTER, A. C., W. H. SCHMIDT, R. E. FLODEN, and D. J. FREEMAN (1978) "Impact on what? the importance of content covered." Research Series No. 2. East Lansing: Michigan State University Institute for Research on Teaching.

PRIMACK, J. and F. Von HIPPLE (1974) Advice and Dissent: Scientists in the
Political Arena. New York: Basic Books.
PROCTOR, C. H. (1976) "Testing for contextual effect." Proceedings of the
American Statistical Association: Social Statistics Section Part II. Washington,
DC: ASA.
PROUDFIT, W. L. (1978) "Criticisms of the VA randomized study of coronary
bypass surgery." Clinical Research 26: 236-240.
REEDER, L. G. [ed.] (1976) Advances in Health Survey Research Methods.
Rockville, MD: National Center for Health Services Research.
RIECKEN, H. W., R. F. BORUCH, D. T. CAMPBELL, N. CAPLAN, T. K.
GLENNAN, J. PRATT, A. REES, and W. WILLIAMS (1974) Social Experi-
mentation. New York: Academic Press.
ROSSI, P. H. (1977) "Some issues in evaluation of human services delivery
programs." Presented at a Conference on Issues in Services Delivery in Human
Services Organizations, Wingspread Johnson Foundation, Racine, WI.
SEARLE, B., P. MATTHEWS, P. SUPPES, and J. FRIEND (1978) "Formal
evaluation of the radio mathematics instructional program, Nicaragua–Grade
1, 1976," pp. 651-672 in T. D. Cook (ed.) Evaluation Studies Review Annual,
Vol. 3. Beverly Hills: Sage.
SLOANE, R. B., F. R. STAPLES, A. H. GRISTOL, N. J. YORKSTON, and K.
SHIPPLE (1975) "Short term analytically oriented psychotherapy versus
behavior therapy." American Journal of Psychiatry 132: 373-377.
SUDMAN, S. and N. M. BRADBURN (1974) Response Effects in Surveys: A
Review and Synthesis. Chicago: Aldine.
SULLIVAN, J. H. (1976) "Foreign affairs oversight: role of the staff survey
mission," pp. 173-185 in U.S. Senate, Subcommitte on Oversight procedures,
Committee on Government Operations. Legislative Oversight and Program
Evaluation. 94th Congress, 2nd Session, Washington, DC: U.S. Government
Printing Office.
TYLER, R. W. (1978) "Comments," pp. 324-330 in M. J. Wargo and D. R. Green
(eds.) Achievement Testing of Disadvantaged and Minority Students for Edu-
cational Program Evaluation. Monterey, CA.: CTB/McGraw-Hill.
U.S. General Accounting Office (1968) Need to Improve Regulatory Enforcement
Procedures Involving Pesticides. B-133192. Washington, DC: USGAO.
WALBERG, H. J. [ed.] (1974) Evaluating Educational Performance: A Source
Book of Methods, Instruments, and Examples. Berkeley, CA: McCutchan.
WALDO, G. P. and T. G. CHIRICOS (1977) "Work release and recidivism."
Evaluation Quarterly 1: 87-108.
WALKER, D. F. and J. SCHAFFARZICK (1974) "Comparing curricula." Review
of Educational Research 44: 83-112.
WARGO, M. and R. GREEN [eds.] (1978) Achievement Testing of Disadvan-
taged and Minority Students for Educational Program Evaluation. New York:
McGraw-Hill.
WEAVER, R. (1975) "Failure of the parent effectiveness training (P.E.T.) evalua-
tion." Evanston: Northwestern University Psychology Department.
WEIKART, D. P. and D. P. BANET (1975) "Planned variation from the perspec-
tive of a model sponsor." Policy Analysis 1: 485-510.

WHOLEY, J. S., J. N. NAY, J. W. SCANLON, and R. E. SCHMIDT (1975) "Evaluation: when is it really needed?" Evaluation Magazine 2: 89-93.

WILEY, D. E. (1976) "Another hour, another day: quantity of school, a potent path for policy," pp. 225-265 in W. H. Sewall, R. M. Hauser, and D. L. Featherman (eds.) Schooling and Achievement in American Society.

WILLIAMS, W. (1976) "Implementation analysis and assessment," pp. 267-290 in W. Williams and R. F. Elmore (eds.) Social Program Implementation. New York: Academic Press.

YATES, F. (1952) "Principle governing the amount of experimentation in developmental work." Nature 138-140.

# APPENDIX I: SMALL THEORY OF MEASUREMENT IN FIELD EVALUATION

| In Symbols | In Words |
|---|---|

### A. The Linkage

$$\eta = \tau + e$$
$$e \sim (0, \sigma^2)$$

Response, $\eta$, is a simple additive function of treatment, $\tau$, and of unspecified, possibly unknowable influences, e.

### B. The Response

$$Y = K\eta + \phi$$
$$\phi \sim (0, \sigma^2_\phi)$$

The response variable, Y, is only a partially valid indicator of response to treatment, $0 < K < 1$.

$$Y' = K\eta + \phi + \xi$$
$$\xi \sim (0, \sigma^2_\xi)$$

The response variable, Y', is not only partially valid, but is subject to random errors in measurement, $\xi$.

### C. The Treatment

$$T = \gamma\tau$$

The treatment $\tau$ is imposed incompletely, $0 < K < 1$.

$$T' = \gamma\tau + \delta$$
$$\delta \sim (0, \sigma^2_\delta)$$

Not only is treatment structurally incomplete but it varies along a continuum for each individual.

D.  In the laboratory or low noise setting, we have:

$\eta = \tau + e$ with noncentrality parameter $\lambda_\eta = \dfrac{N\Sigma\tau^2}{\sigma^2}$

In the field, we have:

$Y' = K\gamma\tau + K\delta + Ke + \phi + \xi,$

$\lambda'_y = \dfrac{NK^2\gamma^2\Sigma\tau^2}{K^2\sigma^2 + K^2\sigma_\delta^2 + \sigma_\phi^2 + \sigma_\xi^2}.$

**EXAMPLE FOR APPENDIX: NONCENTRALITY PARAMETERS ($\lambda$) AND PROBABILITY OF TYPE II ERRORS, (P(II))**

A.  Linkage

$\lambda = \dfrac{N\Sigma\tau^2}{\sigma^2}$            Let $N = 40, \tau = .5, \sigma_\eta^2 = 1, = 1.25$

$\lambda_\eta = 10 \Rightarrow P(II) = .08$            $df_1 = 1, df_2 = 39, \alpha = .01$

B.  Response Variable

$\lambda_y = \dfrac{K^2N\Sigma\tau^2}{K^2\sigma^2 + \sigma_\phi^2}$            Let $K = 3/4$ = validity of Y, so

$\sigma_\phi^2 = 35/64$

$\lambda_y = 5.07 \Rightarrow P(II) \doteq .35$

$\lambda'_y = \dfrac{K^2N\Sigma\tau^2}{K^2\sigma^2 + \sigma_\phi^2 + \sigma_\xi^2}$            Let reliability of Y' = .80 so,

$\sigma_\xi^2 = 10/32$

$= 3.96 \Rightarrow P(II) = .46$

C.  Integrity of Treatment

$\lambda'_y = \dfrac{NK^2\gamma^2\Sigma\tau^2}{K^2\sigma^2 + K^2\sigma_\delta^2 + \sigma_\phi^2 + \sigma_\xi^2}$            Let $\gamma = 3/4, \sigma_\delta^2 = \dfrac{\sigma_\tau^2}{4} = \dfrac{1}{16}$

$= 2.17 \Rightarrow P(II) \doteq .72.$

# 11

## AGAINST THEM OR FOR ME:
## COMMUNITY IMPACT EVALUATIONS

### Harris M. Allen, Jr. and David O. Sears

Evaluation researchers typically apply an economic model to assessing program impact on individual attitudes. This model emphasizes aggregate analyses of cost-benefit ratios that are products of the current life situation of the population in question. Often, evaluators seem inclined to stress those factors which reflect immediate, situationally-specific concerns that become operative with the threatened or actual implementation of the program. For instance, when assessing community reactions to a rapid transit system, they are likely to suggest that aggregate perceptions about the relative increase in mobility afforded by the system relative to the increase in income taxes incurred by its maintenance will be the critical variables. Thus, evaluators apparently prefer to see the individual as part of a rationally calculating group which balances the perceived gains and losses accumulating from contact with the program. The product of this balancing process, in turn, is said to determine the aggregate's response to that program.

Social psychologists, most notably Katz (1960), have incorporated this cost-benefit model in what is called the functionalist approach to attitude formation: attitudes are created and maintained by the goals they are intended to serve. In the case of cost-benefit considerations, attitudes are said to be adopted out of a Benthamite utilitarian motive. Because individuals intend to maximize their gains and minimize their losses, they will adopt those predispositions that are most instrumental to achieving these ends. Thus, the individual's self-interest governs the orientation toward a particular stimulus object.

An alternative view of attitude formation has been proposed by socialization theorists. In the socialization model, individuals acquire stable predispositions toward certain key stimulus objects by the time they have reached adolescence. Typically the product of familial and early educational influences, these predispositions maintain a high degree of resilience and stability throughout the individual's life-time. The affective nature of these predispositions causes them to generalize toward related stimulus objects with the passage of time. As a result, the symbolic aspects of related stimuli tend to evoke the generalized predisposition even during adulthood. Of particular interest is the prediction that these socialization residues, when evoked, will over-power the effects of more functional, self-interest factors as determinants of the individual's response.

## BUSING IN LOS ANGELES

A number of studies on various political issues have investigated the comparative utility of the functionalist and socialization models as determinants of individual attitudes. One such study concerns the controversial use of busing to achieve court-ordered desegregation in Los Angeles public schools. This study of white Los Angeleno attitudes toward busing presented an opportunity for a direct test of the competing models. At the time of data collection (December 1976), the school district was under court order to produce a proposal that demonstrated "reasonable and feasible progress" toward school desegregation. The discussion of the proposals submitted by citizen action groups to the school board was marked by a high degree of controversy and publicity. The proposals covered a wide range of alternatives. Several called for the mandatory busing of white children that would entail over an hour's worth of busing time. In sum, the situation seemed quite fertile for activation of both the self-interest and the socialization residue components of attitudes.

The strategy, then, was to pit the relative predictive power of impersonal, abstract socialization residues against more personal, concrete, issue-related factors as predictors of busing sentiment. The data were obtained from a local survey sample of 899 white adult residents randomly selected from the Los Angeles County area and interviewed by telephone during a time of considerable debate over the proposals (December 1976). The survey instrument was a 77-item questionnaire designed to probe variables pertinent to the formation of busing opinions.

Seven independent variables were identified. The purest and most reliable measure of the self-interest dimension was a five-point variable indicating whether or not the respondent had school age children in Los Angeles city public schools. Other measures reflecting more subjective self-interest were the respondents' perceptions about the likelihood of busing. One of these measures asked whether or not the respondents felt that the busing of their own child or of children in their neighborhood was likely. The other measure indicated the extent to which the respondents thought the busing of minority children into their neighborhood was likely.

The socialization residue dimension was measured by two factors, general racial intolerance and political conservatism. Generalized racial intolerance was assessed by a standardized, highly reliable scale constructed from five attitudinal items, all of which loaded highly on the same factor in a varimax rotated factor analysis. Two three-point variables assessed the respondents' opinions about the government's special treatment of blacks and the pace at which civil rights advocates are moving. The other variables measured agreement with the statements "Blacks shouldn't push themselves where they are not wanted," "Over the past few years blacks are getting more than they deserve," and "Whites don't have the right to keep blacks out of their neighborhood." Political conservatism was a single item assessing the respondent's self-designated position on the liberal-conservative continuum. Respondents also were asked about their age and education.

The dependent variable was another standardized, highly reliable scale composed of five items, all of which loaded on the second factor of the above factor analysis. One item reflected the respondents' attitudes toward the general use of busing for integration, and another reflected their reactions to the implementation of a local plan. The other three variables were Likert scale items reflecting the respondents' agreement with the statements "Busing will improve education," "Busing will not increase violence," and "Integration justifies busing."

A series of multiple regression equations tested the relative power of the seven independent variables in predicting opposition to busing. The racial intolerance scale was by far the most potent predictor item, with a standardized beta equaling .39, twice that of any other variable. The political conservatism item was likewise quite significant. In contrast, among the self-interest items, only the composite variable about children in public schools was a reliable predictor. The two likelihood items washed out almost completely, as did age and education. The percentage of variance accounted for by these seven predictors was a .23, a result which, in view of the $R^2$s associated with most contemporary survey analysis, attests to the predictive power of the overall model.

Other analyses did not substantially alter this constellation of results. For example, when the likelihood of future in-busing and future out-busing was controlled, racial prejudice continued to contribute nearly twice as much toward the regression equation as the self-interest composite item. Moreover in crosstabular analyses, the strengths of associations for racial prejudice and busing opposition and for political conservatism and busing opposition were .51 and .37, respectively; the comparable gamma statistic for self-interest and the busing dependent variable was only .18.

With regard to the demographic variables, further analyses corroborated previous work in the socialization literature, linking old age and little education with the two symbolic attitudinal variables. The older and less educated the respondents, the more likely they were to be racially prejudiced, politically conservative, and opposed to busing. Said another way, the variance associated with the main effects of age and education in the multiple regression equation was absorbed by the two statistically independent socialization residue items.

## IN CONCLUSION

In this Los Angeles study, the socialization residues, generalized racial intolerance, and political conservatism, whose antecedents are old age and little education, were substantially more influential in determining busing attitudes than the self-interest variables. These results have been substantiated elsewhere. The Sears et al. (1979) analysis of busing attitudes in the 1972 CPS National Election sample, the McConahay and Hawley (1977) study on busing sentiment in Louisville, the report by Kinder and Kiewiet (forthcoming) on personal economic discontents and voting, and Tyler's (1977) study of adolescents' symbolic reactions to the energy crisis come to essentially the same conclusion. Symbolic political attitudes, acquired at an earlier age, continue to exert considerably more impact on adult policy positions than do the relevant, current, more situation-specific self-interest variables.

These data call into question the purely utilitarian approach to the formation of attitudes. Extrapolating these results to trends in program evaluation research, the economic cost-benefit model may present at best a semiaccurate picture of both the community impacts of social programs and their influences on these outcomes. Consideration of self-interest factors is not regarded as being without merit. Rather, the conception of people as rational beings who react to a program primarily on the basis of what they stand to gain or lose by it may not be enough. This may be the case particularly when the program attempts to address a politically sensitive issue such as busing or, more generally, any concrete attempt to achieve school desegregation. Examining the effects of more irrational forces, themselves the product of a socialization process that took place in a context perhaps unrelated to the program objectives, may be more appropriate. People seem, at least in current studies, to be more against others than for themselves in their response to social change.

## REFERENCES

KATZ, D. (1960) "The functional approach to the study of attitudes." Public Opinion Quarterly 24: 163-204.
KINDER, D. R. and D. R. KIEWIET (forthcoming) "Economic grievances and political behavior: the role of personal discontents and collective judgments in congressional voting." American Journal of Political Science 23.
McCONAHAY, J. B. and W. D. HAWLEY (1977) "Is it the buses or the blacks?" Presented to the American Psychological Association.
SEARS, D. O., C. P. HENSLER, and L. K. SPEER (1979) "Whites' opposition to 'busing': self-interest or symbolic politics." American Political Science Review 73: 369-384.
TYLER, T. R. (1977) "Adolescents' symbolic reactions to the energy crisis". Presented to the American Psychological Association.

# 12

## COST-EFFECTIVE MEDICAID MENTAL HEALTH POLICIES: DESIGN AND TESTING

### Barbara C. Davenport and Ronald L. Nuttall

Faced with virtually uncontrolled mental health care costs, an ineffectual payment decision-making system, and rapid increases in the number of Medicaid clients receiving psychiatric day treatment, the Massachusetts Department of Public Welfare is seeking a cost-effective policy for mental health care services. Such a policy would permit publicly assisted clients to receive adequate, appropriate, and effective treatment at fiscally responsible levels.

The Massachusetts Department of Public Welfare spent nearly four million dollars last year for ambulatory health services with little idea of what these funds actually purchased. A full range of mental health services were available to recipients, including inpatient, day treatment, clinic and nonclinic therapy. Day treatment costs were increasing most rapidly, because of the Department of Mental Health's deinstitutionalization policy. It was estimated that this policy alone could cost Medicaid nine million dollars yearly. Assessment of community-based facilities, particularly psychiatric day treatment, thus became a focal point of the effort to design cost-effective policies for mental health services.

# THE SYSTEM AS A WHOLE

A first step in design was to consider the system as a whole, particularly clients' treatment, costs, and outcomes in different care settings. Obtaining this information proved enormously complex since different state agencies are responsible for different aspects of mental health care, including the departments of mental health, public health, and welfare. Even within the Medicaid program, hospital, clinic, and nonclinic services are administered by different directors, have different policies, use different reimbursement structures, collect different data, and are processed through different computer systems. Determining patterns of client care becomes virtually impossible. Even comparing the services offered in clinic versus nonclinic settings is difficult because of varying policies and reimbursement rates.

As an example, policies for clinic and physician-provided therapy are entirely different. Therapy offered in clinics is subject to some constraints on length. In order to provide over twelve sessions of therapy, prior approval by welfare department consultants is required. In clinic settings, therapy may be given by a variety of mental health professionals: psychiatrists, psychologists, social workers, and psychiatric nurses. Individual sessions are reimbursed at the rate of $30.00 an hour.

In nonclinic settings, no constraints are placed on the amount of therapy and no prior approval is required. However, only physicians can provide therapy in nonclinic settings. Before March 1976, reimbursement was $25.00 an hour, but a 30% legislative cut on all physicians' fees reduced this to the current $17.50.

Psychiatric day treatment, a recently offered service, requires prior approval for over sixty days of treatment in free-standing clinics. The reimbursement rate, ranging from $17.00 to $29.00 a day, is set individually and varies according to each facility's staffing pattern and other factors. In contrast, hospital-based day treatment is not subject to length controls, and the rate is the same as that for the hospital's daily base, ranging from $56.00 to $76.00 a day.

## RESULTS AND COMPARISONS

The system-as-a-whole studies sought to compare types of clients being served, types of professionals serving clients, diagnoses and treatment modalities, medications and referral sources for different settings. Since the clinic patients were all Medicaid and the private patients were largely (94%) non-Medicaid, these groups represented different socio-economic populations.

No substantial differences were found for sex, race, or medications. Age, referral source, diagnoses, and treatment modality and length differed.

Medicaid clinic patients were more likely to be diagnosed as schizophrenic and depressed; private patients were more often diagnosed as neurotic or as having personality disorders. For the nonclinic group, depression and neurosis each occurred for about 30% of the clients. In clinics, the incidence of neurosis was only 18%. In the nonclinic population, there was a positive relationship between Medicaid status and a diagnosis of schizophrenia and a negative correlation with a diagnosis of neurosis. Thus Medicaid patients were reported by physicians to be more disturbed psychologically than non-Medicaid patients.

In terms of medication, slightly less than half of the clients in both clinic and nonclinic settings received no medication (when adults only were used in the clinic population). When children were included in the clinic population, clinic patients received less medication than nonclinic patients.

Regarding treatment modality, both clinic and nonclinic patients generally received individual therapy, 59% and 66% respectively. Group therapy was provided 21% of the time in clinics and only 5% of the time in nonclinic settings. Diagnostic services were offered during 10% of all visits in clinics and 13% of all visits in private settings. Referral sources also differed. Private patients were referred primarily (47%) from physicians, whereas clinic patients mainly were referred (30%) from social service agencies and schools. In clinics, therapy was provided by psychiatric social workers, psychologists, and psychiatrists with about equal frequency (26%, 25%, and 24% respectively). In nonclinical settings, only physicians delivered services.

Treatment lengths for clinic patients were shorter than for nonclinic patients. Nearly 60% of the clinic patients but only 30% of the nonclinic patients were in therapy for six months or less. On an average, patients were seen 3.5 times a month; the range was from 2 to 11 visits. Overall, patients received only seven therapy sessions during the six-month sample billing period, with a range of 1 to 138 sessions. The average therapist charged for 70 sessions of therapy and had ten patients during this time. Most surprising was the finding that 30% of all clients received 2 or fewer sessions in a six-months' period.

# THE IMPACT OF REIMBURSEMENT STRATEGIES

A second step in designing cost-effective mental health service policies was tracing the impact of some prior policy changes or differences, particularly reimbursement strategies. The impact of the previously mentioned 30% fee cuts, of the unlimited psychotherapy policy, and of the prior approval system were examined.

## THE IMPACT OF THE 30% CUT IN FEES

In Massachusetts all rates are set by a state commission. Although protected from political pressures, the commission is not wholly immune to them. The 30% cut in physicians' fees was authorized by the governor and did not originate from the commission. Fees for primary care services since have been restored, but not those for speciality services such as psychotherapy. Thus psychiatrists are now reimbursed at $17.00 an hour, whereas before March 1976 they received $25.00 from Medicaid.

The fee cut led to a sudden drop in reimbursements, which was followed by a gradual increase. After six months, reimbursements decreased 35% relative to precut levels while number of claims increased 7%. After twelve months, the amount paid increased by 22% relative to precut levels while the number of claims had decreased by 11%. Eighteen months later, there was a 22% drop in reimbursements and claims decreased by 5%. These data suggest that a fee cut in the absence of other controls only partially achieves the desired cost control outcomes. First, there are displacement effects: cuts may result in shifts to other more costly services such as clinic visits at $30 each. Second, cuts may encourage fraud. In the Massachusetts instance, a number of psychiatrists hired less trained mental health workers to provide therapy and illegally billed Medicaid under their M.D. provider number, a ploy enabling the therapist to maintain an income similar to the precut level.

## LIMITED VERSUS UNLIMITED THERAPY POLICIES

Maximum limits or arbitrary cutoffs are the most common reimbursement control mechanism used by third-party carriers. Among the problems with these limits are: (1) a tendency to provide the maximum amount to all clients whether services are needed or not so that the ceiling becomes the floor; (2) insensitivity of such policies to individual needs for longer treatment; (3) encourgement of revolving-door clients who present themselves each year for $500 worth of therapy; (4) inability to treat clients in need after the yearly limit is reached; (5) openness of the system to individuals who have little likelihood of benefiting from the services; and (6) that documentation of outcomes in not required.

Another common form of cost containment is the prior approval system. Problems with the prior approval system include: (1) lengthy treatment plans are required of the provider, but are rarely used clinically; (2) treatment plans tend to reflect ability to state the case well, not actual need for treatment; (3) consultants find it extremely difficult to make decisions on treatment plans, because no objective criteria for decision making are available; (4) treatment tends to be approved for the equivalent of the maximum period, regardless of problems, adding the inefficiency of paying professionals to make yes decisions when, operationally, restrictions are based on treatment length; and (5) the lag time between request and approval may delay treatment.

Comparing clinic (prior approval) and nonclinic (no prior approval) settings permitted some assessment of the impact of these different policies. In the clinic setting, interviews with providers suggested that most providers requested prior approval for continued care routinely. In comparison, 40% of the nonclinic Medicaid patients were seen for four or fewer visits. Absence of an approval mechanism did not appear to increase utilization, at least not among physicians paid $17.50 an hour. Conversely, the prior approval system did not appear to limit or shorten length of therapy.

### REIMBURSEMENT RATES

Another policy difference the consequences of which could be examined was the impact of different rates of reimbursement for similar services. The clinic reimbursement rate is $30.00 an hour; the rate for private psychiatrists was $17.50. Provision of services in mental health clinics has been increasing more rapidly than services in nonclinic settings. This might be due to other factors, such as the expansion of clinic facilities. Interviews suggest, however, that the fee disparity has made it more attractive for psychiatrists to ally themselves with clinics as therapists, diagnosticians, or administrators. Respondents in the survey of psychiatrists indicated a tendency to refer patients to mental health centers and sometimes treat them there, in part to avoid absorbing costs of missed or cancelled appointments and also in part to avoid having to deal with the Medicaid forms.

# DESIGNING AND TESTING A COST-EFFECTIVE POLICY

Taking into account the findings from the study of the system as a whole and the analyses of the impact of specific policies, the following principles guided development of a prototype cost-effective Medicaid mental health reimbursement system:

(1) The reimbursement system should be applicable throughout the delivery system as a whole. This implies some mechanism for determining appropriate client placement on a continuum of services.

(2) The system should be based on an instrument meeting both clinical and administrative needs. Such an instrument should be simple to administer; usable at intake, review, and outcome stages; and appropriate for ongoing studies of which services are achieving what type of results and at what cost.

(3) The system should place clinical decision making as close to the client as possible. Under the current Medicaid prior approval system, decision are made at the state level for clients who are never seen by the consultants.

(4) The system should involve only forms maximizing clinical and administrative communication, which are uniform across programs, avoiding unnecessary duplication.

(5) The system should place as much responsibility as possible on the provider facility for conducting self- clinical and utilization review. With adequate guidelines, responsibility for such a review should be shifted from reimbursers to providers.

(6) Data should be aggregated in ways facilitating planning and evaluation at program, area, region and state levels.

(7) Feedback should be given comparing program practice patterns across providers.

## THE MODEL BEING TESTED

Psychiatric day treatment was selected as the area for pilot testing the system. In the next few years, a rapid increase in number of psychiatric day treatment providers is expected because of the state deinstitutionalization policy. The number of state hospital patients dropped from 13,000 in 1969 to 4,900 in 1976. Facilities offering psychiatric day treatment are proliferating. Most clients of the 43 programs already operating are Medicaid-eligible, yet only a few of the programs have met licensing standards for Medicaid providers. The still relatively small number of providers, the anticipated growth, and the newness of this service contributed to the decision to begin the pilot test with this setting. Also, the day treatment program directors were cooperative and concerned about client assessment.

In developing a psychiatric day treatment policy, the overall goal was to eliminate the prior approval system, replacing it with a client-centered clinical and fiscal management approach that would cost Medicaid less than the existing system and maintain or improve effectiveness. Specific objectives included: limiting services to clients likely to be helped by this form of treatment; documenting level of functioning in behavioral terms; linking client need to program capability; charting progress over time in terms of client functionality; developing length-of-treatment norms in relation to functionality; developing a peer review mechanism; and establishing ongoing cost-effectiveness analysis systems.

Program guidelines were prepared by a committee of professional therapists, consisting of day treatment program directors selected for their diverse orientations and complementary skills, with representation from various stakeholder groups. Although the guidelines were developed for Medicaid use, they were designed to encompass all day treatment clients and to be used in any program.

Implementation was begun by training three program staffs who were most willing and ready to use the guidelines. External trainers helped minimize provider feelings of having a Medicaid policy forced on them. The trainers had been involved in developing levels of functioning instruments for use in day treatment, and were extremely knowledgeable about day treatment conditions (Carter and Newman, 1976). In one program, selected to be a model project, staff were trained more intensively.

As other programs have become Medicaid-eligible providers, training in the new reimbursement system has been offered to clinicians and administrators. Providers have been given the option of using the prior approval system or the levels-of-functioning system. All have chosen the

latter. A good deal of provider feedback is sought regarding the usefulness of the system to their facility, as unhappy providers can sabotage
almost any reimbursement policy.

## UTILIZATION REVIEW AND QUANTITATIVE NORMS

During the one-year pilot test period, and, if successful, thereafter,
retrospective monitoring by Medicaid will provide cost control and
quality assurance. This is less costly than prospective review when cases
are many and objective criteria for clinical decision making are few.
Norms are being developed to serve as such criteria, linking length of
treatment to level of functioning. Siegel et al. (1978) had earlier
compared length and frequency of treatment to diagnosis in an effort
to develop quantitative norms. They did not, however, assess client
outcomes or costs. The policy being pilot tested permits such quantitative norms to be established.

Review procedures could then be changed. If quantitative norms
could be developed on the basis of provider practice patterns, deviant
cases could be flagged in routine reports gathered by the system.
First-level review of such cases could involve evidence that the process
criteria specified in the guidelines had been met, including intake
screening, appropriate review, goal-setting and termination planning.
Such a first-level review could be made by trained clerical staff at the
state level and would not require clinical judgments. Cases requiring
clinical assessments would be reviewed on site, with peers assessing level
of functioning and reasons for the type and length of treatment.

This approach substitutes retrospective review for prior approval.
Providers would submit monthly reports listing the clients, their baseline level of functioning, the current level, and their termination levels.
Quarterly reports comparing providers with each other would be prepared by Medicaid and shared with the providers, who presumably
would have strong incentives to take corrective action if their performance seemed unfavorably deviant. Comparative utilization feedback
thus is seen as a first step in controlling excessively long treatments.

It is true that intake screening in mental health care has not been
used widely as a baseline against which to assess improvement in
functioning in relation to treatment length. Tieing reimbursements to
improvement in functionality is even more innovative. As a safeguard
against denying reimbursement to clients who might not seem to fit the
criteria but who the provider feels should receive services, provisions

have been made for individual consideration and exemptions: one example might be individuals relying on the day care center for maintenance of functioning.

The guidelines will be evaluated in terms of the cost savings and quality of care. To help determine the latter, Medicaid records of all clients in day treatment are being studied. The data base will be client records for five years before the guidelines were implemented and two years after implementation.

## SUMMARY

The Massachusetts Department of Public Welfare is trying out a client-centered cost outcome system of reimbursement. Reimbursement is based on client improvement in terms of functionality over time, following intake screening to identify clients most likely to be helped by different kinds of services. The policy is being pilot tested in psychiatric day treatment programs. Expansion to the entire mental health system is planned, contingent on the results of the pilot test evaluation. It is hoped that by evaluating the total system, then considering the impact of various reimbursement strategies, next selecting a small portion of the system in which to try out the change, and finally monitoring the impact of the new policies, Massachusetts will provide its publicly-assisted clients with quality mental health services at reasonable cost.

## REFERENCES

CARTER, D. and F. NEWMAN (1976) A Client-Oriented System of Mental Health Service Delivery and Program Management. U.S. DHEW Series C, No. 12, 76-307. Rockville, MD: National Institute of Mental Health, Division of Biometry and Epidemiology.
SIEGEL, C., LASKA. E., GRIFFIS, A. and WANDERLING, J. (1978) "Quantitative care norms for psychiatric ambulatory population in a county medical assistance program." American Journal of Public Health 68: 352-358.

# 13

## COUNTING ACTIONS LOUDER THAN WORDS:
## BEHAVIOR SCALES OF JOB PERFORMANCE

Hermann F. Schwind

Although personality traits are still dominant criteria for personnel appraisal, behavior-oriented measures of job performance are becoming more popular (Campbell et al., 1970). In one of the first applications, Flanagan (1954) defined the critical requirements of a job as those behaviors crucial in making a difference between doing a job effectively and doing it ineffectively. This technique, modified by Smith and Kendall (1963) and Campbell et al. (1970), is now better known as the Behaviorally Anchored Rating Scale (BARS), or Behavior Expectation Scale (BES; see Zedeck and Baker, 1972).

The behavioral approach to performance appraisal avoids much of the ambiguity of trait ratings by reducing the performance construction to the job itself (Dunnette, 1966; and Zedeck and Baker, 1972). This notional characteristic of behavioral scales is supported empirically by reports of Fogli, Hulin, and Blood (1971) and Smith and Kendall (1963) that interrater agreement generally is high ($r \geqslant .97$) on the scale value assigned to behavioral descriptions. Additional support comes from Campbell et al.'s (1970) analysis of the conceptual unidemensionality of behavioral incidents within scales.

Blood (1974) points to several positive spin-off effects from the use of behaviorally oriented scales. First, they can extend the domain of evaluated performance. Using as many organizational perspectives as possible (e.g., even clients') could considerably broaden the job behavior domain. Second, behavioral scales can help in developing training programs (Cambell et al., 1973). Since skills required on the job are described in behavioral terms—as compared with the name of a skill domain—shortcomings are more easily identified and task-specific training programs initiated. Also, since behavioral descriptions can be stated negatively, unwanted behaviors which trainees should learn to avoid can be pinpointed. Third, behavioral scales can assess agreement on organizational policy. In scale development, behavioral items are rated according to the level of performance described; items with a large variance usually are discarded. However, these items may be important for organizational development, identifying unclear organizational policy or areas of conflict.

Despite the intuitive appeal of behavior oriented scales, recent reviews of the literature (Schwab, Heneman, and DeCotiis, 1975; Schwind, 1977) have not been encouraging. Comparing behavior-oriented scales with Graphic Rating Scales (GRS) and/or Summated Rating Scales (SRS), researchers have found either no or only modest superiority of BARS over GRS or SRS and thus have questioned the investment of the time and effort required for development of BARS (Borman and Dunnette, 1975).

One of the major shortcomings of BARS seems to be a waste of costly information. Critical incidents for a job are subject to an elaborate validation, retranslation, and rating process, and they must meet a standard deviation criterion (Smith and Kendall, 1963). Usually twenty to fifty critical incidents per job dimension survive. Yet only between five and ten, depending on the number of anchoring points of the scale, are utilized; all others are discarded. Discarded items may contain valuable information about the job dimension. The decision to eliminate them usually is made on the basis of arbitrarily chosen criteria: a convenient mean value to fit the scale points, and the degree of agreement between raters as measured by the standard deviation.

# A NEW PERFORMANCE EVALUATION SCALE: THE BEHAVIOR DESCRIPTION INDEX

To improve the rating characteristics of behavior-oriented scales and reduce their shortcomings, a new scale is proposed, based on descriptions of critical job behavior incidents. The development of these incidents is similar to the procedures for BARS (write-up, validation, retranslation), but the rating of the incidents from very ineffective to extremely effective is dropped. Instead of selecting five, seven, or nine incidents per job dimension (depending on the number of scale points chosen), a larger number of behavioral incidents is selected, the limit being determined only by the capacity—and willingness—of raters to read the more extensive behavior descriptions. Raters seem willing to respond to about twenty or thirty items per scale on a five-scale measure. About thirty items per scale may be optimal, since increasing the numbers of items may lead to rater fatigue, halo, and leniency.

In the scale itself, the behavioral incidents are listed randomly. The rater responds to the question: "Does the ratee exhibit the described behavior *consistently* (all the time)?" The responses (ratings) can be evaluated individually to determine specific weaknesses or converted into point scores. The responses can be given any weight the rater (or the evaluator of the ratings) desires. A supervisor could determine in advance what scores would be acceptable or unacceptable. For example, out of thirty possible points (assuming that thirty behavior samples were chosen per scale),

0-15 may mean: urgent training required (or, if measured after training, training ineffective)

16-20 may mean: training recommended

21-25 may mean: refresher course may be useful

26-30 may mean: no training required.

## AN APPLICATION OF THE APPROACH

Five large Canadian chartered banks participated in this application. Assistant branch managers comprised the focal group, since their positions required a large amount of continual training. Training managers, themselves having been for at least two years in an assistant branch manager's position, determined that this job had five main aspects: Administration, Customer Relations, Marketing, Personnel Administration and Training.

In all five banks, branch managers, assistant branch managers, and bank clerks and tellers were asked to describe examples of effective and ineffective job behaviors of an assistant branch manager. After editing and removal of redundant items, there were approximately 300 to 400 items per bank. Judges from each bank then determined whether each item was a valid description of an assistant branch manager's job behavior. They also categorized each item into one of the job dimensions mentioned above. Items were retained if 80% of the judges agreed on their validity and category. Approximately 80 to 150 behavior samples survived this process. These items were listed again, this time ordered into their respective categories, and sent to a group of judges from all banks. These judges rated each item on a 1 to 7 scale as to the degree of effectiveness the item described, ranging from very very ineffective to extremely effective. Items were retained if the standard deviation of their ratings did not exceed 1.0. Approximately 50 to 80 behavior samples per dimension remained from each bank's initial sample pool. Those items were used to develop Behaviorally Anchored Rating Scales for each bank.

From the residual behavior samples, 50 items per job dimension were selected according to the lowest standard deviation criterion (i.e., highest degree of agreement among judges). A total of 1,000 judges (200 from each bank) assessed the validity of each item as a typical job behavior of an assistant branch manager, and rated it on the 1 to 7 effectiveness scale. Items were retained if 80% of all judges and 60% of the judges of the individual banks agreed on the validity of the item and if the standard deviation of the item did not exceed 1.5.

## GOOD COMPARED TO WHAT

In addition to the Behaviorally Anchored Rating Scale (BARS), a Graphic Rating Scale (GRS), and a Behavior Description Index (BDI) were developed. The GRS was an adaptation of a 7-point global rating scale of performance acceptability in the five areas that was used by the banks for their regular performance appraisal. The BARS and the BDI instruments involved job behavior samples. BARS items were selected according to (a) ratings closest to a scale point (1 to 7), and (b) lowest possible standard deviation. No items could be found for the midpoint range of the scales, a problem discussed by Landy and Guion (1970), who suggest that polarization is a necessary consequence of eliminating items which do not have meaning to individuals. The BDI instrument involved 20 job behavior samples per job dimension, or 100 in total. Examples of effective and ineffective behavior were selected according to the lowest standard deviation and listed in random order.

A group of 25 assistant branch managers of one of the five Canadian banks were rated by their superiors, using the GRS, BARS, and the BDI as appraisal instruments. The GRS scores had a significantly higher halo effect than both BARS and BDI scores. The GRS scores contained no ratings in the two lowest scale ranges ("unacceptable" and "moderate") or in the highest scale range ("excellent"); for the BARS and the BDI instruments only the lowest scale ranges are not utilized.

Using the multitrait-multimethod approach suggested by Campbell and Fiske (1959), convergent validity was significant for almost all entries. Discriminant validity was highest for the BARS/BDI correlations. Since both convergent and discriminant validity are established for the BARS and BDI instruments, it can be concluded that both showed evidence of construct validity, while the GRS format compared less favorably.

## IN CONCLUSION

First, behaviorally oriented scales need not be organization-specific. Goodale and Burke (1975) earlier demonstrated that BARS need not be job-specific. The extension of the use of behavior-oriented scales to other, but similar, jobs in the same organization and now even to similar jobs in different organizations in the same industry should make the significantly higher investment in time and effort for the development of behavior oriented scales more worthwhile. Organizations could pool their resources to develop such instruments, or delegate this task to an institution of which related organizations are members.

Second, the psychometric characteristics of behavior-oriented scales can be improved in several ways. One of the major shortcomings of the BARS format was the severely limited utilization of the total pool of information available on the job behavior domain. The switch from a Likert-type scale—which limited the number of behavior samples used per scale to the number of anchor points—to an anchorless format allows, theoretically, the use of the total job behavior domain.

Third, because of the favorable rating characteristics, the increased utilization of job information, and the specific feedback to raters, evaluators, and ratees, it is possible that the BDI can be used as the basis of an evaluation system offering both information to trainers and managers alike.

## REFERENCES

BERNARDIN, H. J. and C. S. WALTER (1977) "Effects of rater training and diary-keeping on psychometric error in ratings." Journal of Applied Psychology 62: 64-69.
BLOOD, M. R. (1974) "Spin-offs from behavioral expectation scale procedures." Journal of Applied Psychology 59: 513-515.
BORMAN, W. C. and M. D. DUNNETTE (1975) "Behavior-based vs. trait-oriented performance ratings: an empirical study." Journal of Applied Psychology 60: 561-566.
CAMPBELL, J. P., M. D. DUNNETTE, R. D. ARVEY, and L. W. HELLERVIK (1973) "The development and evaluation of behaviorally based rating scales." Journal of Applied Psychology 58: 15-22.
CAMPBELL, J. P., M. D. DUNNETTE, E. E. LAWLER, and K. E. WEICK (1970) Managerial Behavior, Performance, and Effectiveness. New York: McGraw-Hill.
DUNNETTE, M. D. (1966) Personnel Selection and Placement. Belmont, CA: Wadsworth.
FLANAGAN, J. C. (1954) "The critical incident technique." Psychological Bulletin 51: 327-358.
FOGLI, L., C. L. HULIN, and M. R. BLOOD (1971) "Development of first-level behavioral criteria." Journal of Applied Psychology 55: 3-8.
GOODALE, J. G. and R. J. BURKE (1975) "Behaviorally based rating scales need not to be job specific." Journal of Applied Psychology 60: 389-391.
LANDY, F. J. and R. M. GUION (1970) "Development of scales for the measurement of work motivation," Organizational Behavior and Human Performance 5: 93-103.
SCHWAB, D. P., H. G. HENEMAN, and T. A. De COTIIS (1975) "Behaviorally Anchored Rating Scales: A Review of the Literature," Personnel Psychology 28: 549-562.
SCHWIND, H. F. (1977) "New ways to evaluate teaching and training effectiveness." Presented at the Adult Education Research Association meeting in Minneapolis, April.

SMITH, P. C. and L. M. KENDALL (1963) "Retranslation of expectations: an approach to the construction of unambiguous anchors for rating scales." Journal of Applied Psychology 47: 149-155.

ZEDECK, S. and T. BAKER (1972) "Nursing performance by behavioral expectation scales: a multitrait-multirater analysis." Organizational Behavior and Human Performance 7: 457-466.

# 14

## NEW HEALTH TECHNOLOGIES:

## ASSESSING THE COSTS AND BENEFITS

Selma J. Mushkin

In a study for the National Institutes of Health, one of our preliminary report findings came to be a datum in the controversy on technology control. As a consequence, we became interested in that controversy. Cost-benefit analysis is central to the debate.

Proposals are being advanced to regulate technology or, at a minimum, to provide an organizational structure for assessing the costs and benefits of technology, extending back in the process to the requirements for cost-benefit assessment that accompany research grants. Rational behavior in funding research and paying for medical care requires informed choice among possible options. Those making the decisions require information on what can be expected by way of benefits and costs. The framework of policy analysis has proved most

AUTHOR'S NOTE: The research in this study was carried out by the Public Services Laboratory of Georgetown University under contract # NO1-OD-5-2121 with the Division of Program Analysis of the National Institutes of Health, Project Manager: Dr. Herbert B. Woolley, and Principal Investigator: Selma J. Mushkin, Director of Public Services Laboratory.

useful in gaining at least a clearer articulation of objectives. Further, analyses that have been made have forced a critical appraisal of criteria for assessing progress in health (Mushkin, 1977). It has become plainer that the measures of impact which are based on the application of biostatistics on mortality and morbidity derived from concepts developed perhaps over a century ago are incomplete and often misleading.

# OBJECTIVES OF TECHNOLOGY ASSESSMENT

Three separate purposes are scrambled in the discussion of technology assessment. These three objectives need to be distinguished and the criteria of progress toward each defined in terms of the specific objective. The proposals and hearings before Congress and other relevant discussions jump from one objective to another as if the approaches to deal with them were the same.

Safety, efficacy (or effectiveness), and cost containment are the three objectives that are sought.

**Safety.** Safety is used here in the special sense of the potential hazards that might be unleashed in scientific probing. Traditions of free inquiry are challenged by recombinant DNA research. Is some research to be barred or rigidly controlled because of hazards, or not? As one commentator posed the question, "Should certain lines of inquiry simply be ruled out of bounds as too perilous for frail mankind?" (Greenberg, 1977).

The purpose of safety controls is to prevent illness. Scientists raised the issue of inadvertent creation of hazardous organisms in the course of research. And the scientists participated in a voluntary moratorium on recombinant DNA research, pending development of safety guidelines by NIH. Clarity in the formulation of safety standards would help answer the critical questions. What research is to be monitored? By whom? Who is to decide? How are decisions on enforcement to be made? With what sanctions?

Less basic safety questions are defined here to be encompassed within the objective of "effectiveness." These include the challenges on safety arising from statistics on unnecessary patient deaths and such studies as Illich's (1976) that charge, "Doctoring may be hazardous to your health."

194IMPROVING EVALUATIONS

**Effectiveness.** A second objective is effectiveness of health care and biomedical research embodied in such care. The purpose here is to (a) better inform providers of care, (b) inform consumers of care, and (c) improve the regulation of drugs, instruments, and so forth on safety and efficacy.

Despite a decade or more of urging, the assessment of comparative therapies for their effectiveness is still very deficient. Medical protocols are established, but the kind of information that could document the effectiveness of these and other alternatives is often lacking, especially information defining effectiveness in terms of the functional status of the patient. Information now available to physicians and other providers of medical care about the probabilities of outcomes in applying alternative therapies is seriously deficient. Physicians do not have the necessary facts, and patients can hardly receive answers to such questions as: What good will this medicine or procedure do? What are the chances that it will cure? What are the chances it will control the disease? What are the adverse effects? What are the probabilities of different reactions? How does one modality compare with other possible procedures?

Part of the explanation for the lack of information on medical treatments lies in the physicians' control over medical care decisions. Yet, it is clear that the characteristics of the patient comprise one input into the effectiveness of medical care, and certainly the patient's compliance with a medical regimen is another. As long as a physician continues to decide about care as guardian for the patient, the need to know about the probabilities of consequences is muted. However, a series of factors is converging to give new emphasis to the need for information for patients to make decisions. Those factors include medical malpractice suits, the higher education levels of today's patients, and the awakened sense of consumer participation.

Deficiencies in information about optional modalities are being addressed. Scholars at the School of Public Health (Bunker, 1976; Weinstein, 1976) at Harvard University, and at the School of Hygiene of Johns Hopkins University (Williamson, forthcoming), among others, are engaged in the type of research that will yield assessments of therapies. University-based centers such as the cancer centers throughout the nation, and the heart centers, are intended to provide a base of data along with their examinations of consequences of alternative modalities. However, the imprecision of medical research is perhaps suggested by the study of statistical procedures in medical manuscripts by Gifford and Feinstein (1977).

Corrective action to provide basic data on optional therapies to deal with diseases makes ordinary common sense for both providers of care and patients. In the absence of such information, therapies are prescribed in shades of darkness. Machinery for collecting the necessary data on therapies from practitioners has been put in place for some disease categories. More machinery of this kind is needed. Biostatistical and biometric techniques applied to the therapeutic data should help establish probabilities of cures, and of control of disease, at various functional levels. A number of questions remain to be resolved: How large an effort? Over what time period? With what incentives? Administered by whom? And with what machinery for dissemination?

Assessments of the effectiveness of known therapies need to be carefully distinguished from assessments for cost-control purposes that would extend to proposed new biomedical research. Confusion in purpose seems widespread, with resulting ambiguity on what is feasible and on what methods are appropriate for policy implementation.

**Cost containment.** Examples of large capital equipment costs, such as the cost of CAT scanners or cardiac intensive care units in hospitals, emphasize the role of new technology as a factor in the rise of health care costs. In a little over a decade, health care costs have escalated to just under 9% of the GNP, without an end in sight for the growth in commitment of resources. Given this large and rapid growth, it is not surprising to find concern about any factor that is thought to contribute to the inflation. In the material presented here, studies of the Public Services Laboratory (PSL) at Georgetown University are used to assess biomedical research costs.

## THE NEED FOR
## RESTRICTION ON TECHNOLOGY

One PSL study asks: Is technology the villain in causing medical care costs to skyrocket? (Rycroft and Vehorn, 1977). Against the backdrop of testimony before the President's Biomedical Research Panel, which claimed that "at least half of the increase in hospital expenditures (between 1965 and 1975) is related to more intensive use of real resources" (Gaus, 1975), a review was undertaken of what is known about technology's impact on costs.

As a starter, technology is not consistently defined in the literature. A technological change is used at times to encompass any change in resources used, ranging from additional laboratory tests (including more frequent use of the same kind of test) to wholly equipped intensive care units. New drug therapies, new surgical instruments, new hearing aids or prosthetic devices are included. At other times, discussions of technology seem to be restricted to capital-intensive equipment. But sometimes any factor "not otherwise accounted for" is technology.

In principle, changes in patient outcome along with inputs need to be considered. If the outcome has changed, the product is different, and quality improvement should be deducted in assessing cost increases. The Council on Wage and Price Stability, in its 1976 report on rising health care costs, distinguishes between interventive technology, which directly alters patient outcome, and supportive technology, which provides information for the operation of interventive technology (Feldstein and Taylor, 1977). As Davis (1973) emphasized several years ago, given the cost pass-through of reimbursement for hospital care, there is little incentive to adopt innovations that reduce costs. Moreover, under third-party finances, demand responds more or less automatically to technological change for new products or more repetitive application of diagnostic or therapeutic methods.

Earlier studies were hampered by the difficulties of measuring changes in output (or patient outcomes) to determine the impact of new technology.

A number of major studies of technology and medical care costs on which the proposals for technology controls are based are fairly old. Most, including some of the more recent studies, deal with hospital costs only. While hospital costs are a substantial part of health care costs, these hospital costs omit sixty cents out of each dollar of health expenditures. The following studies are confined to hospital care: Lave and Lave (1970); Feldstein (1971); Anderson and May (1972); Salkever (1972); Davis (1973 and 1974); Worthington (1975); Feldstein-Taylor (1977) for Council on Wage and Price Stability; and the CBO study (1977). The study by Fuchs and Kramer (1972) deals with physician services, and that of Worthington (1975) for DHEW includes physician services as well as hospital care.

To illustrate the findings, the regression analysis by Davis (1974) shows that demand variables (insurance, real income per capita, population density and other demographic characteristics, and physicians and hospitals per capita) accounted for 45% of the rise in hospital expenses, case-mix variables for 7%, wages (payroll expenses per full-time employee) for 10%, and technology for 38%. Technology in this analysis is a time-trend variable for the period 1962-1968. Feldstein and Taylor (1977) find that technology, measured by non-payroll costs deflated by price, added 7.2% to the annual growth rate of hospital costs. (Hospital labor costs rose 9.0% per year and non-labor costs 11.0%, of which 3.6% was price.)

Economic incentives under insurance plans drive all costs up in the delivery of covered health services. Incentives promote cost-raising rather than cost-saving innovation. In this regard, insurance in health care is similar to procurement in the Department of Defense. Incentives to continually change the product are induced by insurance that allows both physician and patient to demand the "best possible care" with little regard to costs. Fuchs (1974) terms this "the technological imperative."

"Non-payroll expenses" (as reported by the American Hospital Association), the basic data in a number of the studies, are defined to include intern and resident pay, payroll supplements, interest charges, food expenditures, and so forth. Changes in interest over time are influenced by the shift in sources of funds for capital outlays of hospitals from grants to loans and do not reflect a change in real capital use. To the extent that food and laundry are provided under contract, payroll costs associated with food preparation and laundry may be included in non-payroll costs. Until comparable data over time are applied in analysis, the results really will remain unclear.

A second approach to technology and its cost impacts is taken in the study following the work done by Scitovsky (1967). Given the interest in technology, Scitovsky and McCall (1976) reanalyzed data on the cost of care in the Palo Alto Medical Clinic for selected illnesses over the period 1951, 1967, and 1971 to document the change in real inputs (after price adjustment) for those illnesses. Data are given for treatments for otitis media, acute appendicitis, maternity care, breast cancer, forearm fractures, pneumonia, duodenal ulcer, and myocardial infarction.

In the PSL study—still in process—data for 1930 (from the work of Lee Jones, 1933) on use of physician, hospital, drugs, and other medical service for the diagnosis and treatment of selected diseases under high 1930 standards of quality of care is being compared with estimates of use of services in a similar 1970 study by Schonfeld and others (1975) at Yale University. The incompleteness of the 1970 materials requires great caution if it is used without extensive supplementation.

A first cut on findings, however, supports the Scitovsky (1967) analysis that the changes over time in real resource use vary by disease or illness. However, unlike the Scitovsky findings that emphasize increases, the PSL study indicates only that changes in real costs on balance depend on the diseases assessed. The 1930-1970 comparisons show that a large number of diseases with high prevalence in 1930 are similar to otitis media and maternity care in the Scitovsky study, and resources declined rather than increased over the period. Differences in general findings are probably a function of the shift in base year of comparison. In 1930 many infectious and communicable diseases required substantial hospitalization and physician services; preventive measures and drug-specific therapies have reduced costs considerably for those diseases.

A third approach that seeks to narrow the question to biomedical research is being followed. We are attempting to analyze the share of higher per capita real personal health expenditures and also of improved mortality rates that is attributable to biomedical research.

Several models are being used for the analyses. In Model A—the Behavior Unit Model—real expenditures per capita are assumed to be a function of characteristics of (a) the patient population—measured by real per capita income, (b) providers and provision of care—measured by physician and hospital beds per 100,000 population, (c) method of financing care—or the share financed by insurance, Medicare, and Medicaid, and (d) biomedical research. A similar model of mortality changes is being tested in which real personal health expenditures per capita become an independent variable, capturing many of the characteristics of provision of health care.

In Model B—the Determinant Model—mortality and real expenditures per capita are each analyzed as functions of determinants that fall into four categories: (1) economic variables, (2) societal or stress variables, (3) environmental variables, and (4) medical and biomedical variables.

In Model C—the Residual Model—a residual method was applied that is similar to the models applied almost two decades ago to the residual factor in economic growth. In the residual analysis, determinants of change in health expenditures and in mortality are identified, and technology is defined as a residual. For example, an analysis of the rise in total health expenditures over the period 1930-1975 showed that the more than thirtyfold increase in health expenditures could be accounted for by the rise in population and the aging of that population, medical care price increases, real per capita income growth, and the introduction of third-party payments. In this analysis, the total percentage increase in direct health expenditures is assumed to equal the product of the percentage rise in population (adjusted for the effect of aging of the population), the rise in medical care prices, and a percentage change in demand attributable to the rise in real per capita income and the increased third-party payments or the percent of health expenditures paid by "others." The residual or unaccounted growth in this analysis was very small but negative, not positive in sign; that is, the net impact was cost-reducing rather than cost-increasing. In contrast, the residual method applied to mortality data produces the finding that perhaps 20% of the decline in death rates since 1930 can be attributed to biomedical research. Other models place the contribution of biomedical research even higher (Vehorn et al. 1978).

The results may underestimate the impact of biomedical research because of the interaction of income, biomedical research, medical expenditures, and improved mortality. At the same time, when biomedical research is measured as a residual, other factors, not necessarily research or technology, are part of the effect that is measured.

In the determinant and behavior unit models, biomedical research is measured in a variety of ways. For example, the following data are used: (1) biomedical research personnel (Ph.D.s granted in the biomedical sciences), (2) new drugs (both new drugs marketed as reported by the American Pharmaceutical Association and patents issued for drugs and medicines), (3) other new inventions (with patents issued for health-related professional and scientific instruments as proxy), (4) biomedical research expenditures, and (5) biomedical research literature (number of articles, number of journals, and so on) produced. The analyses carried out so far apply to the first three proxies.

No one of these measures or even a combination of them fully measures biomedical research activity; each is a measure of some aspect of activity. Moreover, none measures quality differences: not all Ph.D.s have the same inventiveness or competence; not all drug patents have the same therapeutic value. A search for the appropriate yardstick for biomedical research is not unique to the studies by PSL. The complex phenomenon of "biomedical research" continues to defy simple measurement or even measurement through the use of multidimensional indicators. Further assessments suggest that some partial indicators come closer to a complete measurement and have greater explanatory powers than others.

While the analyses by PSL are in midstream, with the whole process of study being an iterative one, the tentative findings suggest that, at least over a 45-year period, the costs of illness (especially when costs of death are included) have not been adversely affected by biomedical research and its technology. On the contrary, the cost of death has been reduced markedly.

## ASSESSMENT OF BENEFITS

Unless the objectives of health policies can be defined and progress toward them quantified, the basic tools of benefit-cost analysis cannot be applied. How indeed is progress to be quantified? We earlier applied two measures: (a) changes in direct resources used, and (b) changes in mortality. But neither of these fully captures the basic objectives of biomedical research.

Where market evaluations of outcome exist and are regarded as acceptable, measurement is fairly straightforward. Drug firm R&D expenditures may be a case in point. More difficult are the cases in which market evaluations are likely to be erroneous (because of externalities) or where markets do not exist at all and thus imputations of values are required. Biomedical research by its very characteristics is a pure public good, making market tests generally inoperative and imputations essential.

Traditional human capital measurements have limited usefulness for decision making in biomedical research, especially as "half way" rather than "decisive" or preventive technologies become increasingly representative of biomedical advances.[1] First, the concept understates values through the use of discounting. The method undervalues children's deaths and disabilities in the face of well-recognized family preferences for investment in children. Also, discounting of future earnings in arriving at present values places low value on the risk of life and limb, particularly if a market interest rate is used. Second, it undervalues those who are no longer attached to the work force, such as the aged, and those who have low earnings, such as women, blacks, and other minorities. Third, the concept fails to account for the spillover of the costs of death and illness to family members and to the community. Fourth, several other costs are conveniently omitted: pain, debility, disfigurement, loss of dignity, loss of opportunity, costs of time, and other nonhealth costs, such as special education and transportation. Fifth, the theoretical construct requires that earnings reflect marginal productivity. There are many market imperfections, however, that limit the usefulness of market indicators even as shadow prices of productivity and output. Sixth, the procedure produces unreliable and uncertain estimates because of (a) inclusion or exclusion of consumption—net or gross, (b) period of count—annual or period of illness—used, (c) imputation on risk aversion, and (d) the choice of discount rate. Although methodological improvements are possible, the traditional measure will still be deficient because of the factors described above.

We need to develop concepts of measurement and collect data against new yardsticks in addition to the traditional ones in health care if the payoffs from biomedical research are to be assessed adequately. The gains from biomedical research today are reflected less in saving lives than in making life livelier (i.e., quality of life). Unless we capture the element of improvement in the health status and functionality for the living, we will not be able to tell the full story. At one extreme, the advances in biomedical research may have improved substantially the health status of individuals, with no apparent impact on extension of life.

At a given point in time, the living may be distributed among a set of health states representing an array of conditions that deviates from the "optimum health." In the 1975 health interview survey (probability sample) conducted by the National Center for Health Statistics (1977), the following distribution of the respondents according to activity limitation is observed:

| | |
|---|---|
| With no activity limitation | 85.7% |
| With limitation in major activity | 10.8 |
| With limitation in other activity | 3.5 |
| | 100.0% |

In a probability sample of San Diego County residents consisting of 1,191 residents, it was found that about 15% have dysfunctional status (limited in social or physical activity and mobility) and an additional 50% function with a symptom/problem present (pain, disfigurement, or the like) (Bush, Chen, and Patrick, 1979).

Other survey studies no doubt show similar patterns of dysfunction and symptom/problems among population groups. Again, if biomedical advances are directed toward helping those who do less well in coping with daily activity and have symptom/problems without significantly changing the probability of death, we will seriously underestimate the return of biomedical research if no sensitive measure of health status is used. As more biomedical research effort is spent on halfway technology, the need for other measurement such as functional status becomes more acute.

Essentially two approaches may be followed in formulating alternatives to traditional measurements. One approach is to define quality of life or functionality so that changes in functional status can be related to a biomedical advance and measured in probability or distributional terms, or as average changes. The other is to convert the chances of a change in function, together with the chances of changing survival rates, to a monetary measure by determining "willingness to pay" for the change.

Several tasks require immediate attention by researchers and practitioners in the field. Among them are the following:

(1) Functional states critical to the assessment of biomedical research effectiveness need to be defined in a uniform way. Divergent sets of health states have been proposed by a number of investigators, and the comparability thus becomes troublesome. Strong advocacy of one or another course stands in the way of reconciliation.

(2) Data collection by the National Center for Health Statistics needs to be extended to include more information on functional states.

(3) The costs of care (medical and other) associated with different health or functional states need to be compiled.

(4) The feasibility of estimating the willingness to pay for moving from one functional state to another needs further assessment. Existing studies generally have been confined to the states of life and death, missing many important intermediate steps of health.

(5) Experimentation is needed in the collection of expert opinion on the impact of biomedical advances on movement among health states. Although expert opinions need to be supported by objective data, the opinions themselves are useful in understanding the consequences of biomedical advances on functionality.

(6) Political requirements on the criteria for assessments need to be identified, including determination of the problems of information overload and value-revealing components of functional states.

(7) Methods need to be designed for making operational the recent theoretical advances on demand-revealing processes for a public good such as biomedical research.

Until analysis establishes that R&D controls are important to cost containment (that is, that optional methods are not more effective) and until benefit measurements are compatible with the actual outcome of health research, it would appear desirable to move slowly toward any new offices charged with assessment of biomedical research projects. Proposals for cost-benefit analysis of biomedical research that leave the analysis to the principal investigator (PI) of the project may not be significant. The PI is clearly enthusiastic about the project and believes in it. If, however, a central large assessment effort is considered, with a substantial commitment of new funds, then much preliminary work is required on outcome measurement and understanding cost impacts over time.

## NOTE

1. As a shorthand, benefits are defined here to include effectiveness (or nonmonetary measures) as well as monetary measures.

## REFERENCES

ANDERSEN, R. and J. J. MAY, (1972) "Factors associated with the increasing cost of hospital care." Annals of the American Academy 399: 62-72.
BUNKER, J., F. MOSTELLER, and B. BARNES [eds.] (1976) Costs, Risks and Benefits of Surgery. New York: Oxford University Press.

BUSH, J. W., M. M. CHEN, and D. L. PATRICK (1979) Health Status and Health Policy. San Diego: University of California Health Index Project. (processed)

CHEN, M. M. and D. P. WAGNER (1978) "Gains in mortality from biomedical research, 1930-1975: an initial assessment," pp. 73-81 in Social Science and Medicine, Vol. 12c. Oxford, England: Pergamon.

Congressional Budget Office (1977) Staff Study. Washington, DC: CBO.

DAVIS, K. (1974) "The role of technology, demand, and labor market costs in the determination of hospital costs," pp. 283-301 in M. Perlman (ed.) The Economics of Health and Medical Care. New York: John Wiley.

——— (1973) "Theories of hospital inflation: some empirical evidence." Journal of Human Resources 8 (Spring): 181-201.

FELDSTEIN, M. (1971) The Rising Cost of Hospital Care. Washington, DC: Information Resources Press.

FELDSTEIN, M. and A. TAYLOR (1977) The Rapid Rise of Hospital Costs. Executive Office of the President, Council on Wage and Price Stability (January) Staff Report. Washington, DC.

FUCHS, V. R. (1974) Who Shall Live? New York: Basic Books.

——— and M. J. KRAMER (1972) Determinants of Expenditures for Physicians Services in the U.S. Washington, DC: U.S. Public Health Service, National Center for Health Services Research and Development (December).

GAUS, C. R. (1975) "Biomedical research and health care costs." Testimony of the Social Security Administration before the President's Biomedical Research Panel (September).

GIFFORD, R. H. and A. R. FEINSTEIN (1977) Remarks on a critique of methodology in studies of entro-coagulant therapy quoted in Medical Practice Information. Washington, DC: Policy Research Inc., Demonstration Project.

GREENBERG, D. S. (1977) "Dangerous Knowledge: Should It Be Controlled?" Washington Post (October 11), A-19.

ILLICH, I. (1976) Medical Nemesis, The Expropriation of Health. New York: Random House.

LAVE, J. and L. LAVE (1970) "Hospital cost functions." American Economic Review 50: 379-395.

LEE, R. I., L. W. JONES, and B. JONES (1933) The Fundamentals of Good Medical Care. Chicago: University of Chicago Press.

McGINNIS, J. M. (1977) Medical Technology: Some Efficiency Considerations. Cambridge: Harvard Center for Community Health and Medical Care (February).

MUSHKIN, S. J. (1977) "Criteria for program evaluation," ch. X in Respiratory Diseases: Task Force Report on Prevention, Control, Education. Washington, DC: DHEW Division of Lung Diseases, National Heart, Lung, and Blood Institute (March).

———, L. C. PARINGER, and M. M. CHEN (1978) "Returns to biomedical research 1900-1975: an initial assessment of impacts on health expenditures," pp. 105-120 in R. H. Egdahl and P. M. Gertman (eds.) Technology and the Quality of Health Care. Germantown, MD: Aspen Systems.

Public Services Laboratory conference on Functional Health Status and Biomedical Research and Technology (1977) Washington, DC: Georgetown University, September 23 and 24.

RYCROFT, R. and C. VEHORN (1977) Medical Costs and Medical Technology: A Review of Selected Literature. Washington, DC: Georgetown University Public Services Laboratory. (processed)

SALKEVER, D. (1972) "A micro-economic study of hospital cost inflation." Journal of Political Economy 80: 1144-1166.

SCHONFELD, H. K., J. F. HESTON, and I. S. FALK (1975) Standards for Good Medical Care. DHEW publication number (SSA) 75-11926. Washington, DC: Office of Research and Statistics, Social Security Administration, Department of Health, Education, and Welfare.

SCITOVSKY, A. A. (1967) "Changes in the costs of treatment of selected illnesses, 1951-1965." American Economic Review 57: 1182-1195.

——— and N. McCALL (1976) Changes in the Costs of Treatment of Selected Illnesses, 1951-1964-1971. National Center for Health Services Research (July).

VEHORN, C. L., S. LANDENFELD, and D. WAGNER (1978) Estimating the Returns form Biomedical Research. Presented for Public Services Laboratory at the Atlantic Economic Association Meeting, Washington, DC (October 19).

WEINSTEIN, M. C. and W. B. STASON (1976) Hypertension, A Policy Perspective. Cambridge: Harvard University Press.

WILLIAMSON, H. W. (forthcoming) Medical Care Outcomes: Assessment and Improvement.

WORTHINGTON, N. (1975) "Expenditures for hospital care and physicians services: factors affecting annual changes." Social Security Bulletin 38 (November): 3-15.

# SECTION IV
# THE ROLE OF EVALUATION

# 15

## ASSUMPTIONAL ANALYSIS: A METHODOLOGY FOR STRATEGIC PROBLEM SOLVING

Ian I. Mitroff, James R. Emshoff,
and Ralph H. Kilmann

The recent work of several students of organizations shed light on the actual working environment in which managers and decision makers operate and the characteristic kinds of problems they typically face (Emery and Trist, 1965; Lyles and Mitroff, forthcoming; Mintzberg, 1971; Mintzberg, Raisingham, and Theoret, 1976). In a word, the environment is more often one of constantly changing conditions, uncertainty, and turbulence than one of certainty, stability, and predictability. Little wonder that under these conditions problem forming and problem defining become at least as important as problem solving by means of conventional techniques. The manager who can formulate problems effectively is in a position to take advantage of such turbulence and thus to convert a problem into an opportunity.

Both the environment in which she operates and the kinds of problems she faces typically place the manager or decision maker in a

This chapter is a revised version of a paper in press to appear in *Management Science*. It is reprinted here with permission from the Institute of Management Sciences.

real dilemma or paradox. The manager constantly faces problems for which there is a real need for the best available evidence just to define the nature of the problem. At the same time, the manager is beset with extensive pressures to act both immediately and decisively (Mintzberg, 1971). She cannot afford the luxury of waiting indefinitely for all the evidence to come in before taking action. Just the reverse is often the case. If she or the organization wishes to survive, then she must take action in order to find out if the actions taken were the correct ones. Thus, succinctly put, the paradox is: the manager is often required to act in order to uncover the evidence as to whether the action she *took* is the one she *should have* taken. Instead of data always guiding action, the taking of action often guides the collection of data in the sense that the proper data often cannot be uncovered except through the risking of action (Churchman, 1971).[1] The questions, then, are: What *can* the manager do in this not uncommon case? and What *should* she do?

It was in order to handle this very set of conditions that Churchman (1976), Mason (1969), and Mitroff (and Kilmann, 1978) proposed a special problem solving technique known as the Dialectic. Essentially the Dialectic is an adversarial problem-forming methodology which is especially suited to treating intensely ill-structured, i.e., difficult-to-define, issues. It does so by attempting to set up at least two very different (antithetical) and maximally challenging views (definitions, policies) of a problem situation so that everything the one view takes for granted as a basic and reasonable assumption, the other challenges as intensely as it can. The intent is not to confuse a decision or policy maker who is witness to this dialectic interplay or debate between opposing views, but rather to assist the decision or policy maker in understanding the critical role that the postulation of very different assumptions about the nature of a problem plays in the basic definition of the problem and, hence, in its ultimate disposition. The intent is thus to allow the manager to take advantage of turbulent environments and thereby to convert a problematic situation into an opportunity (Ackoff, 1974).

This paper represents an attempt to carry the Dialectic a significant step further in its development. It attempts to go beyond previous formulations by outlining a detailed operational procedure whereby one can systematically construct a Dialectic. That is, previous formulations did not answer such questions as: Where do the opposing views (issues) that constitute a Dialectic come from? Are there only two opposing views, as in the Mason (1969) article, or can one formulate several different views on some strategic policy question? How can they be constructed? In earlier versions, the reader is merely presented with an already formed set of Dialectic policies on an issue. Further, earlier formulations did not address themselves to the exceedingly important issue of how the opposing views which constitute a Dialectic can be synthesized at all. In sum, the intent of this paper is to add to the development of an operational methodology for forming a Dialectic and for synthesizing the resultant conflicting views.

## THE METHODOLOGY

Table 1 outlines three of the more basic steps or phases which constitute the methodology. As will become clear, there are many more steps than three. For ease and convenience of presentation, we have focused on the three most major parts of the methodology. We comment in turn on each step.

### GROUP FORMATION

Ackoff (1974) and Churchman (1971, 1968), among others (Pounds, 1969; Rittel, 1971), have argued that problems only exist in relation to purposeful individuals; i.e., only persons who are thwarted in the attainment of desired goals have problems. The first step in the methodology thus consists of the bringing together of as many individuals as possible who have a potential bearing on the definition of the proposed solution, and who have as different definitions of the problem as possible. To do this, we have found it both necessary and desirable to bring together managers from different functional perspectives and organizational levels. The intent of this step is to attempt to insure that as many important perceptions of a problem will be included in its formulation as possible, and that important aspects will not be overlooked or excluded outright. Indeed, it is precisely because they are so critically important to the organization as a whole that ill-structured strategic policy issues will tend to receive the attention of more than one individual (Mason, 1969; Mintzberg, 1971; Mintzberg et al., 1976). In fact, the more a problem or issue is felt to be critical to an organization, the more it will be felt to be necessary to secure the views of as many different individuals as possible in managing its definition and ultimate disposition. The initial step of the methodology thus concerns the important twin issues of how to assemble an appropriate collection of diverse individuals in the first place and how to work with them in the second place for the purpose of problem formulation and problem solving.

In previous papers, Mitroff and Kilmann (1978, 1976; Kilmann and Mitroff, forthcoming; Kilmann, Lyles, and Mitroff, 1976; Kilmann, 1977) have described various methods (behavioral technologies) for sorting a relatively large and *hetero*geneous collection of twenty or more individuals into relatively small and *homo*geneous groups of six to eight individuals per group. In order to help insure that important aspects of the problem will not be overlooked, one wants to assemble as large and as heterogeneous an initial collection as possible across the entire organization. This is also supported by the literature on small groups and problem solving (Kilmann and Seltzer, 1976).

These behavioral technologies essentially attempt to accomplish two things: (1) maximization of different problem perspectives *between* groups so that what one group takes as a "given" or "natural" definition (perception) of a problem, another group will be moved to challenge as a tenuous if not unwarranted assumption; whatever the definition of a problem or issue produced by a particular group we want to take explicit action to insure that it will be challenged *by at least one other* group; (2) maximization of interpersonal similarity and liking *within* any particular group in order to insure that each group can function effectively, i.e., in order to remove as much as is possible the

TABLE 1:  **Steps in the Methodology**

| Step | Activity | Means for Accomplishing |
|---|---|---|
| 1. | Formation of Different Groups | MAPS[a] Design Technology<br>Personality Type Technology<br>Ad Hoc Group Technology<br>Vested Interests Technology |
| 2. | Assumption Surfacing | Stakeholder Analysis<br>Assumption Sorting |
| 3. | Dialectical Debate Between<br>Group Policies and Synthesis | Assumption Negotiation<br>Assumptional Decision Theory |

a.  Multivariate Analysis and Participative Structure

interpersonal conflicts *within* groups that often interfere with effective group behavior (Kilmann, 1977). For example, some of the groups naturally adopt a short-term operational approach to a problem; others, a longer-term strategic approach. In this way, individuals are sorted into groups on the basis of their cognitive style and their preference for certain kinds of issues rather than on their level in the organization or functional expertise. (For a detailed discussion of the multivariate procedures by which groups are created, see Kilmann, 1977.)

It should be noted that *without the creation of opposing groups the above procedure can be dangerous and for this reason is not to be recommended in general.* If the extreme homogeneity of each group is a blessing in that it reinforces the natural strengths and similar tendencies of each individual in the group, then the extreme homogeneity is also a danger in that it magnifies the weaknesses (i.e., the one-sidedness of perceptions) of the individuals. On the other hand, this procedure is desirable in the present context because by creating extreme groups we have explicitly insured ourselves that a dialectical debate will be produced between positions that are as different from one another as possible. If anything, the danger of one-sidedness that often occurs naturally in organizations through the process of selective filtration of members (and hence homogeneity of viewpoints) is lessened in this process since we have taken explicit steps to maximize the challenging of views.

Since the various techniques for sorting groups have been extensively discussed elsewhere (Saaty and Rogers, 1976) we shall not pursue them here. We merely wish to stress that since it is people who have and create problems, every step of methodology is of necessity grounded in behavioral science. Clear recognition must be given to the interpersonal dynamics that govern the behavior of people in groups. Otherwise, the proper behavioral conditions will not be fostered which permit the open and free discussion and sharing of ideas, feelings, and emotions with regard to the problem at hand.

### ASSUMPTION SURFACING

The heart of the assumption surfacing or specification process is a set of techniques for helping decision makers to uncover and analyze the critical key assumptions upon which their policies rest. This process can best be illustrated by discussing an example drawn from an actual case in which the techniques were applied. The situation in this case concerned a drug company faced with a major pricing policy decision on one of its most important products. The decision was so significant that it affected the economic structure of the entire company. As a result, the decision required analysis of the entire internal financial structure of the company as well as various market considerations.

When the problem surfaced, there were three already existing groups of managers within the drug company, each of whom had a significantly different policy with respect to the pricing of the drug. For easy identification, the groups were: (1) the high-price group; (2) the low-price group; and (3) the mid-price group. All three groups were making, unbeknownst to themselves and to the other groups, entirely different macro-assumptions regarding who were the important stakeholders, and all had very different detailed micro-assumptions about the nature of the problem.

A technique known as "Stakeholder Analysis" (Ackoff, 1974) was used to identify the assumptions of each group. In contrast to *stock*-holder analysis, *stake*holder analysis asks a decision maker or manager to consider all the parties who will be affected by or who affect an important decision. It asks the manager to list as many parties or interest groups as she can who have a stake in the policy under consideration. This list of parties is typically much broader than the single category of stockholders. While important to be sure, the stockholders are only one of many contending groups which have an impact on and a stake in a corporation. They are neither the only group nor always the single most important group.

Each group was asked to list the stakeholders which were most important to its particular policy (see Figure 1). In this example, all three groups listed substantially the same parties. (In general, this will not be the case and a dialectical debate described later will occur at this step). For the most part, the categories are generic, and hence, with little modification, apply to most business situations. For example, in the present case, the retailers are pharmacists, although it turned out that it was important to differentiate between large chain retailers and small, singly-owned pharmaceutical outlets.

It can easily be seen from Figure 1 that depending upon what is assumed about each of the stakeholder categories, the resultant policy is greatly affected. In fact, the whole point of getting managers to identify who are the important stakeholders in their situation is to help them confront the important question "What is it that you *have been* assuming about the stakeholders or that you *have had* to assume about them so that *starting from* these assumptions you are able to *derive* your policy?" Stakeholder analysis thus asks a manager to work backwards. Instead of regarding the problem at the level of the resultant policy, it asks the manager to focus on the underlying assumptions and to regard the real problem as being at this level. What assumptions has she been making, and why? What is the effect of making other assumptions? Can her policy stand up to other assumptions; can it tolerate them? Is it compatible with them? Is the current set of assumptions internally consistent with other assumptions? These are only a few of the uses to which stakeholder analysis can be put.

As an example, we were able to see that the physician was one of the most important stakeholder categories for each group. We were also able to see that the groups were making very different assumptions about the attributes of the physician. The high-price group was assuming that the general category of physicians was primarily motivated by high quality and thus would prescribe a drug independently of its cost. The low-price group, on the other hand, was assuming that the physician was primarily price-sensitive. These two assumptions were in direct opposition.

There is no single decisive test to guarantee the completeness of a set of assumptions. But it is possible to test the relevancy of assumptions that have been specified. This is done through a negation of the assumptions. If the basic statement of an assumption is read in a negated form and it does not lead to a change in some aspect of the strategy, then the assumption is possibly irrelevant to the strategy. This one operational test is provided in the assumption specification process to insure that the list of assumptions does not grow in number without bound for the wrong reasons.

The next step in the process involves the prioritization or ranking of the assumptions with respect to two criteria: (1) the relative *importance* of the assumptions which underlie a policy, and (2) their relative *certainty*. A powerful technique which can be used for prioritizing assumptions has been invented by Saaty (and Rogers, 1976). Essentially, the technique allows a decision maker to derive a ratio scale weighting of the importance of an entire set of objectives, goals, means, assumptions, objects, and so forth from a pair-wise ordinal comparison of each element of the set. Table 2 illustrates the mathematics of the procedure for the simplest possible case of two assumptions, $A_1$ and

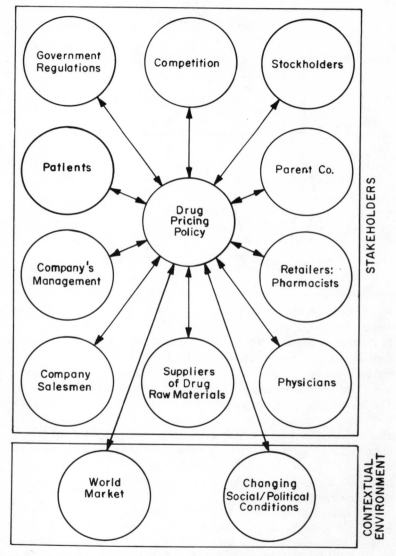

Figure 1 Functional Stakeholder Analysis for a Pharmaceutical Company.

TABLE 2:  Prioritization for a Two-Assumption Case

|         | $A_1$ | $A_2$ |
|---------|-------|-------|
| $A_1$ | $\dfrac{W_1}{W_1} = 1$ | $\dfrac{W_1}{W_2}$ |
| $A_2$ | $\dfrac{W_2}{W_1}$ | $\dfrac{W_2}{W_2} = 1$ |

$$A = \begin{pmatrix} \dfrac{W_1}{W_1} & \dfrac{W_1}{W_2} \\ \dfrac{W_2}{W_1} & \dfrac{W_2}{W_2} \end{pmatrix} \quad w = \begin{pmatrix} w_1 \\ w_2 \end{pmatrix}$$

$\therefore$ , Aw = 2w, an eigenvalue problem

$A_2$. The procedure assumes not only that it is easier for a decision maker (dm) to compare each objectives' relative importance with regard to each of the other objectives one at a time ($w_i/w_j$), but that a dm can actually make such comparisons. Under this procedure, a dm need only say that $A_1$, for instance, when compared with $A_2$ is nine[2] times more important for the derivation or support of a resultant policy than $A_2$. The assumption of the procedure is that a dm can more easily supply the relative ratios of the weights ($w_i/w_j$) of importance than the absolute weights ($w_i$) themselves. Starting with the ratios of relative importance $w_i/w_j$, it can easily be shown that the determination of the $w_i$ reduces to an eigenvalue-eigenvector problem. Starting with the matrix A of relative weight in Table 2, one can derive the vector w of absolute weights.

It is important to point out that the mathematics of this procedure is relevant only because it allows a dm to investigate the effect of varying the weights of her assumptions. The first author and Professor Richard O. Mason have constructed a short computer routine which allows a dm to examine different weights. The procedure outlined in

Table 2 is only a part of the total methodology, not the whole, and, further, only a means, not an end in itself.

The significance of the procedure lies with Figure 2. Going through the Belief Assessment procedure twice (Table 1), i.e., rating the assumptions with regard to their relative importance and certainty, allows one to determine which assumptions fall into which quadrant of Figure 2. For obvious reasons, we are not as interested in those assumptions falling in the extreme left-hand half of Figure 2. Even stronger, while the assumptions falling in the upper right-hand quadrant are important, those falling in the lower right-hand quadrant are the most critical. They are precisely the assumptions one looks to the Belief Assessment process, and the methodology as a whole, to identify. Because the assumptions in the lower right-hand quadrant are important and yet because decision makers are uncertain of their plausibility, truth, reasonableness, and so on, they deserve the most intensive discussion with regard to what if anything could be done to make their occurrence or their validation more certain. The identification and verification of such assumptions are at the heart of strategic planning.

There is an important reason for prioritizing assumptions in the above way. We have found that individual policies not only differ with regard to the detailed assumptions they make regarding stakeholders

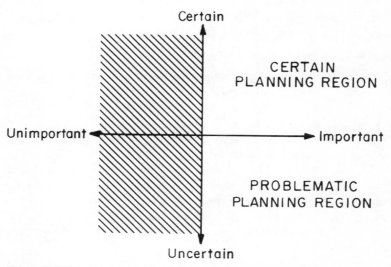

Figure 2 Belief Assessment of the Importance Versus the Certainty of Critical Assumptions.

but that typically they assume very different stakeholder categories altogether. What one group or policy sees as an important or potentially important party, another sees as relatively unimportant. The strongest way of putting this is to say that we have found that when one prioritizes in terms of Belief Assessment, the assumptions of the different policies pertaining to the different stakeholder categories typically fall into diametrically opposite quadrants of Figure 2. What one group or policy takes as a relatively unimportant and certain assumption, another often takes as important and uncertain. The stage is thus typically set for an intense dialectical debate between the proponents of the different policies regarding their respective assumptions.

The purpose of the dialectical debate is not, at least at this point in the methodology, for each group to convince the other of the uncontested truth of its position, but rather to show how and why each group views the situation as it does and what its viewpoint entails. The purpose is to show both parties that there are different ways of viewing the situation and that what each takes as a natural set of "givens" (natural assumptions), the other takes as an unnatural set of "takens" (unwarranted assumptions). The whole point of this procedure is to demonstrate to all the groups that there really are no "givens" in the first place; there are only "takens." Since this is the case, we want to make sure we have done everything in our power to locate, expose, and challenge these "takens." We know of no better way of doing this than through conducting a dialectical debate with regard to key assumptions.

### DIALECTICAL DEBATE

The dialectical debate proceeds much through the manner described by Mason (1969) although with some important additions. Through Belief Assessment analysis, we are able to identify for each policy its key underlying assumptions, i.e., those assumptions falling in the "important" quadrants of Figure 2. Typically we have found that it is possible to reduce these assumptions down to one or two really critical or key assumptions. These generally fall into the "important" and "uncertain" quadrant. This shortens immensely the debate between policies. Instead of having to debate then to fifteen assumptions, one can, because of the power of the Belief Assessment analysis, focus on the critical items and hence make the debate both more manageable and productive.

Up to the point of the dialectic debate, we have found it advisable to work with each group separately. We have found that this helps each group to develop the best case for its position. Otherwise, groups spend too much time thinking about each other and tend to soften their position rather than building the strongest, and this means the most extreme case for their position. In our culture, we are unconsciously trained for compromise or even the avoidance of conflict. We therefore find it necessary to consciously train managers to appreciate the value of adversarial policy making. The danger is not of reaching compromise, but of reaching it too soon and for the wrong reasons, e.g., because of the inability to tolerate conflict as a sometimes necessary and valuable tool for policy making. Notice that we are not saying that in itself conflict is always desirable. We are saying that the outright rejection and unconsidered avoidance of conflict is undesirable and may be counterproductive.

The conduct of the debate proceeds by having the spokesperson of each group list the one or two key assumptions associated with its policy. Each spokesperson then argues why the group's assumptions are critical to its policy, why the policy is dependent upon them. Only after each group has made its presentation and every group has under-stood why the assumptions of each individual group are critical to that group's policy does the methodology enter the last, the most difficult, and the most critical phase—the negotiation of assumptions. Before this can proceed, however, it is vital that each group understand the assumptions of the other groups and why they are critical for those groups. Each group is not asked to necessarily accept alternative assumptions; it is merely asked to attempt to understand them. We have found, as a rule, that the more a group can begin to "understand" the assumptions underlying an opposing group, the closer it will be to later "appreciating" the value of entertaining alternative assumptions and, hence, achieving compromise.

The most difficult part of the methodology is admittedly that of achieving compromise between assumptions. Even more difficult is coming up with an entirely new, synthetic set of assumptions that bridge the old policies and go beyond them as well. For example, every now and then the active discussions of spokespersons lead to a statement of assumptions which everyone can endorse. In fact, every opposing view with regard to assumptions has been incorporated into a "final," synthesized set. While difficult to achieve, it is nevertheless possible for a synergistic solution to emerge.

In an attempt to achieve synthesis, and at the very least compromise, an assumption-negotiation procedure has been worked out. After each group has listed its key assumptions on a chalkboard for public inspection by all of the other groups, each group is asked individually to identify the assumptions from the other groups which most perturb its policy, i.e., those assumptions (key or otherwise) which are the hardest for each group to live with. After each group has done this, all of the groups are asked to engage, to the extent they can, in assumption modification. Each group is asked to soften its assumptions to the point where they just barely support its policies; i.e., where if they relaxed their assumptions any further, they could no longer derive or support their own policy. Alternatively, groups are asked to restate their assumptions in ways to incorporate all differences as in a synergistic solution. In this way, it is hoped that by successively working back and forth between the assumptions of the different groups to obtain a zone of compromise, if one is possible, and from this zone to extract a set of compromise assumptions or a synthesized set of assumptions.

If such a compromise is not possible or desirable, and it frequently is not, then the participants will at least have achieved a better (i.e., a deeper) understanding of the underlying reasons that have divided them in the past and will continue to divide them in the future. They will have at least achieved the important understanding that if they decide to act on or accept any one of the original policies, then they are in a better position to consider what might happen if the assumptions of the policy they have chosen to implement no longer prove valid. They can at least defend their choice to their superiors by arguing that they have made their choice under the most critically challenging test conditions. This does not mean or guarantee that their choice was the "right" one, for in the realm of ill-structured problems there may be no single "best" or "right" solution, merely relatively "better" ones (Rittel, 1971), where "better" means awareness of one's assumptions. If ignorance of assumptions is not a desirable property for well-structured problems, it is even less a desirable property for ill-structured problems where even more is at stake and dependent upon examining key assumptions.

## ASSUMPTIONAL DECISION THEORY

What if assumption negotiation cannot be achieved? What if a compromise set of assumptions and a policy based on a common set of assumptions cannot be achieved? Or, what if the groups as a whole feel that a compromise solution is not feasible or desirable? What does one do in this not untypical situation? In case this occurs, we have found that it is useful to take decision makers through a variant of the typical action-truth table of statistical decision theory. Table 3 illustrates the procedure.

Suppose that there are three policies (as there were for the situation represented in Figure 1) and that compromise proves impossible—i.e., it is not possible to modify the assumptions in the three policies so as to make them acceptable to each of the other groups. Since some sort of action must eventually be agreed upon—at some point assumption examination has to terminate and action take place—if we cannot achieve compromise or synthesis between the policies, then one of them must be chosen to implement. The question is how that choice should be made.

**TABLE 3:  The Costs of Implementing Policies Compared with One Another**

| | | Implementation/Action | | | |
|---|---|---|---|---|---|
| | | $P_1$ | $P_2$ | $P_3$ | |
| x | $P_1$ Assumptions | correct | error RC=? VC=? R =? | error RC=? VC=? R =? | lower price |
| x x | $P_2$ Assumptions | error RC=? VC=? R =? | correct | error RC=? VC=? R =? | raise price |
| x x | $P_3$ Assumptions | error RC=? VC=? R =? | error RC=? VC=? R =? | correct | middle price |

RC = the real cost of a policy assumption
VC = the visible cost of a policy assumption
R   = the reversibility of a policy assumption

Table 3 says that the choice should be made by considering the effects of implementing any one policy with regard to each of the others. Suppose for example that $P_1$ turns out to be "true" (i.e., in this case this means that a set of assumptions which were important but uncertain at the time of choice ultimately turns out to be "correct" in the sense of being verified by resultant market data, say, within three to six months of putting the policy into action). Table 3 asks what the errors are which are made in turn by implementing policies $P_1$, $P_2$, and $P_3$. If $P_1$ is true, and $P_1$ is implemented, then there is no error. If $P_2$ and $P_3$ are implemented, however, then there will be certain costs associated with these two cases. We have split these costs into two parts: a "real" cost (RC) and "visible" cost (VC). In addition, there is another factor to be considered, the "reversibility" (R) of an action or error. By "real," we mean a cost that is easily determined through normal market data.

In the case of the drug company referred to earlier (Figure 1), the three policies were: $P_1$ = lower the current price of the drug; $P_2$ = raise the current price of the drug; and $P_3$ = steer a middle course between $P_1$ and $P_2$. By taking the representatives of all three policies through Table 3, we were able to get common agreement between them as to the RCs, VCs and Rs associated with the off-diagonal cells. The RCs were the estimated real losses in profits which would occur if one adopted $P_i$ when $P_j$ were "true."

The VCs, on the other hand, are a bit more subtle and, hence, a bit trickier to determine. They are best explained as follows. Suppose that the policy $P_2$ is, in fact, the correct one. That is, suppose that because of competitive conditions, the quality of the product, advertising, and so forth one can actually raise the price of one's product—an action that many executives would be afraid to do. Because of this fear, suppose that it was decided to adopt policy $P_1$. There would then not only be an obvious real cost associated with this action (the obvious loss of profits), but we contend that there would be a less visible cost as well. If one lowers the price when one could have raised it, then it may be impossible for management to know this. By lowering the price, one has precluded the opportunity of finding out whether this was possible. One precludes the data, so to speak. By the same token, the reversibility of this action may also be rather low. It may be very difficult to come in later and raise prices once one has lowered them. That is, the VC of $P_1$ is low or conversely the invisible cost of $P_1$ is high. Visibility thus refers to the ease and possibility of observing the cost of a policy if some other policy is in fact correct. By means of this reasoning process, it was decided (counter to initial intuition) that the "best" policy from the company's point of view was to recommend price increases.

If the process in Table 3 is so valuable, why, one might ask, did we not proceed directly to it? The answer is that everything in Table 3 presupposes the previous steps. All of the various "costs" in Table 3 are made with respect to the assessment of the assumptions which have come before. The presumed "truth" of the policies is with respect to the key assumptions underlying each policy. The actions are with respect to what it takes to implement the assumptions, to act on their truth—indeed, to make them come true. The costs are determined relative to the assumptions; i.e., what is the cost of considering one assumption as true or false when another is true or false? To the authors' knowledge, this is very different from conventional statistical decision theory.

There is also another reason for not proceeding directly to Table 3. Table 3 not only embodies but reinforces a win-lose competitive mentality between the various strategies. While we do not want to preclude the possibility that one of the pure strategies is actually best, we wish to insure that every serious consideration will be given to the search for a synthetic policy before opting for any pure policy. Only after serious consideration has been given to synthesis do we wish to fall back upon one of the pure strategies. This derives from our basic belief that rarely in complex social and managerial problems will any one pure strategy pick up and integrate the multitude of considerations which are necessary for successful problem management.

## CONCLUDING REMARKS

The purpose of this paper has been to add to the "development" of a methodology for ill-structured problems. We deliberately stress the word *development,* for such a methodology is still in its infancy. We lay no claims here to having provided the last word with regard to it. Indeed, in the spirit of this paper, the methodology we have outlined may be regarded as embodying the assumptions of the authors. As such, our assumptions deserve to be taken to task by others with alternate assumptions.

# NOTES

1. This point will be illustrated in the later parts of this paper.

2. If the two objectives are judged to be of equal importance, then one assigns a relative ratio of 1 to $w_i/w_j$. If $A_i$ is absolutely more important than $A_j$, one assigns a ratio of 9.

# REFERENCES

ACKOFF, R. L. (1974) Redesigning the Future. New York: John Wiley.

CHURCHMAN, C. W. (1971) The Design of Inquiring Systems. New York: Basic Books.

––– (1968) The Systems Approach. New York: Delacorte.

EMERY, F. E. and E. L. TRIST (1965) "The causal texture of organizational environments." Human Relations 18: 21-32.

KILMANN, R. H. (1977) Social Systems Design: Normative Theory and the MAPS Design Technology. New York: Elsevier, North-Holland.

––– (1977) "Structural designs for OD diagnosis: alternatives and consequences." Working Paper #231. University of Pittsburgh Graduate School of Business.

––– and I. I. MITROFF (forthcoming) Organizational Problem Solving: A Social Science Approach. New York: Elsevier, Horth-Holland.

KILMANN, R. H. and J. SELTZER (1976) "An experimental test of organization design theory and the MAPS design technology: homogeneous versus heterogeneous composition of organizational subsystems." Proceedings of the Eastern Academy of Management.

KILMANN, R. H., M. LYLES, and I. I. MITROFF (1976) "Designing an effective problem solving organization with the MAPS design technology." Journal of Management 2, 2: 1-10.

LYLES, M. and I. I. MITROFF (forthcoming) "On organizational problem forming: an empirical study." Administrative Science Quarterly.

MASON, R. O. 1969 "A dialectical approach to strategic planning." Management Science 15: B-403-B-414.

MINTZBERG, H. (1971) "Managerial work: analyses from observation." Management Science 18: 97-110.

–––, D. RAISINGHAM, and A. THEORET (1976) "The structure of 'unstructured' decision processes." Administration Science Quarterly 21: 246-275.

MITROFF, I. I. and R. H. KILMANN (1978) "On integrating behavioral and philosophical systems: towards a unified theory of problem solving," pp. 207-236 in Research on the Sociology of Knowledge, Sciences, and Art. Vol. I. Greenwich, CT: Jai.

––– (1976) "On organizational stories: an approach to the design and analysis of organizations through myths and stories," pp. 189-207 in R. H. Kilmann, L.

Pondy, and D. Slevin (eds) The Management of Organization Design New York: North Holland.

POUNDS, W. F. (1969) "The process of problem finding." Industrial Management Review 11: 1-19.

RITTEL, H. (1971) "Some principles for the design of an educational system for design." Journal of Architectural Education 26: 16-27.

SAATY, T. L. and P. C. ROGERS (1976) "Higher education in the United States (1985-2000), scenario construction using a hierarchical framework with eigenvector weighting." Socio-Economic Planning 10: 251-263.

# 16

## TINKERING WITH OPEN SYSTEMS: ORGANIZATIONAL THEORY PERSPECTIVES ON EDUCATIONAL PROGRAM EVALUATION

Michael S. Knapp

Writers advocating strategies for the systematic evaluation of social programs are not the only people who think about evaluation processes in complex organizational settings. Organizational sociologists have recently focused attention on evaluation as a basic organizational process. Looking in structural terms at organizations and their relationship to their surrounding environments, writers such as Thompson (1967), Dornbusch and Scott (1975), and Meyer and Rowen (1977, 1978) have suggested key variables within organizations which shape the evaluation processes taking place within them.

The evaluation literature has yet to develop a careful analysis of the organizational forces surrounding the enterprise of program evaluation. Caro's (1971) review of the evaluation research literature, for example, devotes much attention to the "organizational context" of program evaluation and to the problematic role of the evaluation researcher. Caro's discussion describes the tensions in the encounter between administrator and researcher and suggests ways of facilitating this

226

relationship, but fails to take into account the larger forces and structural conditions which impinge on the evaluation effort. The evaluation literature contains much practical experience with the problem of fitting formal program evaluation into established organizational settings. But more powerful conceptual tools need to be brought to interpret that experience.

There have been some provocative exceptions to the lack of a systematic organizational analysis in the evaluation literature. Burnham (1973), Bice, Eichorn, and Klein (1975), and Wergin (1976) have taken advantage of the insights of organizational sociology in building evaluation models. Weiss (1977) has brought organizational concepts to bear on understanding the limitations on research utilization in public agencies. These pieces and others beginning to be heard at evaluation conferences suggest that a productive dialogue between organizational analysis and evaluation theory is developing.

This paper brings to the developing dialogue one set of organizational theories. To keep the discussion manageable and concrete, illustrations will be drawn from one particular kind of program setting—that of innovative educational programs embedded within established educational organizations such as public schools—although the theoretical principles apply more broadly to many kinds of organizations. The paper will first discuss the organizational elements and assumptions of typical program evaluation efforts, then review three theories concerning organizational evaluation processes, and finally assess the assumptions in the light of the theories.

## COMMON FEATURES AND ORGANIZATIONAL ASSUMPTIONS OF FORMAL PROGRAM EVALUATION APPROACHES

In practice, most approaches to formal program evaluation share the following organizational elements. (1) Resources from a sponsoring authority are allocated to an activity labeled "program evaluation," "cost-benefit analysis," or the like. (2) A person or team, usually external to the program, is designated as the evaluator. (3) A programmatic activity, which may or may not have taken place already, is selected as the object of the evaluation. (4) The evaluator coordinates systematic data collection concerning program inputs, activities, or outcomes. (5) The data are recorded in some reproducible form. (6) At a later time, a synthesized and interpreted form of the data is communicated formally to various audiences, usually including those who make policy and resource allocation decisions affecting the program.

At some point evaluative criteria become established; by implication, other criteria are excluded. These criteria vary in terms of their source, number, clarity, degree of explicitness, or relationship to stated program goals, but they must exist. They direct attention towards certain areas of program functioning, imply that certain measures of program functioning are more important than others, and established reference points for determining program success or failure. The aspects of program attended to, the relative weightings given each measure, and the points of reference by which measures are interpreted imply choices among evaluative criteria. Formal program evaluation models to date have tended to urge that such choices be explicit, public, and relatively fixed.

Program evaluation efforts with the characteristics just described make implicit assumptions about the nature of the organizational setting in which the evaluation is performed. Using innovative programs within established educational organizations as a specific case, some of the important assumptions are as follows.

## ASSUMPTIONS ABOUT PROGRAMS AND THEIR EFFECTS

• Educational programs are discrete definable entities within the organization. In most cases, the "program" is treated as a separate organizational subunit (or set of units) with its own staff, resource allocation, and time and space allocation, as in the case of a minischool, an outdoor education program, or a K-3 open classroom arrangement.

• Cause-effect relationships exist between program activities and educational outcomes, as indicated primarily by the behavior or performance of students. What goes on in reading classes is thought of as the primary determinant of students' reading ability, or a high school career exploration program is thought of as a causal influence on students' career preferences or manner of choosing careers.

• Cause-effect relationships can be measured with social science research techniques. Students' mental abilities, attitudes, or motivational levels, for example, are assessed with tests, interviews, or observations. Structured interviews or observational instruments measure the degree and nature of program implementation by classroom teachers, counselors, or administrators.

## ASSUMPTIONS ABOUT DECISION MAKING AND THE ROLE OF INFORMATION IN IT

- Decisions made by people in charge of educational organizations are among the primary determinants of what goes on in these organizations. Principals, superintendents, and various high-level program coordinators are thus thought to have substantial control over the activities and functioning of the programs they manage.
- Explicit information about program functioning is a primary input into decisions made about such programs. Program evaluation is thus seen as meeting a preexisting "need" for sound information by decision makers, who are assumed to want the "best" information available.
- As educational organizations presently operate, people with management responsibility have little systematic information on the functioning of the organization or its subunits. Without some formal process for gathering evaluative information, principals and superintendents are regarded as having only impressionistic or unverifiable information to go on.
- The additional information generated by a systematic program evaluation process is both attended to and understood by potential users. Implicit in any evaluation report, for example, is the assumption that the conclusions and data on which these are based will be both read and assimilated by the principal, the school board member, higher-level administrator, or even the classroom teacher.

## ASSUMPTIONS ABOUT IMPLEMENTING A SYSTEMATIC EVALUATION PROCESS

- Consensus can be generated concerning the choice of appropriate evaluative criteria. Typically, educational program evaluations take the stated program goals (in a more operationalized form) as a reflection of presumed consensus, although alternative criteria may be employed. It is the rare case which interprets data from the points of view of program staff, parent groups, top administrators, and teachers' union, especially where these groups hold conflicting views.
- Formal program evaluation processes require specialized skills and trained personnel. In other words, people with training in the social sciences or related disciplines are assumed to be the most appropriate staff for conducting an evaluation process.

• A systematic evaluation process can be conducted without counterproductive side effects by specialists who are outsiders to the organization containing the program. Personnel brought in to evaluate school programs are thus assumed to be able—in principle, at least—to measure student outcomes, gain access to necessary records, and report findings to administrators without unduly disrupting the operation of program or organization.

• The program evaluation process can be managed to produce information at times when interested audiences most want it and can make use of it. In other words, when the school board debates the continuation of a learning disabilities program, for example, or more accurately in the month leading up to that debate, the program evaluation process will have come up with some relevant data regarding the program's effects or operation.

This list does not exhaust the kinds of organizational assumptions underlying educational evaluation schemes, nor does it do justice to the significant divergence of evaluation models one from the other. But it is sufficient to demonstrate that fundamental organizational processes are involved: the definition of organizational subunits, their interdependence and coordination, decision-making and control processes, the differentiation of roles within an organized setting, the relationship of the organization to its surrounding environment, and the relationship of organizational structure to the behavior of participants.

## THREE PERSPECTIVES FROM ORGANIZATIONAL THEORY

Recent work in organizational theory provides a way of analyzing the adequacy of these assumptions. Although many branches of organizational theory have potential bearing on the problem, this paper restricts itself to three related structural theories, each of which deals explicitly with evaluation processes.

The first perspective, principally advanced by Thompson (1967), treats evaluation as a double process: (a) the means by which organizations determine their fitness, and that of their component units, for future action; (b) the means by which the organization as a whole and each subunit within it seeks to *demonstrate* fitness for future action to its respective surrounding environment.

The second perspective, reflected primarily in the work of Dorn-busch and Scott (1975), treats evaluation as the principal mechanism by which the organization's authority structure is maintained and the activities of members kept in line with organizational purposes.

The third perspective, developed by Meyer and Rowen (1977, 1978) and closely related to the work of Weick (1976), sees evaluation as a device by which a "loosely-coupled" organizational system is made more tightly coupled with dysfunctional implications for the system.

The perspectives share a conception of the organization as an "open system," that is, an interrelated set of roles, resources, and activities in continual dynamic interchange with the environment outside organiza-tional boundaries (see Katz and Kahn, 1966). All three treat evaluation as a controlling process, by which parts of the organizational system are bound more tightly together. The organization is assumed by each theory to be a purposeful entity, though none insists that stated organizational goals are the primary determinants of action. Finally, all three perspectives focus on structural features—that is, on the pattern-ing of roles and functions within the organizational system irrespective of the specific personalities involved.

The key concepts of each perspective will first be summarized; then their implications for the assumptions made implicitly by most program evaluation activity will be examined.

### EVALUATION AS THE RATIONAL DETERMINATION OF FITNESS FOR FUTURE ACTION

At the heart of this perspective is the premise that all organizations seek to act as rationally as they can in the face of continual environ-mental uncertainty; that is, they try to render things as predictable as possible for the technical core of the organization where its work is carried on. Schools, which are highly dependent on dynamic environ-ments, are especially interested in reducing environmental uncertainty.

The nature of the work done by the organization has much to do with the extent to which technical perfection can be reached. Given favorable environmental conditions, the ideal can be approached in assembly-line production enterprises, where the nature of the object worked on and the technology of production are both fully known. But in the case of schools, where the "objects" worked on are human beings and the "technology" for bringing about desired changes poorly under-stood, those who carry out the organization's core tasks face a good deal of uncertainty. Schools do what they can to make these tasks as predictable as possible, by judiciously grouping students, by developing regular routines, by retaining experienced personnel, and so on.

As suggested by Thompson (1967: 83-98), assessment within organizations is a continuing and two-sided process. On the one hand, subunits seek to demonstrate their capacity to meet organizational needs by scoring favorably on those criteria which are most salient and visible. Correspondingly, the organization as a whole attempts to score favorably in those areas visible to the most important groups in its surrounding environment. In educational organizations, where clear internal measures of technical performance do not exist or are not agreed upon, demonstration of fitness for the future tends to rely on external measures such as the nature of facilities, external achievements or honors accruing to school personnel, or parent testimonials.

The other side of the two-sided assessment process is the continual examination by the organization of itself and its component parts for evidence—whatever evidence can be found—that it is as fit as possible to cope with the uncertain future. The kinds of evidence employed, argues Thompson, depend principally on the beliefs held by key organizational actors about causation—the degree to which organizational efforts affect outcomes—and on the level of consensus about criteria by which outcomes will be judged. Evaluation of effectiveness by precise measurement is most likely where causal relationships are believed certain and a common standard of desirable outcomes exists. But in organizations such as schools, where participants hold multiple and often conflicting criteria of effectiveness and have poor understanding of causal processes, such procedures are not favored. Instead, Thompson argues, pressure develops to find evidence that the organization compares favorably with other similar organizations (on any criteria). Within the organization, subunit performance tends to be judged on the basis of conformity to rules, fulfillment of quota expectations, and the creation of favorable impressions on coordinate subunits.

Consider as an example a school evaluating a new team teaching arrangement in the fourth through sixth grades. It is unlikely that anyone would claim to understand the relationship between such an arrangement and student learning. Measuring learning precisely simply compounds the existing lack of understanding. But the school needs some way of assessing the new arrangement, and there exist alternatives which are readily available: the conformity of the new program to disciplinary rules, its ability to meet organizational quotas (e.g., occupying a specified amount of students' time in a schedule or covering a certain portion of curriculum in a given unit of time), or its capacity to inspire confidence among school personnel outside the program. Simultaneously, with an eye toward the reaction of key elements in the surrounding environment, the school has reason to look for evidence that the most visible aspects of the teaching arrangement (the appearance of instructional spaces, the activities of students outside the school, student work taken home) meet the criteria of groups on which the school is most dependent for support—especially vocal parent groups and district personnel. The school may also try to show itself in a favorable light by comparison with other schools near at hand— whether or not there is justifiable basis for making comparisons.

In short, the organization's search for evidence of effective functioning depends heavily on what is believed to be within its control and on what is held to be a desirable outcome both by organizational members and outsiders. Various forms of evidence fulfill the *organizational* need for increased predictability of events and for continued demonstration of effectiveness to environmental elements.

This perspective stops short of spelling out in more precise terms the mechanisms by which the evaluation process takes place. Whose standards and beliefs about causation are most influential? What is the link between the assessment process and subsequent decisions? What consequences does evaluation have for organizational members, and how do they react to these consequences? The next perspective explores these questions more directly.

## EVALUATION AS THE MECHANISM FOR
## MAINTAINING AUTHORITY WITHIN THE ORGANIZATION

This perspective, as developed by Dornbusch and Scott (1975), treats the organization as a structure of authority, maintained principally by the mechanism of performance evaluation. Those in positions of authority allocate tasks to be performed, including the task of evaluating performance. By monitoring task performance and bringing rewards and penalties to bear on organizational members as a result of the evaluations, the activities of everyone within the organizational system are controlled and kept in line with its purposes.

At first glance, this appears to be a theoretical model concerned with the evaluation of *personnel* rather than programs. But the two are never so easily separated as the literature on program evaluation implies. To the extent that program evaluation takes place within a single authority system—as is the case with educational programs which are subunits of schools or school districts—any assessment of "program" activities may influence the rewards and penalties brought to bear on individual staff. This is often true of innovative programs, where the firing or reassignment of teachers, to take an extreme example, may follow judgments, by those allocating resources, that the program did not "work."

Dornbusch and Scott distinguish four analytical elements in the internal process of evaluation. (1) Tasks, including that of evaluating, are allocated to various organizational members. (2) Criteria are determined specifying performance aspects to be examined, the relative importance of measures, and the standards by which measurements will be appraised. (3) Performances are sampled in some fashion. (4) Samplings of performance are judged relative to a standard, with varying degrees of discretion exercised by the ones doing the judging.

At the heart of this view of evaluation is the notion that the process consists of a series of choices (not necessarily conscious) made by one or more individuals in positions of authority—choices of tasks to be allocated, of criteria brought to bear on task performance, of activities or outcomes sampled, of rewards or penalties associated with given appraisals. Evaluation is thus a decision-making process in itself, directed at every facet of organizational functioning.

Several organizational variables critically influence the evaluation process, making it more problematic in certain kinds of organizations. First, the characteristics of the tasks themselves make evaluation more or less easy. Ambiguous task goals, interdependent tasks, or complex tasks with unpredictable outcomes—all characteristics of most educational programs—make the work of the authority and control system more difficult. Second, work arrangments may not permit performance to be observed easily. Also, the number of people in the authority system and the power differences between them bear directly on the smoothness with which the evaluation process operates (Dornbusch and Scott, 1975: 149-158).

The key point is that task complexity and organizational arrangements influence the way members view the authority system. Their perceptions ultimately affect the stability of the system. The unpredictability of school tasks leads teachers and other personnel to expect considerable autonomy. Where sufficient autonomy is not granted, staff members view the authority system as improper, and are likely to resist it and pressure it to change. In particular, they will resent and resist careful inspection of their activities, fearing that they will be held accountable for outcomes that their own efforts may not have produced.

This perspective is describing fundamental processes at work within any organization, whether or not a formal program evaluation process is taking place. Staff performance in schools is routinely evaluated by those in authority, often by one cursory visit by the principal each year or even by less formal means. Almost inescapably, a formal program evaluation feeds into the authority maintenance process, by providing new data on effects which may be attributed to individual performance. This is most noticeably the case with innovative programs, where those conditions most associated with an intrusive authority system pertain: ambitious and ill-specified evaluative criteria, combined with complex, interdependent tasks the outcomes of which are least well understood. Not surprisingly, the resistance to the perceived intrusion—which program evaluation represents—tends to be high with such programs.

In its focus on the assessment of individual task performance of organizational members, this perspective pays little attention to the powerful elements external to the school which profoundly affect evaluative processes taking place within it. The third perspective, described below, addresses this latter concern.

## EVALUATION AS A TIGHT COUPLING DEVICE
## IN A LOOSELY COUPLED SYSTEM

The third perspective, reflected in the work of Meyer and Rowen (1977, 1978), assumes that publicly established institutions such as schools are extremely open systems, heavily influenced by their external environments. Not only does the outside society influence the actual inputs, activities, and outputs of the school, but it also legitimizes and gives social meaning to schooling. From this point of view, the school as an organization is not only a set of interrelated activities and roles, but also a set of representations of societal ideas about education. The school moves students through a sequence of "ritual" categories, which give social meaning to the end products of schooling: the "graduate" and the "educated person."

In order to accomplish this mission of transforming people into educated persons, the school has evolved a "loosely coupled" structure, as originally described by Weick (1976). In other words, schools have developed a structure in which the parts are purposefully *not* closely coordinated with one another and do little to determine or control each other's activities. This lack of tight coupling of activities is seen not only between subunits at the same hierarchical level, but also between higher and lower levels within the organization. A study by Deal, Meyer, and Scott (1975) illustrates this principle in the case of elementary schools: neither district personnel nor school principals were found to have much impact on curricular innovation or the adoption of new teaching practices at the classroom level.

Lest the idea of loose coupling seem like a description of a tight structure under poor management, it is useful to consider some of its special advantages. The loosely-coupled organization responds more flexibly to environmental threats, allows localized adaptations to special needs, seals off problem areas (Weick, 1976: 6-9). Furthermore, it allows a greater number of *local* innovations, though it resists their diffusion. Finally, it reduces coordination costs and at the same time increases the sense of efficacy and autonomy felt by organizational members.

Within this conception of an educational organization, formal evaluation of activities or their presumed outcomes acts as an instrument of communication, coordination, and control. By inspecting the outcomes or process of a new open classroom arrangement, for example, its manner of operation becomes known to outside groups in more detail, its attributed effects are on display, and it is potentially more susceptible to efforts by outside groups (school administration, community elements, or others) to control it. Many program evaluators would argue that this is precisely what they intend to do: to help audiences to whom the program is deemed accountable see what it does and with what results. But the loose coupling theorists warn that doing so may have detrimental effects on the organization. In other words, there are limits to the extent to which educational programs can be made visible without destroying critical aspects of their operation or of their host organizations.

The dilemma facing the schools, as argued by Meyer and Rowen (1978: 79-87), is that they must *tightly* control the categorical structure of the educational system—the classification of students, the array of curricular topics, the certification of teachers, and the progression of students through an orderly sequence of ranks. At the same time, the school *loosely* controls the substance and actual implementation of education in the classroom: teachers work in relative isolation, and no one outside the classroom knows with any precision what goes on within classroom walls. To the state, community, school board, administrators, and even non-math teachers, for example, it is important to know that "ninth-grade mathematics" is taught for a certain number of hours, with appropriately credentialled teachers, with some assessment of student efforts. But, Meyer and Rowen would argue, what actually transpires within a given ninth-grade classroom, or even inside the students' heads, is of relatively little concern to those parties just named. If they were to look closely, the various parties would be likely to discover that they had different ideas about the content of ninth-grade math. Systematic evaluation of instruction leads to such a discovery. In other words, schools draw support, their institutional reason for being, from pluralistic constituencies by resisting overly specific definitions of what it is they are supposed to do.

The loose coupling perspective goes on to argue that the formal organization of the school is, in fact, a symbolic structure of socially generated categories, which defines the product of a school, namely an "educated person." This symbolic structure is held together within the organization by a network of mutual confidence between teacher and student ("What Mr. J teaches us is ninth-grade math"), between teacher and teacher or between teacher and administration ("Mr. J is covering his part of the ninth-grade curriculum"). A similar network of confidence connects school to the surrounding community. Each component or level in the system assumes that the other levels are doing what is appropriate and that they *know* what is appropriate.

According to this perspective, efforts to gather systematic information on program functioning—including most forms of program evaluation as now practiced—destroy these networks of mutual confidence. Increased information leads to *in*creased uncertainty and to the possibility that the school is not fulfilling its social mandate. Also, increased information leads to the recognition that competing constituencies do not agree on the operational nature of the school's mission; they only agree at a more categorical level. But by contrast, precise information on teacher credentials demonstrates that a categorical requirement of schools is fulfilled: that it be staffed by trained professionals who are presumed competent by virtue of training.

The loose coupling perspective leads to a very simple prediction: organizations such as schools are likely to resist the collection of precise, systematic information about instructional programs or their effects. Or, where this information is required (e.g., for the receipt of federal funding), the results tend to be ignored or suppressed. Symbolic or ritual inspection of instruction or its outcomes, however, are likely to occur, as part of the school's demonstration of professional good faith.

There is some evidence for these predictions from loose coupling theory: the extensive resistance to program evaluation efforts and the nonutilization of findings (e.g., Guba, 1972, with reference to educational evaluations) or historical analyses of recurring calls for accountability and reform (e.g., Meyer and Rowen, 1978: 88). Although far from conclusive, enough evidence exists to make one wonder about unintended effects of any systematic program evaluation effort.

The loose coupling perspective is somewhat extreme, and it leaves many questions unanswered. It views schools from a distance in terms of the schools' relationship to society. From this vantage point, individual differences between schools and programs are difficult to see. The perspective does not consider whether precise evaluation can be performed more informally and less publicly than tends to be the case with most formal program evaluations. Finally, with its focus on the symbolic structure of schools, the perspective tends to lose sight of actual behavior of organizational members.

## IMPLICATIONS FOR THE ORGANIZATIONAL ASSUMPTIONS OF PROGRAM EVALUATION

Taken together, the three perspectives just described provide us with a picture of the evaluative processes at work in organizations such as schools. In any organization, evaluative processes exist which help maintain a stable authority system and help secure the organization's relationship with its environment. Key conditions, especially those associated with the complexity and unpredictability of task performance, shape the evaluative process used, the kinds of measures used, and the reactions of organizational members. In many respects, organizations such as schools strategically avoid evaluating themselves and cope more flexibly with internal and external uncertainties by doing so.

As has been suggested throughout the review, systematic program evaluation inevitably becomes entangled with these evaluative processes. First, new data are generated with which various parties can assess and demonstrate (or refute) the organization's fitness for future action. Second, the performances of program staff or others are sampled, and by implication are appraised (even if in aggregate form), in such a way that staff careers and the stability of the authority system may be affected. Third, systematic accounts of program performance threaten the loosely coupled structure of the organization and the networks of mutual confidence which permit it to fulfill its mandate.

This theoretical picture of organizational dynamics surrounding evaluation calls into question a number of the assumptions typically made or implied by program evaluation activity, which were listed at the beginning of this paper. Implications of the organizational principles are reviewed below.

## IMPLICATIONS FOR ASSUMPTIONS ABOUT PROGRAMS AND THEIR EFFECTS

From the point of view of these organizational perspectives, the "program" being evaluated may or may not be a definable organizational entity, as is usually assumed in program evaluation efforts. The program might be a set of tasks, a grouping of positions or functions, or a symbolic response to an environmental demand with no necessary link to actual activities. Or, the program might be *part* of the jobs of various people, inextricably linked with other "nonprogram" activities or positions. To the extent that the program cannot be structurally defined, it is less likely to be the focus of the evaluative processes these theories describe.

The three perspectives make it clear that the beliefs about causation held by key actors influence the kinds of evaluation processes acceptable to the organization. Although much current program evaluation presumes that causal relationships can be found, the organizational theories note the tremendous uncertainty inherent in the technology of educational organizations. This uncertainty contributes to pressure for measures of performance which do *not* specify outcomes precisely or which (falsely) attribute outcomes to the performance of specific individuals. Also the uncertainty about what efforts lead to what outcomes increases staff desires for increased autonomy and decentralized decision making. In other words, given that causal processes are believed to be unclear, organizational members prefer that their work be neither well exposed nor carefully measured.

Nothing in the organizational principles described here would dispute the assumption that causal relationships are technically *possible* to detect with sophisticated techniques from social science (though Weick would question the degree to which relationships between variables are as determinate as social scientists have tended to presume; see Weick, 1976: 9-11, 18). However, the three perspectives do make clear that precise information may be dysfunctional, by inviting unjustified attributions of responsibility for outcomes, increasing information management costs, and exposing the organization unnecessarily to hostile environmental elements.

### IMPLICATIONS FOR ASSUMPTIONS ABOUT DECISION MAKING AND THE ROLE OF INFORMATION IN IT

The assumption that higher levels in the organization control the activities of those lower down is questioned by these perspectives in the case of organizations with uncertain technologies, such as schools. The loose coupling perspective makes this point most strongly, by asserting that inspection of one unit's activities by another destroys the mutual assumption of confidence in each other's work. The other two perspectives imply that the organization seeks tighter controls, but is severely constrained by the dynamic nature of the "objects" worked on, the lack of causal certainty, and the lack of consensus about desirable outcomes.

Explicit information about organizational functioning seems to play a less important role in organizational decision making than most program evaluation activity assumes. Again, such information is important from an *organizational* point of view for what it communicates about individual task performance (when tasks bear some causal relationship to outcomes), about organizational fitness for the future, about the correspondence between the organizational structure and external expectations of it. Given the nature of the educational organization's work and environmental dependencies, the rational decision-making model assumed by much program evaluation activity is, from the point of view of these three theories, less important to the organization. In this regard, the three perspectives would assert that decision makers at any level in educational organizations tend to have little detailed information, of a formally recorded nature, on program functioning—on this point the perspectives agree with the assumption of little information!

The three perspectives do not address directly assumptions about the capacity of key organizational members to comprehend, absorb, and make use of the additional information generated by program evaluation activities. Other organizational research deals centrally with that issue, suggesting among other things that the time and attention of decision makers are much more limited than program evaluation efforts have assumed (see Sproull and Larkey, forthcoming).

## IMPLICATIONS FOR ASSUMPTIONS
## ABOUT IMPLEMENTING EVALUATION PROCESSES

The presumed consensus on evaluative criteria underlying many program evaluation approaches is unlikely to emerge in the organizational setting as described by the three perspectives. The plural environment of the school alluded to by Meyer and Rowen contains many competing interests, as does the coalition of interests which constitutes the organization's primary decision-making group, according to Thompson (1967: 132-133). Ultimately, the choice of evaluative criteria in any effort to determine organizational effectiveness becomes a political process, in which the interests of various parties conflict and cannot all be satisfied (Scott, 1977: 71-74). This argument states theoretically what some writers have suggested more pragmatically in discussions of the politics of evaluation (see, e.g., House, 1973, regarding the politics of educational evaluation).

Regarding the assumptions that external evaluation specialists are necessary for program evaluation and that they can manage their activities with minimal counterproductive side effects, the perspectives point to two potential complications. Where evaluation specialists come temporarily from outside the organization, at the request of external bodies, a potential communication link is set up between the organization and its environment. This may run counter to the organization's efforts to control the evaluative image held of it by external groups. Evaluation specialists who are formally part of the organization, as in the case of the program evaluator retained permanently by a school district, create a different complication: they tend to become an additional, often unwitting, element in the organization's authority

system. In other words, the presence of a formally designated evaluation specialist may make the organization more vulnerable to the
outside or make its internal authority system more complex and problematic.

## IN SUMMARY

Four themes run through the discussion of organizational assumptions implicit in most current program evaluation activity. First, new
evaluative information almost inevitably plays a role in the organization's system of authority and control. Program evaluations set in
motion forces which can influence the stability of the authority system,
alter the ability of staff to work together, and affect staff jobs. Second,
organizations as open systems exist in delicate balance with a complex
environment. Program evaluation has the potential to alter that balance,
often without intending to do so. Third, the choices made consciously
or unconsciously as part of the program evaluation process are funda-
mentally political: the criteria on which the evaluation is based favor
certain interests to the exclusion of others. Lack of consensus about
desirable outcomes makes precise measurement less relevant to organizational needs. Fourth, the lack of clarity about causal processes, at
least as believed by organizational members, decreases the usefulness of
systematic evaluative information to the organization.

The processes described in this paper may seem to imply that
program evaluation has little place in the organizational settings where
it is frequently practiced. Clearly, program evaluation activities tinker
with the subtle system of relationships which constitutes an established
organization. At least in the case of educational organizations, program
evaluation efforts run counter to some of the fundamental tendencies
described by organizational theories reviewed here. There are several
implications of this state of affairs for further development in the
theory and practice of evaluation.

In many cases, it can be argued that organizations need some degree
of disruption. Program evaluation may raise to public consciousness and
scrutiny aspects of organizational operations long neglected or taken
for granted. Or, program evaluation may help to stimulate a needed
crisis of authority within an organization locked into old, unproductive
ways of operating. To the extent that it creates these kinds of dysfunc-

tions, program evaluation may perform a valuable service. But it is probably better for program evaluators to be aware of the full range of dysfunctions they help to create. Otherwise, in the name of improvement, they may hinder as often as they help.

Nonetheless, the evaluation community will need to confront more directly that fact that *im*precision and lack of systematization have important roles to play in organizations providing human services. Systematic program evaluation can tamper with subtle networks of authority, communication, and confidence which allow organizations to deliver their services in a complex environment. The important challenge for program evaluators is to discover those kinds of situations in which additional systematic information can improve specific programs and at the same time meet basic organizational needs.

Finally, the dialogue between organizational theory and the program evaluation community has only begun. The three perspectives reviewed here have distinct limitations. For one, these theories attend to general structural tendencies of organizations; other potentially important factors are left out. Furthermore, the theories presented here have less to say about the dynamics of evaluation outside the boundaries of a single organizational system, as is the case with much federal-level evaluative research. Also, organizational theory is formulated at a level of abstraction which gives the practicing evaluator few clues about what he should do next week. Finally, there is the danger of reading into the formulations of organizational theory too much wisdom and the temptation to reify "the organization" as if it had a life of its own apart from the actions and motivations of its members.

But at the least, the perspectives reviewed here and other research in the emerging field of organizational theory describe systematically the context in which program evaluation activity takes place. The description raises important questions about the nature of evaluation processes. By responding to these questions, the evaluation community may ultimately improve both its own work and the organizations it seeks to help.

## REFERENCES

BICE, T. W., R. L. EICHORN, and D. A. KLEIN (1975) "Evaluation of public health programs," in M. Guttentag and E. Struening (eds.) Handbook of Evaluation Research. Beverly Hills: Sage.

BURNHAM, R. A. (1973) "Systems Evaluation and Goal Disagreement," in E. House (ed.) School Evaluation: the Politics and Process. Berkeley: McCutchan.

CARO, F. G. (1971) "Evaluation research: an overview," in F. Caro (ed.) Readings in Evaluation Research. New York: Russell Sage.

DEAL, T., J. W. MEYER, and W. R. SCOTT (1975) "Organizational influences on educational innovation," in V. Baldridge and T. Deal (eds.) Managing Change in Educational Organizations. Berkeley: McCutchan.

DORNBUSCH, S. M. and W. R. SCOTT (1975) Evaluation and the Exercise of Authority. San Francisco: Jossey-Bass.

GUBA, E. G. (1972) "The failure of educational evaluation," in C. Weiss (ed.) Evaluating Action Programs. Boston: Allyn & Bacon.

HOUSE, E. R. (1973) "Prologue—evaluation in a pluralist society," in E. House (ed.) School Evaluation: The Politics and Process. Berkeley: McCutchan.

KATZ, D. and R. L. KAHN (1966) "Organizations and the system concept," in D. Katz and R. L. Kahn (eds.) The Social Psychology of Organizations. New York: John Wiley.

MEYER, J. W. and B. ROWEN (1978) "The structure of educational organizations, in M. W. Meyer (ed.) Environments and Organizations. San Francisco: Jossey-Bass.

——— (1977) "Institutionalized organizations: formal structure as myth and ceremony. " American Journal of Sociology 82: 440-463.

SCOTT, W. R. (1977) "On the effectiveness of studies of organizational effectiveness," in P. S. Goodman, J. M. Pennings, and Associates, New Perspectives on Organizational Effectiveness. San Francisco: Jossey-Bass.

SPROULL, L. and P. Larkey (forthcoming) "Managerial Behavior and Evaluator Effectiveness," in H. Schulberg and J. Jerrell (eds.) The Evaluator and Management. Beverly Hills: Sage.

THOMPSON, J. D. (1967) Organizations in Action, (New York: McGraw-Hill, 1967).

WEICK, K. E. (1976) "Educational organizations as loosely-coupled systems." Administrative Science Quarterly 21: 1-19.

WEISS, C. (1977) "Limits on bureaucracy's use of research: constrained repertoire theory." Presented at the American Psychological Association annual meeting, San Francisco, August.

WERGIN, J. F. (1976) "The evaluation of organizational policy making: a political model." Review of Educational Research (Winter).

# 17

## EMERGING ISSUES FOR
## EVALUATORS AND EVALUATION USERS

Robert F. Rich

Within the last decade, program evaluation, or evaluation research, has matured into a discipline with specific training programs, journals, professional societies, and continuing education programs. It has received recognition by the federal government, particularly the legislative and executive branches, and has been legitimated through legislatively mandated requirements and special offices of departments (e.g., the Assistant Secretary for Policy, Planning, and Evaluation), as well as divisions of the Office of Management and Budget and the General Accounting Office. Academics and practitioners alike think of evaluation as a formal component of the problem-solving/policy-making process.

Evaluation is thought of as a formal component of the problem-solving/policy-making process by academics and practitioners alike. In academic circles, there is a concern for training professional evaluators or, at a minimum, professionals who understand evaluation and can assess the quality and viability of its findings. These professionals are hired in government agencies, large research institutions, and in the expanding number of for-profit consulting firms.

As evaluation research expands, several issues need to be addressed: (1) Are the appropriate methodological tools available, and are they being applied? (2) What types of professional training and continuing education programs consistent with the realities of program evaluation, as a field, should be developed? (3) Are evaluation research results effectively being translated into policy/action? (4) What can be done to decrease the abuse and misutilization of evaluation data? (5) What ethical standards should be developed for evaluators; and who will enforce these standards?

This list of issues is by no means exhaustive. It does, however, point to a core set of concerns that deserve attention. This essay is devoted to exploring each of these issues, what is at stake, and in what directions the field is developing?

## METHODOLOGICAL TOOLS—THE-STATE-OF-THE-ART

Evaluation research gained relatively rapid legitimacy in academic circles through adapting traditional, proven methodologies to the evaluation process. Evaluators often learn how to use a set of complex, sophisticated techniques (e.g., regression analysis, interrupted time-series analysis, log-linear models, path analysis) as part of their professional training. Not infrequently, these become tools in the search of a problem, applied without sufficient discrimination to many questions. Such application of models and techniques developed for other problems (and by other disciplines) may produce long-term difficulties.

For example, if one is concerned with the performance of minority students in selective institutions of higher education in the United States, the classical evaluation model would stipulate that data be collected on cumulative grade point average, rank in class, post-graduate placement, high school class rank, high school grade point average, and scores on a national aptitude test. These data would then form the core of the variables to be examined. Inputs (e.g., aptitude test scores, high school grade point average) would then be correlated with outputs (e.g., college cumulative grade point average), and outputs would be examined in the context of a regression analysis.

Similarly, if one were interested in the impact of a change in the legal drinking age from 21 to 18 years of age, one would first define an appropriate output/performance measure (e.g., rate of deaths in the 18-21 age category due to drunken driving). Data on this criterion variable would be collected over time along with a set of variables that might be correlated with the outcome measure.

As Marcia Guttentag pointed out in her testimony before the Senate Committee on Human Resources, experimental designs and classical statistics, where applied to social programs, often either force a set of assumptions on a program or attempt to change the program to be similar to what the research model requires. The literature on the sociology of professions teaches us that this is not atypical to the maturation process of a relatively new professional field.

Evaluation research, which is not being conducted primarily for scholarly purposes (e.g., secondary analysis of data), is seldom in the position of simply being able to develop *eloquent* statistical models. There are users who need to know whether their programs or projects are "successful." They want to *understand* what is working well and what might be done to improve unsuccessful or problematic programmatic components.

Thus, it seems logical that evaluators should concern themselves with *understanding* the program to be evaluated as well as the *structure* and *environment* in which the program is located. This type of understanding may not be provided by the mechanical application of classical statistical techniques to the day-to-day operations of a program. If evaluators are to possess the capacity to suggest or actually prescribe treatments for improving programs, they must understand what the ultimate programmatic goals are in addition to what means are being used to reach those goals.

In his famous article "Reforms as Experiments," D. T. Campbell (1969) contends:

> The political stance should be: this is a serious problem. We propose to initiate policy A on an experimental basis. If after five years there has been no significant improvement, we will shift to policy B. By making explicit that a given situation is only one of several that the administrator . . . could in good conscience advocate, . . . the administrator can afford honest evaluation of outcomes. Negative results . . . do not jeopardize his job for his job is to keep after the problem until something is found that works.

One does not simply want to move from policy A to policy B in a mechanical fashion—i.e., "A has not worked, so let us move on to B."

The adoption of policy B should be made with an understanding of the reasons why "A" failed in contrast to a simple determination that "the performance measures reveal that A was not successful."

In trying to understand structure, environment, and context, evaluation research needs to become more interdisciplinary than it is at the present time. There is a good deal that can be learned, for instance, from anthropologists and their notion of an organizational ethnography. Operations research, systems analysis, and management information designers have developed techniques which produce detailed descriptions of the formal structure of an organization as well as the process that is followed (actors, decision criteria) while engaging in problem-solving activities.

The decision-theoretic approach is an example of a new method which "recognizes the dynamics and multiple levels of decision-making in human service program" (Guttentag, 1978). This method applies a simplified form of multiattribute utility scaling and Bayesian statistics to increase its sensitivity to the expressed goals and alternative options of decision makers.

Successful evaluation teams will avail themselves of the variety of techniques now available and/or in the process of being developed. The more traditional techniques allow one to be confident, in terms of statistical levels of significance, of the findings presented. However, do these "significant findings" speak to the formative problem-solving needs of decision makers? More important, is the evaluator confident that he/she understands the operations of the program being evaluated? In the evaluation area, we may have to face the challenge posed by Quade: Do social scientists want to be approximately correct or precisely wrong?

## TRAINING PROGRAMS

The discussion of appropriate methodological tools has a direct bearing on the substantive training programs designed for professional evaluators. What skills do we want the graduates of these programs to possess? In addition to the tools of classical statistics and experimental design, several other skills are important:

(1) **The ability to structure problems and to train clients to do so.** There is a large body of literature on the problems associated with ill-defined objectives and goals in the program evaluation process. Lack of consensus between evaluators and clients tends to discredit the evaluation, creating an atmosphere of suspicion, distrust, and anxiety.

Some of the responsibility for ill-defined objectives lies with Congress in the legislative process, some with the bureaucracy in the implementation process (rules, regulations, program development), and some with evaluators who, in many cases, only evaluate on the basis of what is given to them. If there is not a clear understanding of what objectives and goals are being evaluated on the part of all interested parties (i.e., stakeholders) in the evaluation process, then the evaluators are sure to encounter resistance to the presentation of findings and to their ultimate utilization.

(2) **A strong sense of ethics and values.** The most important dimension of this type of training (to be discussed in more detail in a later section) is coming to grips with some difficult questions early on in one's professional career: At what point does the evaluator advise a client that it is not appropriate to take on an evaluation at this time? Does the evaluator ever work him/herself out of a job? Are there conditions under which the evaluation process should be terminated?

(3) **An ability to synthesize evaluation results.** Evaluators should be familiar with the form in which most of their users (i.e., government officials) prefer to receive research findings. Graduates should be expected to know how to (a) write a short, relevant memo; (b) present an oral briefing; and (c) write an intelligible executive summary.

(4) **An understanding of the "users' environment."** Evaluators should also be sensitive to the environment (structure, incentive system) in which users operate. This requires an understanding of the civil service system, the operating rewards/incentives in government (federal, state, local), the leverage/pressure points used by Congress and executive branch officials alike to attain desirable objectives, and successful strategies for promoting innovation and change. In addition, training in this area would include an understanding of how information is used in governmental agencies and in Congress/legislatures.

The necessity of this training is based on the premise that evaluators should/must understand the environment in which their findings will be disseminated. Potential professional evaluators should, at least, be sensitive to the concrete realities of the policy-making process.

# ARE EVALUATION RESULTS
# BEING EFFECTIVELY TRANSLATED INTO ACTION?

These training outcomes are based on the knowledge utilization literature, which indicates that policy makers are receptive to program evaluation results; they do not feel that the best information is being made available to them; and they do not feel that evaluators are receptive and responsive to their needs (Caplan, 1976). There is, it would seem, a need to create effective knowledge-transfer mechanisms for translating evaluation information into action/policy.

The knowledge-utilization literature is not, however, a guide in clarifying who should be engaged in translating, what types of knowledge-transfer mechanisms should be created, and who should be responsible for the effective application of these mechanisms. Most of the programs to translate knowledge into action reflect a belief that if information is timely, relevant, in the proper form, and oriented toward the decision maker's agenda, utilization (i.e., action) will follow (Rich, 1979a). Those who subscribe to this belief attempt to change what might be called knowledge-specific characteristics.

Those with a different perspective contend that knowledge-specific characteristics (timeliness, relevance, form) are important but insufficient for producing utilization. Instead, one should be concentrating on organization design, bureaucratic structures, and incentive/reward systems (Rich, 1979a, 1979b). There are, however, few examples of projects or programs which have acted out of a commitment to this belief.

If successful knowledge-transfer mechanisms are more dependent upon bureaucratic rules and procedures than they are on knowledge-specific characteristics, then it will be important to orient utilization programs in this direction. The resolution of this issue, even on a tentative basis, seems to be critical for the future development of evaluation research. To the extent that one is concerned with usability of evaluation results, it would be important to determine what factors are most influential in determining whether knowledge-transfer mechanisms will be successful.

# ABUSE, MISUSE OF EVALUATION RESULTS

At the same time that one is concerned with developing effective measures for the application of evaluation research results, it is worth noting that utilization is not a priori valuable. Presumably, effective knowledge-transfer mechanisms are not being developed because it is believed that utilization/applications are worthwhile in and of themselves.

A use can be found of any study, if it becomes necessary to do so. Thus, a professional evaluator must be concerned with the quality of utilization. Cook (1978) distinquishes between intentional and unintentional abuse of evaluation research results. He also has introduced the concept of premature use of information.

One example of premature use of evaluation results is the case of the Westinghouse-Ohio OEO study. As Williams (1975) reports it, a preliminary draft report released exclusively for purposes of OEO internal staff review was disseminated to the White House; the findings were subsequently used in a major policy address delivered by President Nixon. These preliminary results were then debated in the public arena. When the final report was released, it received little attention although it illuminated some of the issues raised in the Nixon speech and the ensuing debate.

Unintentional misutilization is pervasive. Evaluations may be misunderstood or selectively cited. It may also be that secondary analysis of data adds dimensions to an overall understanding of a program that was not previously available. It may also be the case that policy makers draw policy conclusions which are not warranted on the basis of the data presented or the levels of statistical significance of the data. These types of activities (e.g., overgeneralization) are not fully under control of the evaluator or the staff aide originally responsible for transmitting the data.

D. T. Campbell, Philip Hauser, Andrew Gordon, and others have studied the intentional abuse/misutilization of information. This phenomenon has most often been documented in cases where the organizational incentive system encourages such activity. Philip Hauser suggests that statistics are becoming increasingly important for decision-making purposes; thus, they will be particularly open to "the temptation to use statistics for administration, agency or other interests, as distinguished from the public interest."

Jerome Skolnick describes the administrative pressure put on police officers to increase clearance rates (the number of crimes solved over the number of crimes committed) and, thus, show what a good job the police department is doing. In response to this pressure, officers will falsify reports so that they can show what a reduced rate of crime has occurred in the categories their superiors are most concerned with. The same phenomena has been illustrated in the New York City Police Department.

> A Vassar College freshman . . . dashed into the West 100th police station last July 11 to gasp out an account of being robbed of her purse at knife point in Central Park.
>
> To her astonishment, she says, the officer who took her statement told her he was going to record the crime not as felonious assault but as a larceny which is much less serious.
>
> The Officer . . . told her frankly that he was falsifying the report so that the 24th precinct—widely hailed as the city's model precinct—would show a reduction in the rate of violent crime in its area [Sibley, 1972].

Campbell (1971b) cites two other examples of statistics being used for political ends:

> To return to an earlier example, Chicago's reform policy superintendent, Orlando Wilson, was wise when he rendered the police records incomparable with previous periods. This may have been necessary as mutinous subordinates might have inflated the records just to embarrass him, easily done when a sizeable portion of crimes have been going unreported. Similarly, in these days many school systems are less vulnerable because their records and summary figures are color-blind; they in fact do not know which pupils and which teachers are Negro, nor in which schools Negroes are present. Records of overall achievement and trends over time can be selectively cited by politicians for their political ends.

Alternatively, agencies under pressure may simply not collect information which could prove to be harmful. Andrew Gordon et al. (1975) studies this phenomena and reports:

> The Bureau of Labor Statistics abolished the urban poverty survey in the 1972 election year, and the federal administration, embarrassed at the numbers of people defined as poor, has been

accused of trying to discontinue the poverty-level index, One wry critic has suggested that to protect themselves fully some agencies would have to conduct business by word of mouth.

This study also suggests that even if the information is collected, it may serve the interests of the organization to store it in an unretrievable form:

> The data may even be collected in appropriate ways, but only be released after being made useless. For example, the sought information can be coded or presented in ways that render it harmless for investigative purposes. Data are frequently stored and/or presented in irreducible aggregates thus not allowing some questions to be asked of them; for example, policy budget data could be available by policy district, but unavailable by precinct or census tract or it could be reducible to only categories like 'violence control' rather than to the specific amounts for 'juvenile gang controls.' Unless data are stored in their rawest form, which is quite unusual, some coding decisions must be made. The interests represented by those who determine the structure of the data files, and thus fundamentally affect what what is retrievable (or retrievable at acceptable costs) are most likely to be the interests of the top agency personnel [Gordon, 1975].

Clearly, the incentive system—the system of rewards and punishments in bureaucracy—affects the way in which information is ultimately used.

## ETHICAL STANDARDS FOR EVALUATION

A discussion of abuse and misuse as well as the description of a training program leads one to focus on ethical standards.

What ethical standards should be developed, and who (if anyone) should enforce them? It is not surprising that a field that has grown in recognition and legitimacy as quickly as evaluation research, has not devoted very much attention to questions of ethical standards and behavior.

As Congress continues to mandate evaluation, as it takes Sunset legislation more seriously, and budgets of Offices of Policy, Planning, and Evaluation become larger, the issue of ethical standards is critical.

One dimension of concern is the dependence of agencies on evaluators. Agencies are dependent because legislators are demanding evaluation, and because of the fact that an agency who sponsors evaluations is (from the perspective of government officials) considered to be legitimate. The dependence relationship is, to some extent, also based on the mystique of evaluation research. It is not clear how these professionals produce the sophisticated, fancy numbers they do; but is it clear that important policy makers take them into account.

Professional evaluators should consider several issues:

- At what point in the evaluation process do they advise a client that their services are no longer needed?
- Is it ethical to advise a client not to fund an evaluation study because of the current policy environment?
- Should the evaluator accept the definition of the objectives given to them, or should he/she work with clients to gain a clear consensus on objectives?
- Similarly, who determines what the evaluation criteria should be?
- Is this the sole responsibility of a third-party evaluator, or should he/she attempt to gain a consensus among all interested parties?
- If evaluators engage in these consensus seeking activities, to what extent are they losing their objectivity as outside evaluators?
- Is objectivity exclusively a function of distance from the process of program/project decision making? In other words, do the evaluators need (as many would contend) to be an outsider for them to conduct a truly objective evaluation?
- What are the limits of an evaluator's responsibilities—at the time a report is submitted or after a decision concerning the effectiveness and/or continuation of the program being assessed? If one adheres to the latter position, does this mean that evaluators should assist agency staff in writing summaries for their superiors? Should evaluators be part of agency briefings? Should they make concrete policy recommendations?
- What can the evaluator do to minimize misuse/and abuse of research findings? On the basis of the OEO experience, for example, should preliminary results be withheld? If so, how is one to get valuable feedback from agency· participants? Does close collaboration with agency staff in translating evaluation findings in recommendations minimize the chances for unintentional misutilization?

These ethical issues relate to existing bureaucratic structures and reward systems in the public sector. If evaluation is to affect the policy process, professional evaluators must address questions having to do with the limits of objectivity, the limits of direct involvement in the policy-making process, and the ability of evaluators to limit abuse and misuse of research findings.

## CONCLUSION

When and if we move closer to Campbell's (1971a) notion of an experimenting society, the professional evaluator will take on an increasingly important role basically because evaluation will be so important.

Even if we never realize the dream of an experimenting society, it is clear that evaluation activities are a vital part of the policy-making process at all levels of government and in the private sector as well. Further expansion should not continue without a careful assessment of where we are as a field, where we want to go, and how we might arrive at our objectives in a manner which appears to agree upon professional standards. In other words, the evaluators need to evaluate themselves.

## REFERENCES

CAMPBELL, D. T. (1971a) "Methods for the experimenting society." Presented before the Eastern Psychological Association, April 17.
――― (1971b) "Administrative experiments, institutional records, and non-reactive measures," in William Evans (ed.) Organizational Experiments. New York: Harper and Row.
――― (1969) "Reforms as experiments." American Psychologist 24: 409-428.
CAPLAN, N. (1976) "The use of program evaluation by federal policy makers at the national level." Presented at a NIMH-sponsored meeting of the Network of Consultants on Knowledge Transfer, New Orleans.
――― et al. (1975) The Use of Social Science Knowledge in Policy Decisions at the National Level. Ann Arbor: Institute for Social Research.
COOK, T. (1978) "The abuse, misuse, and premature utilization of information." Presented at a conference on "Research Utilization," University of Pittsburgh, Graduate School of Business, September 20-22.
GORDON, A. and D. T. CAMPBELL, (1970) "Recommended accountability

guidelines for the evaluation of improvements in the delivery of state social services." (unpublished).

GORDON, A. et al., "Public access to information." Northwestern Law Review 68, 2: 285-286.

GUTTENTAG, M. (1978) Testimony before the Senate Committee on Human Resources. (as quoted in Evaluation and Change, Special Issue, p. 18)

HAUSER, P. M. (1972) "Statistics and politics." Prepared for the annual meetings of the American Statistical Association, August 15.

ILCHMAN, W. and T. UPHOFF (1971) The Political Economy of Change. Berkeley: University of California Press.

KITUSE, J. and A. V. CICOUREL (1969) "A note on the use of official statistics." Social Problems 11 (Fall): 131-139.

LEVINE, R. A. (1972) Public Planning: Failure and Redirection. New York: Basic Books.

MORSS, E. and R. F. Rich (1979) Government Information Management. Boulder: Westview.

RICH, R. F. (1979a) "Editor's introduction." American Behavioral Scientist 22: 327-337. January/February, 1979.

――― (1979b) The Use of Social Science Information and Public Policy Making. San Francisco: Jossey-Bass.

――― (1977) "The use of social science information by federal bureaucrats: knowledge for action versus knowledge for understanding", pp. 199-212 in C. Weiss (ed.) The Uses of Social Research in Public Policy Making. Lexington, MA: Lexington-Heath.

SIBLEY, J. "Students say a policeman tried to falsify a report of a holdup. New York Times (November 23): 5 and 40.

SKOLNICK, J. H. (1975) Justice Without Trial. New York: John Wiley.

WEISS, C. H. (1978) "The use of evaluation research." Presented at a conference on "Research Utilization," University of Pittsburgh, School of Business, September 20-22.

WILLIAMS, W. (1975) Social Policy Research and Analysis. New York: Elsevier.

# 18

## EVALUATION AND CHANGE

Howard Davis and Susan Salasin

There has been reason to question whether evaluation will make a beneficial impact on change. We asked William Niskanen, who had been assistant director for evaluation at the Office of Management and Budgeting from 1970 to 1972: "What is your impression about the extent to which evaluation findings, the outcomes of analytic studies, were used in reaching decisions about programs?" Niskanen's answer: "It would be difficult in many cases to attribute more than 5 percent of the ultimate changes that are made to any analytic contribution whatsoever." Attkison and coworkers visited evaluators in sixty community mental health centers (CMHC). They found a growing demoralization among persons involved with evaluation, partly because they fail to see that their work has any impact on decisions. Windle and Volkman reported on apparent disenchantment on the part of CMHC administrators with respect to the utilization payoff from evaluation. Weiss (1972) found evaluators' "most common complaint is that their findings are ignored." Wholey (1976) concluded that "the recent literature is unanimous in announcing the general failure of evaluation to affect decisionmaking in a significant way." Cohen (1975) states, "There is little evidence to indicate that government planning offices have succeeded in linking social research and decisionmaking." And Weidman et al.(1973) remark that on those rare occasions when evaluation studies have been used, "the little use that has occurred (has been) fortuitous rather than planned."

We are not questioning that these observations are sound. But it has become something of a pastime recently to bemoan the recklessness of evaluation efforts. What is important to point out is that the references just cited are all at least four years old.

## MORE RECENT EVIDENCE

There is mounting evidence that evaluations are having more impact than was earlier seen. Former National Institute of Mental Health Director Bertram Brown (1977), in his prepared testimony on program evaluation before the Committee on Human Resources, points out that a series of evaluations have examined the CMHC "seed money" concept and centers' ability to find other sources of funds as the federal grants decline. Recommendations to require improvement in centers' internal fiscal management, accounting, and billing systems were consequently incorporated into the CMHC Amendments of 1975. A study of Institute programs on aging pointed out deficiencies in CMHC service to the elderly and recommended increased emphasis in this area. The Amendments added the requirement that services especially designed for the elderly be a part of every CMHC. An evaluation of citizen participation in CMHCs was very critical of this aspect of centers' operation, and specific provision requiring representative citizen governing boards for CMHCs was included as directed policy. These and other program evaluations provided useful input to development of legislation. Even though they were not the full contributors to specific provision of the CMHC law, they in each case added to the cumulative weight of evidence bearing on one side or the other of specific decisions.

Lynn (Salasin, 1977) provides dramatic examples of the impact of evaluation and analysis in federal agencies ranging from Department of Defense, through the National Security Council, HEW, to the Department of the Interior. These influences on policy decisions actually occurred earlier, though some of us are only now sitting up and taking notice.

As we meet with evaluators throughout the country, they increasingly rise to dispute the intimation that evaluation results are not leading to direct impact.

# DIFFERENT EXPECTATIONS

However encouraging the evidence of direct impact may be, there seems to be an emerging awareness that we have been looking for a direct immediate coupling of evaluation and decision making. Perhaps this is a wrong measure of the effectiveness of evaluation research. Should there be a toe-to-toe alignment of evaluation results and program decisions? Some time ago, a leading researcher on evaluation in Colorado suggested that an agreement be demanded that program administrators would guarantee the use of evaluation results before studies were initiated. Understandably, evaluators would have a desire for immediate reinforcing feedback; however, two emerging phenomena suggest that evaluations would do better to delay that reinforcement, allowing more appropriate and penetrating contributions to become evident.

# THE EXAMPLE OF CORROBORATING FINDINGS

Patton et al. (1975) found in their research on the actual use of a sample of Federal evaluation projects that the matter of impact was considerably more complex and less dismal than their original thinking had led them to expect. Evaluation research was used by decision makers but not in the clear-cut and organization-shaking ways that social scientists sometimes believe research should be used. Weiss and Bucuvalas (1976) in a rigorously controlled study of determinants of utilization, observed that the cumulative effect of multiple studies over time can be significant. Perhaps in defense of Nietzsche's raindrops, a sufficient number can mold even granted policies. Evaluation research, as applied to decision making, probably still is of insufficient age to present many evidences of the cumulative phenomenon. But an illustration can be drawn from the applied research field, where the application of decision making precedes the history of evaluation research by perhaps a decade. A rising major program at NIMH, already receiving congressional endorsement, is the Community Support Program. It entails the marshaling of human services resources in the interests of the mentally disabled. The architect of that policy decision, underway for approximately two years, did not consciously draw upon any previous specific evaluation researchers. However, it is more than interesting that

NIMH project No. OM-29, funded in 1957, involved a comprehensive evaluation of an identical program at the local level. Since that time some 200 studies have been funded on community services for the chronically mentally ill. It would be difficult to document successful marketing of the results from many of those specific studies. But what has happened instead, it at least can be inferred, is that a culture has evolved, one in which there is a wide awareness of the urgency of the problem, and one in which there has been a saturating diffusion of knowledge and skills on mobilizing community resources. Finally, it seems, that the right agglutination of factors was brought together by Judy Turner, the primary creator of the program. But time also helped in bringing together circumstances that would render a nationwide system possible.

## THE EXAMPLE OF CORROBORATING INFLUENCERS

It is not only the accumulation of corroborating studies that influenced change. Corroborating influencers may spring from seeds beyond evaluation researchers' doing. When Ciarlo (1977) began adding suggested directions of decisions based upon evaluation studies at Denver General Hospital, he felt the same sense of ineffectiveness reported by many early evaluators. But after a period of quiescence, which interestingly seemed to follow a nine-month period, policy decisions were adopted that bore a remarkable resemblance to suggestions in the evaluation reports. Yet on inquiry, he was unable to gain confirmation that the determinant of decision had been the evaluation recommendation. Did this mean that sources of ideas were merely forgotten? Does it only confirm that decisions are much slower in growing than we sometimes assume? Or was there accumulating evidence for a decision emerging from many sources? We do not know. What it does seem to confirm is what has been observed in the field of research utilization, namely, that results drop into underground rivers, there mating with other knowledge, often reemerging miles away in a form allowing scant recognition of the original sources of the outcropping. Certainly one conclusion can be drawn from this observation: evaluators can find solace in knowing that their work may prove to be far more impactful than early and direct feedback would lead them to believe.

# THE EXAMPLE OF CHALLENGES TO ASSUMPTIONS

Weiss and Bucuvalas (1976) call attention to a second major phenomenon of evaluation utilization.

"Research is useful not only when it helps to solve problems, when it provides ideas and information that can be instrumentally applied to recognized problems. Research is also useful when it questions existing perspectives and definitions of the problematic. [The] decisionmakers are indicating that research can make substantial contributions to their work by challenging the ideas currently in vogue and providing alternative cognitive maps. Even if the implications are not feasible or politically acceptable at present, such research helps to develop alternative constructions of reality. In time these alternative images of reality can yield new ways of addressing policy problems and new programs of procedures for coping with needs."

This contribution might be called *Enlightenment.* How this can be employed to document the worth of evaluation and how it can provide reinforcing feedback to evaluators remain obscure. But at least awareness of it can be expanded, and its significance recognized in classical major evaluations, such as that in Head Start, through which Dr. Julius Richmond contributed so greatly. The heuristic ramifications are evident, quite in addition to the consequent traceable social innovations that take place.

The evidence is difficult to turn away from: evaluation is more profoundly significant in its contributions than many have realized. It is indeed maturing toward an immensely important, and enduring, role in the human services world.

A peripheral observation on the accelerating contribution of evaluation is that one hears and reads concern now with not just promoting the impact of evaluation on change, but of reining it in, of holding back, of controlling misutilizations.

# MORE RAPID MATURATION

There is an urgent cry for the rapid maturation of evaluation. The mission ahead is staggering. Even in fiscal year 1977, the reported obligations for program evaluations in the major departments whose mission responsibilities may be broadly categorized in the human resources area amounted to $148.3 million dollars, requiring the resources of 676 staff years. That was $83.4 million, and 335 staff years for HEW alone (Granquist, 1977). The total for the federal government was $243 million with 2,176 staff years. On top of this is the OMB plan for a major role of evaluation in its zero-based budgeting context. The Government Accounting Office increasingly is demanding effectiveness evaluation of programs. At this time, the U.S. Senate Committee on Human Resources is midway through hearings on program evaluation toward consideration of its role in sunset legislation, with the probability that both formative and summative evaluations will be employed to assist with decisions on possible future policies as the sunset hour approaches.

## AN EXTENDED ROLE CONCEPT

The call for evaluators to encompass knowledge and skills beyond scientific methodology is being echoed in many quarters. Stockdill and Sharfstein (1976) underscore the view that evaluation is as much political material as scientific, so evaluators should reach beyond the role of being providers of truth. GAO's (1976) manual on evaluation and analysis to support decision making outlines a range of recommended functions extending from ascertaining decision makers' needs to reassessment of decision makers' alternative decisions. The document, "Public Policy and Evaluation Research," prepared by Powers and Holland (1976), calls for specific guidance in the art of evaluation theory activities. These span decision analysis in the early evaluation planning stages, and involve addressing the value assumptions underlying public programs, reconciling the conflict between the respective researchers and public administrators, and fostering wide, explicit, public and private discussion of the often difficult questions or interpretations of evaluation information and results.

Lynn says:

> The most interesting thing we are observing is the interaction between the process of implementation and change, on the one hand, and the political process on the other. The two are just

inextricable, and that's very important to understand. The lesson, then, would be that the change agent (evaluator?) attempting a change on this scale had better well understand the political significance of the changes that he or she is concerned about. Be prepared to cope with the sorts of situations that are going to arise, and anticipate them well enough to prevent them from arising in the first place [quoted in Salasin, 1977].

Patton et al. (1975) advise,

> It would appear to us that it behooves social scientists to inform themselves fully about the political context of the evaluations in which they work. It is precisely through such a heightened awareness of the political implications and consequences of their research that social scientists can reduce their own uncertainty about the uses to which their work is put without impairing their ability to state their "truth" as they see it.

Of course, many evaluators already have expertise pertinent to, and are addressing in their work, the political context of social programs. But the arena of knowledge and skills of all responsible evaluators should encompass not only the methods of science but also relevant portions of the fields of planning, of change, and of decision making, perhaps even reaching into the realm of political science. One way of picturing the expanded role is through a Venn diagram with evaluation as the center circle, with its perimeter overlapping the fields mentioned. In order to gauge the extent to which this occurs at the present time, bibliographies in the respective fields (except for political science) were examined for overlap of topics and of authors. Overlap appeared to be approximately 20% in terms of topics, but under 5% for authors contributing to the literature in the respective topics. Expansion of the evaluation ring will come hard, but it is seen as essential if evaluation is to reach optimum maturity in its potential role contribution.

## EVALUATORS' PERSPECTIVES

How do evaluators feel about this proposal? So far, there are only small samples on which to base guesses. In the first issue of the *ERS Newsletter* a simple quasi-semantic differential scale was presented, pertaining to seven factors deemed relevant to the soundness of the notion. The profile derived from the first 59 responses was presented in the second issue of the *Newsletter*. Happily, it bears close fidelity with two additional profiles obtained from evaluators at NIMH Staff College sessions in Atlanta and Kansas City. (On these occasions, the role extension was labeled "Consultation on Planned Change or Stability," though already second thoughts have been given regarding the limitations of that definition.)

Evaluators felt that the role extension was consistent with their values, that there is a sense of obligation, a high motivation for the extended role, that current circumstances and timing are appropriate for considering the extension, and that the yield or payoff would be notable. However, they were somewhat less sure that they had the abilities, in terms of time resources and sanctions. There seem to be serious concern about the resistances that such a role would evoke. And with small wonder. The threat that evaluation already poses in the role of auditor of adequacy regularly is reported in the literature. But if evaluators are seen as being instrumental in consequent response to evaluations, the sky darkens. Recently it was reported in the Washington Post that the Armed Services Committee has requested of the Library of Congress an evaluation analysis of the relative adequacy of defense capabilities of the United States and Russia respectively. The evaluator not only provided the analysis, but tendered some recommendations on how the imbalance might be rectified. The reaction from the Armed Services Committee was loud: "Here we ask this fellow to do a bean count, and he ends up setting national defense policy for us!" Certainly one caveat about the proposed role extension is that the evaluator should treat gingerly, with the utmost subjunctiveness, offerings that would appear to guide the direction, rather than the process, of assimilation of evaluation results into decision making.

It is hardly likely that decision makers will leap at the opportunity to positively exploit the proferred help of evaluators in decision making. One imagines the following scenario. The evaluator approaches the decision maker's desk with the report, offering, "I would be glad to serve you with my skills in the utilization of this report." "Thanks a lot. Just lay it on the desk there. Don't call us; we'll call you." But that approach is hardly what's advised. Extensive skill can be applied in planning the entire evaluation operation toward rendering it of optimum benefit and desirable change.

But that leads to the most serious doubt about the role extension reported by evaluators: "Sounds OK, but what does it involve?"

One significant lead is given by Kiresuk (1977), who has developed a scale of "Readiness to adopt program evaluation." Analysis of the scale yields a profile allowing an assessment of the determinants of success of program evaluation. Those which appear particularly troublesome would call, it follows, for special attention in overcoming problems that could weaken the effectiveness of evaluation or make it come a cropper altogether, not an unknown experience.

There is more upon which to draw. Chelimsky's (1977) symposium at MITRE called attention to a problem that is endemic among human services agencies, also a situation scolded sternly by Drucker (1974) in contrasting public services with profit-making organizations: goals and objectives seldom lend themselves to evaluation. As a first step, assessment of the evaluability of inferred objectives can, in itself, lead to a sharpening of understanding and to an increase of incentive to turn toward clarified objectives.

To illustrate further what evaluators might consider with regard to the decision-making expansion, still without overt activities toward consulting on planned change as such, one decision-making model is now briefly outlined.

# A CHANGE MODEL

The change model to be used for this example is termed Decision Determinants Analysis. The purpose perhaps might be better served by other models, such as that associated with Guttentag (1973) and Ward Edwards' decision-theoretic, or the multi-attribute model of Shalom Saar and his coworkers. The one chosen is simply more familiar to us. The use of a change model facilitates ordering of the myriad findings and observations about decision making and change. According to Miller (1956), the number of relevant categories of information which can be kept in the mind at the same time is seven plus or minus two. Appropriately, the Decision Determinants Analysis Model contains eight factors, really seven, considering the combination of two overlapping factors. The factors are derived from an algebraic formulation of variables that are considered both necessary and sufficient to account for the success of a decision and its implementation. The determinants have been converted to common language to form the recallable acronym, A VICTORY.

Toward visualizing a framework for this example, consider the given decision appearing on the left side of an equal sign and the A VICTORY factors to the right, of which the predicted success of the decision is a function.

Janis and Mann (1977) summarized six styles through which decisions can be approached:

(1) Rational Optimizing, which is more ideal than practicable;

(2) Satisficing, Simon's (1976) term for decision making in which a course of action is sought that is good enough without comparison with alternative decisions;

(3) Moral decision making, where according to Schwartz (1970), the decision that is more morally justifiable ipso facto is the best;

(4) Elimination by Aspects, described by Tversky (1972) in which decision making becomes an essentially sequential narrowing-down process; all salient alternatives that do not contain the selective aspect are eliminated until a single expedient remains;

(5) Incrementalism or muddling through described by Miller and Starr (1967) in which small changes, each of which is considered "good enough," occur because they are seen as better than leaving the old policy unchanged;

(6) And Mixed Scanning, Etzioni's (1967) term referring to the search, collection, processing, evaluation, and weighing of information and making a choice, but with a degree of rigor that may extend from rational optimizing to slipshod muddling. This mixture of substrategies is said to fit the needs of most democratic governments and organizations. It seems to us, incidentally, in reviewing case examples of decision incidents, that many are made without conscious deliberation. They simply evolve. Suddenly a consensus on a direction of action occurs, but through a new process that approaches the orderliness of those described by Janis and Mann (1977), unless possibly it is muddling-through.

The point here is that whatever style of approach is used in the decision-making process, the likelihood that it will be reached and that an implementation will be successful is a function of the specific determinants on the right side of the equation.

In this example, the decision in question is whether evaluation will have an impact on a later higher-order decision. The example illustrates the use of the model in reporting the factors that have been found to influence the decision, whether conscious or unconscious, to use evaluation results in practice or policy change.

The three reports drawn upon to outline what is known about the determinants of evaluation use are:

(1) Chelimsky's (1977) synthesis of discussions held by over 200 persons involved with evaluation at the federal level;
(2) Patton and coworkers' (1975) study of utilization of 20 major federal evaluations;
(3) And Weiss' (and Bucuvalas, 1976) rigorous study of 250 respondents to questions about the likelihood of use of 50 recently completed studies funded by ADAMHA. (Each respondent rated 2 reports.)

Now, for the individual determinants:

*Abilities*—the resources required to implement the considered decision, sanctions, staff, skills, funding. Weiss found that the factor "Inexpensiveness" was essentially unrelated to the likelihood of use. This would mean that the choice of a decision indicated on the base of evaluation would not be directly influenced by the anticipated costs to implement it. However, she points out that this could be a function of the fact that few of her respondents could estimate the resources required to implement findings. But interestingly, consideration of resources is conspicuously overlooked in the entire literature in planned change. Drucker (1974) refers to a phenomenon of "Buying-Up," in which proponents of a given decision, perhaps unconsciously, failed to consider the wherewithal demands of a favored idea. Yet, on the other hand, Glazer and Ross (1971) found in their experiment on the adoption of an innovation that unavailability of resources can be a most significant factor in the failure to implement decision. (A bit off the dimensions, Patton et al., 1975, could find no relationship between the amount of funds invested in an evaluation and its ultimate utilization.)

*Values*—the set of assumptions that helps to predetermine directions at choice points. Patton's group found that the personal attributes of the potential user of evaluation findings were extremely important. These include interest, aggression, commitment, enthusiasm, and so on. This confirms a common finding in the research utilization field: personal characteristics of potential users—which are now identifiable—may account for the greatest variance in utilization. It follows that an evaluator can make a fair estimate of the likelihood of the use of findings if the potential decision maker is known. It is the attitude of decision makers that we are referring to here, not including such characteristics as highest degree and political orientation Weiss and Bucuvalas (1976) found the extent to which findings conformed to user expectations had a moderately high correlation with likelihood of use. Others have found that the fewer the surprises in results, the more likely utilization will occur. This strengthens the frequent advice for evaluators and potential users to remain in close communication throughout the process of evaluation.

There is a second dimension to values. Weiss and Bucuvalas uncovered an unexpected fact. Specifically, findings that challenge the status quo of the organization, its primary policies, its operating philosophy were considered to be more useful. It had been predicted, understandably enough, that the reverse would be true. The implications of this finding invite speculation.

*Information*—the Plan of Action, the alternative decision itself. Weiss and Bucuvalas found that the clearer a study report signals action steps that can be taken, the more likely it is to have an impact. Ciarlo (1977) has developed an approach termed "Options Evaluation" that allows assessment of the consequences of alternative action steps. Certainly it deserves further inquiry by evaluators. In general, it may be concluded that the more clear the implication for a specific decision, the more legitimization which can be offered to support a decision direction, the clearer it is, the more likely use will occur.

*Circumstances and Timing*—events occurring at the time evaluation results are available, including those that have given rise to the need for the evaluation. Relevance to ongoing circumstances was confirmed by Weiss and Bucuvalas as being positively related with the likelihood of use—hardly surprisingly. But Patton et al. (1975) found that the centrality of evaluation findings to major issues was more complex. In fact, more peripheral findings were more likely to be adopted, perhaps because central issues are more deeply ingrained and therefore more resistant to change. The Chelimsky (1977) discussions, as is so common in the literature, stress the importance of timeliness of evaluation findings. However, both the research studies on utilization fail to find any relatedness between timing and use. The answer seems to lie in the fact that decisions evolve very slowly, and are with us tomorrow, as well as today. That suggests that perhaps we have been overconcerned with timing, as logical as it seems on the surface.

*Obligation*—awareness of a problem, the felt need to do something about it. Chelinsky's discussions asserted that the soundness of evaluation methodology, frankly, had little influence on utilization.

Confirming this was the finding of the Patton group that improving the quality of the evaluation in and of itself would have little effect on increasing utilization. The respondents in Weiss and Bucuvalas' study felt the same when they were judging the likelihood that others would make use of the research results. But in work in their own offices, they gave the highest importance to the quality of research. This fact also has been observed in the general field of research utilization. Users either do not care about the soundness of findings, do not trust them, or are insufficiently sophisticated to judge them. It would seem that this places all the more responsibility on the shoulders of evaluators to ascertain that the results they are purveying meet their own standards—there will be few external checks.

*Resistances*—perceived losses that would occur from making use of evaluation results. The Patton group discovered that negative findings evoked barely more resistance than positive findings. They did learn, however, that surprises in evaluation reports were not well received. Again, this underscores the importance of working with potential users throughout the course of evaluation; perhaps it is a means of reducing resistance by helping to "save face." Fortunately, this measure has become a standard policy with GAO evaluations.

*Yield*—the perceived likelihood that the implementation of a given decision will bring about a state of reward. In this example, we are still talking about the payoff from making use of evaluation findings. We all know that it is a basic tenet of human behavior that the anticipation of a rewarding state of affairs is essential if a specific performance is to be carried out. Yet curiously enough, the researches on the utilization of evaluations remain silent on this point. The evaluator is left to her or his ingenuity to convey to potential users the benefits, even relief from frustration, that could accrue from responding to evaluation results.

This excursion into the factors influencing decisions to use evaluations does not encompass the full richness of sound knowledge in the field, nor has it yet dwelt completely upon the one frustration that all users of research, including evaluation research, encounter: ambiguous, often incomplete, and occasionally contradictory findings. Decision makers with sufficient power sometimes demand that there be no *ifs, ands,* or *buts* in reports. How futile it is trying to meet that demand. Perhaps this is our greatest challenge in evaluation research utilization.

It cannot be denied that there is much room for growth, though there is indeed reason to have confidence in the continuing maturation of evaluation research toward the point where the field can grow toward fuller realization of its potential to meet the heavy responsibility it appears ready to assume at this time. Of course it is a risk. But there is a line in a Yevtushenko poem that goes, "There is such great security in small hope." Let us hope that we can move ahead with the courage to have great hope for evaluation as we withstand the stress of risk.

# REFERENCES

BROWN, B. S. (1977) "Evaluation and change: conflict and detente." Evaluation 4.

CHELIMSKY, E. (1977) An Analysis of the Proceedings of a Symposium on the Use of Evaluation by Federal Agencies. McLean, VA: Mitre, M77-39.

CIARLO, J. (1977) "Options evaluation," Research Progress Report to NIMH, Grant No. MH 20954.

COHEN, D. (1975) "The value of social experiments," in A. M. Rivlin and P. M. Timpane (eds.) Planned Variation: Should We Give Up or Try Harder? Washington, DC: Brookings Institution.

DRUCKER, P. F. (1974) Management. New York: Harper and Row.

ETZIONI, A. (1967) "Mixed scanning: a third approach to decision-making." Public Administration Review 27: 385-92.

GLASER, E. D. and H. L. ROSS (1971) "Increasing the utilization of applied research results," Final Report to NIMH, Grant No. 5-R12, MH09250-02. Los Angeles: Human Interaction Research Institute.

Government Accounting Office (1976) Evaluation and Analysis to Support Decision Making. Washington, DC: Government Printing Office.

GRANQUIST, W. (1977) in "Hearings on the cost, management and utilization of human resources program evaluation." Evaluation.

GUTTENTAG, M. (1973) "Subjectivity and its use in evaluation research," Evaluation 1: 60-65.

JANIS, I. L. and L. MANN (1977) Decision Making. New York: Free Press.

KIRESUK, T. J., S. H. LUND, N. E. LARSEN and S. K. SCHULTZ (1977) "Translating theory into practice: change research at the Program Evaluation Resource Center." Evaluation 4.

MILLER, D. W. and M. K. STARR (1967) The Structure of Human Decisions. Englewood Cliffs, NJ: Prentice-Hall.

MILLER, G. A. (1956) "The magical number seven, plus or minus two," Psychological Review 63: 81-97.

PATTON, M. Q. et al. (1975) In Search of Impact. Minneapolis: Minnesota Center for Social Research.

POWERS, J. and G. HOLLAND (1976) Public Policy and Evaluation Research. Washington, DC: National Science Foundation.

SALASIN, S. (1977) "From national security of mental health: making analysis count in the government." Evaluation 4.

SCHWARTZ, S. (1970) "Moral decision-making and behavior," in J. Macauley and L. Berkowitz (eds.) Altruism and Helping Behavior. New York: Academic Press.

SIMON, H. A. (1976) Administrative Behavior: A Study of Decision-Making Processes in Administrative Organizations. New York: Free Press.

STOCKDILL, J. and S. SHARKSTEIN (1976) "Politics of program evaluation," Hospital and Community Psychiatry, September.

TVERSKY, A. (1972) "Elimination by aspects: a theory of choice." Psychological Review 79: 281-299.

WEIDMAN, D. R., P. HORST, G. TAHER, and J. WHOLEY (1973) "Design of an evaluation system for NIMH." Contract Report 962-7, Washington, DC: Urban Institute.

WEISS, C. (1972) Evaluation Research. Englewood Cliffs, NJ: Prentice-Hall.

——— and M. BUCUVALAS (1976) "The challenge of social research to decision making." Research Progress Report to NIMH, Grant MH 25586.

WHOLEY, J. (1970) Federal Evaluation Policy. Washington, DC: Urban Institute.

## ABOUT THE AUTHORS

CLARK C. ABT is founder and president of Abt Associates Inc. of Cambridge, Massachusetts, one of the largest private social science research firms in the United States. He graduated from M.I.T. in engineering, received an M.A. in philosophy from Johns Hopkins University, and a Ph.D. from M.I.T. in political science. Dr. Abt has over twenty years of experience directing social science research, operations research, systems engineering, and interdisciplinary analysis. He is the author of numerous articles on policy analysis and of two books, *Serious Games* and *Social Audit* and editor of a third, *The Evaluation of Social Programs.* He is also a founder, director, and former president of the Council for Applied Social Research.

HARRIS M. ALLEN Jr. is a doctoral student in the Department of Psychology at the University of California, Los Angeles. His major area is Social Psychology, with minor areas in Program Evaluation, Developmental Psychology, and Psychometrics. His particular interests include the study of political behavior, attitudes, and socialization, the formulation of public policy and intervention strategies as directed toward specific social problems, and the application of advanced statistical techniques (e.g., structural equation models) toward these research topics.

PETER M. BENTLER is Professor of Psychology at the University of California, Los Angeles and Director of a National Institute on Drug

273

Abuse research center on the psychosocial etiological bases of drug and alcohol abuse. He was a recipient of the Cattell Award for Distinguished Multivariate Research. He is President of the Society of Multivariate Experimental Psychology, and the recipient of a USPHS Research Scientist Development Award. His research interests include the development of psychometric and statistical models for multivariate analysis. Professor Bentler is on the editorial board of the journal *Evaluation Quarterly*.

ROBERT F. BORUCH is Director of the Methodology and Evaluation Research Division and Professor in the Department of Psychology of Northwestern University. He is also a past President of the Council for Applied Social Research. He is coauthor of *Social Experimentation* and an editor of *Experimental Tests of Public Policy*. He has published numerous journal articles dealing with methodological, managerial, and ethical problems in research. He is a member of advisory panels of the National Academy of Sciences, the American Psychological Association, and he consults frequently with federal agencies on research planning and design.

LOIS-ELLIN DATTA is Assistant Director of the Teaching and Learning Group of the National Institute of Education, and the 1979 President of the Evaluation Research Society. She has been Chairman of the Joint Dissemination Review Panel and Chief of Head Start Evaluation. Her articles include "The Impact of the Westinghouse Report on the Development of Project Head Start," "Does It Work When It Has Been Tried, and Half Full or Half Empty?" and others on the interplay of technical and contextual influences on evaluation.

BARBARA C. DAVENPORT holds a research position in the Heller School, Brandeis University. She conducts evaluation research studies in health and welfare. She consults with Medicaid and state departments of mental health, specializing in policy development, implementation, and evaluation.

HOWARD DAVIS is Chief of the Mental Health Services Development Branch at the National Institute of Mental Health. He holds an M.S.W. in social work and a Ph.D. in experimental and clinical psychology, both from the University of Denver. In addition to having worked at several mental hospitals and with a number of state and national mental health agencies, he has taught at the University of Minnesota Medical School. The author or coauthor of numerous articles and book chapters, Dr. Davis has made widely recognized contributions in the development and diffusion of information about innovation, organizational change, knowledge transfer, research utilization, and social program evaluation; he recently developed the A-VICTORY model, a tool for the analysis of organizational change. In 1977, Dr. Davis received the Evaluation Research Society's Myrdal Prize (for contributing to evaluation in government).

JAMES R. EMSHOFF is Associate Professor of Management and Director of the Wharton Applied Research Center at the University of Pennsylvania. He has published numerous articles on planning and policy making. He has consulted on strategic planning to numerous organizations.

MICHELLE FINE is Research Associate at the Center for Policy Research in New York City, working on the Vietnam Era Research Project. She is coauthor of *Toward the Experimenting Society: Methods for the Design and Evaluation of Social Experiments,* with Leonard Saxe. Her research interests include the study of domestic violence, social and interpersonal injustice, and the impact of the Vietnam war on the social health of men of the Vietnam generation. She has published in the areas of social experimentation, survey sampling procedures, and evaluation research.

HERNANDO GOMEZ is currently Research Associate for the Human Ecology Research Foundation in Cali, Colombia, and lecturer at the University of the Andes. He has been a Ford Foundation Fellow at Northwestern University and the University of Chicago.

RALPH H. KILMANN is Associate Professor of Business Administration at the University of Pittsburgh. He is the author of numerous articles on organization design and real-world problem solving. He is the author of *Social Systems Design,* published by Elsevier. He consults frequently on organization design and planning.

MICHAEL S. KNAPP is currently a Ph.D. Candidate in the Sociology of Education Program at the Stanford University School of Education. He has been an active member of the Stanford Evaluation Consortium for the past two years, and is also a trainee in the NIMH-sponsored Organizations and Mental Health Research Training Program operated by a consortium of faculty from the Stanford University Sociology Department, Business School, and School of Education. His particular interests include the organizational dimensions of evaluative research, the application of alternative methodologies to the problems of evaluation design, and the synthesis of qualitative and quantitative approaches to evaluation.

IAN I. MITROFF is Professor of Business Administration, Information Science, and Sociology at the University of Pittsburgh. He has published numerous articles on strategic planning, real-world problem solving, and problem structuring. His most recent book, with Ralph H. Kilmann, is *Methodological Approaches to Social Science,* published by Jossey-Bass. He consults frequently with agencies and corporations on planning.

SELMA J. MUSHKIN is a Fellow at the Woodrow Wilson International Center for Scholars. She also is Director of the Public Services Laboratory at Georgetown University. She specializes in studies of human resource and state-local finance. From 1973 to 1975 she was Executive Staff Director of the New Coalition of Mayors, Governors, State Legislators, and County Councilmen. From 1963 to 1968, she was Director of the State-Local Finance Project, George Washington University. Other experience includes Economic Consultant, OECD, Paris; Consultant, U.S. Office of Education; Economist, Public Health Service; and Chief, Division of Financial Studies, Social Security Administration.

RONALD L. NUTTALL is Director of the Laboratory for Statistical and Policy Research at Boston College and Professor in the Educational Research, Measurement and Evaluation Division, Graduate School of Arts and Sciences, Boston College. He is the author of over forty articles and monographs, and coauthor, with Richard Bolan, of *Urban Planning and Politics* (Lexington Books, 1975). His major interests are in policy research, especially in the areas of family, educational achievement, drug abuse, and program evaluation and needs assessment.

ROBERT PERLOFF is Professor of Business Administration and of Psychology at the University of Pittsburgh. A past president of the Evaluation Research Society and of the Association for Consumer Research, Professor Perloff is currently Treasurer and a member of the Board of Directors of the American Psychological Association and of the Board of Directors of the Eastern Psychological Association. He serves on the Mental Health Services Research Review Committee of the National Institute of Mental Health. His research interests are in evaluation, organizational behavior, and consumer behavior. His most recent publications are "Toward an Evaluation of Cooperative Education" (with Edward Sussna, in the *Journal of Cooperative Education*) and "Academia and the *Training of Human Service Delivery Program Evaluators*" (with H.C. Schulberg, in the *American Psychologist*).

ROBERT F. RICH is Assistant Professor of Politics and Public Affairs at the Woodrow Wilson School of Public and International Affairs, Princeton University. He holds a Ph.D. in political science from the University of Chicago, has published extensively on the utilization of social research knowledge, and has served as a consultant for numerous evaluation design and research projects. Rich currently is conducting a study of the determinants of mental health policy making in the state of New Jersey. He is the author of the forthcoming book, *The Power of Social Science Information and Public Policy* (Jossey-Bass, 1979), and will be editor of a new journal, *Knowledge: Creation, Diffusion, Utilization,* to be published by Sage Publications.

PETER H. ROSSI is currently Professor of Sociology and Director of the Social and Demographic Research Center at the University of Massachusetts/Amherst. He has been on the faculties of Harvard, Johns Hopkins, and the University of Chicago, where he also served as Director of the National Opinion Research Center. He has been a consultant on research methods and evaluation to (among others) the National Science Foundation, National Institute of Mental Health, the Federal Trade Commission, and the Russell Sage Foundation. His research has largely been concerned with the application of social research methods to social issues and he is currently engaged in research on natural disasters and criminal justice. His most recent works include *Evaluating Social Programs* (with W. Williams), *Reforming Public Welfare* (with K. Lyall) and *Prison Reform and State Elites* (with R. A. Berk). Professor Rossi is currently coeditor of *Social Science Research.* In 1979-1980, he will be president of the American Sociological Association.

SUSAN SALASIN is Chief of the Research Diffusion and Utilization Section, Mental Health Services Development Branch of the National Institute of Mental Health. She is the founder and Editorial Director for *Evaluation* magazine, an experimental publication designed to further the adoption of program evaluation in human services organizations. Ms. Salasin's primary professional interest is in program evaluation and knowledge utilization as a means of stimulating, facilitating, and guiding organizational change, at both the policy and practice levels. In this capacity, she has written numerous chapters with Dr. Howard Davis for varied groups, including the National Academy of Sciences. She is also engaged in a study of mental health services for women, and is working on the development of services to victims of personal violence.

LEONARD SAXE is Assistant Professor of Psychology and Senior Research Associate of the Center for Applied Social Science at Boston University. His research interests include problems of interpersonal relations and the application of psychology to social problems. He is the author of numerous journal articles in social psychology and is coauthor of a forthcoming text, *Toward the Experimenting Society: Methods for the Design and Evaluation of Social Experiments.* During 1979, he is on leave from Boston University in order to serve as a U.S. Congressional Fellow with the Office of Technology Assessment.

HERMANN F. SCHWIND is Assistant Professor of Business Administration at St. Mary's University in Halifax, Nova Scotia, Canada. He has recently been at the Institute for International Studies and Training in Kamiide, Japan, as a visiting professor. His major teaching and research interests are in organizational behavior and personnel management. He has published in Canada, Germany, and Japan as well as in the United States.

DAVID O. SEARS is Professor of Psychology and Political Science at UCLA. He is also coauthor of *The Politics of Violence: The New Urban*

*Blacks and the Watts Riot, Social Psychology,* and *Public Opinion.* He has published numerous papers on political psychology, attitude change, and problems of racial relations.

MICHAEL SIMMONS is Assistant to the Director of the Office of Management Services, Massachusetts Department of Public Welfare. His particular interests include public administration, policy analysis, evaluation research, and administrative ethics. From 1976 to 1978 he was Systems and Evaluation Specialist of the Cost-Effectiveness Project, Massachusetts Medicaid Program. Other experience includes Consultant, Harvard School of Public Health; Consultant, Boston University Center for Health Planning; Consultant, Massachusetts Office of State Health Planning; and Social Worker, Massachusetts Department of Public Welfare. He is a member of the American Society for Public Administration and the Evaluation Research Society.

BARRY S. TUCHFELD is Director of the Applied Social Research Program in the Department of Sociology at Texas Christian University. His particular interests include the study of alcohol and other drug-related problems and programmatic services directed toward those problems. In addition to publishing in several sociology and alcohol journals, he has produced monographs for the National Institute on Alcohol Abuse and Alcoholism and the National Institute on Drug Abuse.

CHARLES WINDLE is Program Evaluation Specialist in the Division of Mental Health Service Programs, National Institute of Mental Health, Rockville, Maryland. At NIMH he works with research grantees and contractors on development of methods for program evaluation and citizen/consumer participation.

J. ARTHUR WOODWARD is Associate Professor of Psychology at the University of California, Los Angeles. His research interests include the development of multivariate statistical models and their application in theoretical research and applied evaluation research. In 1978, Professor Woodward was recipient of the American Psychological Association's Distinguished Scientific Contribution Award for an Early Career Contribution.

GREGORY WURZBURG is Executive Director of the National Council on Employment Policy and Project Director of the Council's evaluation of federal youth programs. He is coauthor with Sar A. Levitan of *Evaluating Federal Social Programs: An Uncertain Art.*